AROUND THE WORLD

25 YEARS OF SERVICE AS AN OFFICER AND ENLISTED MAN IN THE U.S. ARMY AND U.S. COAST GUARD

BY

Lieutenant Edward Leo Semler Jr., USCG (Retired)

Mel,

I hope you find this a fun and interesting read and it brings back memories of your sailing days!

Enjoy

Ed

First Edition: 2013

Library of Congress Control Number: 2013914658

ISBN: 978-0-615-77701-6

Printed in the United States of America

Front cover: *USCGC Sherman (WHEC-720)* getting ready to replenish at sea in the Persian Gulf 2001

Back cover: Private Edward Semler returning to Camp Pelham Korea after a road march 1983.

Cover design by Doug Benec

Thank you Jana!

INTRODUCTION

This is a memoir of my active duty military career, spanning over 25 years in the United Stated Army and Coast Guard. I decided to try and compile my memories of events, people, and places before they slowly slipped from the moorings of my mind. These are the milestones of my military career to the best of my recollection with the help of letters, photographs, unit newsletters, post cards, unit year books, and personal videos. Everything mentioned actually happened or was told to me first person. The small details may be off compared to someone else's recollection but the meat of the story is real. The names of those I mention are real. Some names I have omitted out of respect for their privacy.

Anybody who served in the military will be able to relate to a lot of the daily routines and stories I am about to tell. Even though we never served together you will more than likely have shared a lot of the same experiences and I hope by sharing my stories it helps you to remember and relive yours.

GETTING READY TO JOIN THE MILITARY

It started out very simply with a desire to follow in my father's footsteps and join the United States Army. He had served in a peace-time Army from 1959 to 1962, mostly in France. My dad was a great story teller and he always knew when to embellish his stories to bring them to life. His stories intrigued me and I dreamed of growing up and experiencing exciting adventures like his.

There wasn't anyone in my immediate family who was currently in the service so the whole experience was bold and new to me. My extended family had a long history of service, with several uncles serving in WWII, my great-great grandfather and his two brothers serving with the Union Army during the Civil War, and my six-time great grandfather serving in the Revolutionary War. But they were all silent about their service or had passed away, so all I had to go on were my dad's tall tales and advice.

While flipping through a magazine when I was in middle school I came across an article on the Coast Guard. I asked my dad if he thought the Coast Guard could be more interesting than the Army, and he told me that he thought they only took people with a college degree. He must have gotten his wires crossed because his older brother Joe was in the Coast Guard during WWII, as an enlisted man, and he never attended college. In fact, I would have never known Uncle Joe had been in the Coast Guard if it hadn't been for a conversation we had at my sister Sarah's wedding in 1991. I was sitting at a table with Uncle Joe and he noticed I was wearing my Coast Guard dress uniform and asked me where I was stationed. I told him I was at the Coast Guard facility at Curtis Bay, Maryland. He replied, "Oh that's where I went to Coast Guard boot camp!"

We had a good long talk after that statement and it seemed like not much had changed in the Coast Guard since he was an electronics technician (ET) in the 1940's during WWII.

My parents had moved to Australia in 1979 where my father's employer, the Central Intelligence Agency, transferred him from Fairfax, Virginia to Alice Springs, Australia. I attended high school in Australia until 1981 and left after completing the 11th grade. My parents thought it would be best to send me back to the states to finish out my 12th year instead of completing it in Australia. It wasn't that the Australian school system was inferior; it was that my parents thought an American High School diploma would translate better in the American workforce.

It was arranged that I would live with my Grandma Semler and Uncle Mike on the Semler family farm located in Gibsonia, Pennsylvania because they had a spare room. My actual legal guardians while I attended school were my Uncle Joe and Aunt Gloria. They lived about 400 yards next door. At the time they had Aunt Gloria's parents living with them and they were tight on room. My grandma had a spare room at the farm so it just seemed easier to stay with her and Uncle Mike.

When I went to Deer Lakes High School to register for my 12th grade year I immediately ran into problems with my Australian schooling. Deer Lakes said my high school credits from Australia would not give me enough credits to graduate after completing the 12th grade in the United States and I would have to complete the 11th grade again in the American school system. Luckily my Cousin Sharon, Uncle Joe and Aunt Gloria's daughter was a teacher in the school district. She was able to somehow demonstrate that I met the requirements for credits to complete the 12th grade and graduate with a diploma.

In February of 1982 while in the middle of my senior year I drove down to New Kensington, PA to visit with my Uncle Harry's family and decided to go see the Army recruiter there in downtown New Kensington. As I walked into the recruiting building I never gave a second thought to the offices of the Navy, Air Force or Marine Corps as I made my way straight to the Army recruiting office. At this point in my life I had no expectations of making a career out of military service. All that was on my mind was fulfilling a desire to follow in my father's footsteps. I looked up to my dad and wanted to experience what he had experienced in the Army.

My recruiter was a young sergeant (SGT) by the name of Ernest Roland, who like any recruiter was very eager to get me signed up and meet his hiring quota. And he didn't even have to go out and drag me off the street; I was a willing applicant that walked right up to his desk! After we started to fill out the required paperwork SGT Roland seemed concerned. When he asked where I had lived and worked the past few years, and I said Australia, it seemed to throw a wrench in the Army's finely tuned recruiting machine. But after much more paperwork I was signed up on the delayed enlistment program. If I passed all my pre-entry requirements I would ship out to basic training in July after I graduated from high school.

In preparation for my deployment in July of 1982 I was routinely contacted by SGT Roland who would drive out to the farm and check in on me. On one occasion he came out in his government vehicle, a tiny little Dodge Horizon. The lane up to the farm was about 200 yards long and about the worst stretch of driveway in the township. When that lane was wet it was like driving through mini lake-sized pot holes all the way up to the house. Well SGT Roland came out after a good rain storm and got that little Dodge Horizon stuck in the lane. Luckily we had a few old farming tractors there on the farm and I started one up and pulled him out.

I had to make several trips into the Pittsburgh Military Entrance Processing Station (MEPS) located at the Federal Building in downtown Pittsburgh. It was about an hour's drive and was pretty much a straight shot down the main drag of Route 8. The trips consisted of the usual pre-entry physicals and an entrance test known as the Armed Services Vocational Aptitude Battery (ASVAB). The ASVAB was an eclectic mixture of subjects to try and find out what career path was best suited for you in the military. Each service has a different minimum score requirement to gain entry into their branch of the service. I passed the Army's required score and was one step closer to shipping out.

When at MEPS I would usually look up my Aunt Betty who worked for the Internal Revenue Service in the same building. I would either visit her office or meet her for lunch down in the cafeteria. She had such an upbeat personality that always put a positive spin on the visits.

On one of these visits to MEPS I had to decide what my job field would be in the Army. The female Army counselor who was assigned to me sat me down and asked me what I wanted to do. My reply was, "I don't know. What does the Army need?" Now I was putting a lot of trust in her hands! She said "How about being a combat bridge crewman, your ASVAB general technical (GT) score of 100 shows you're pretty strong in this job field." And she followed that question up with, "I can even get you a guaranteed assignment to Korea." Now I thought this all sounded just peachy! Little did I know that a combat engineer was just one step up from an infantryman and no one wanted to go to Korea!

On another trip to MEPS I had to take my physical. This is an all-day affair going from one room to another and waiting for your turn to be seen to give blood, have your eyes checked, provide a urine sample, and so on. At one point in the physical they piled the 40 or so of us military candidates into a room and told us to line up in rows and get undressed down to our underwear. After complying with the command a doctor with his assistant walked up and down the rows. As the doctor made comments his assistant took notes. The doctor had walked past the front of me without much fuss and continued down the row. I heard him walking up the row behind me, heard him talking, and then felt his cold hands on my back. He told me I had a curvature of the spine and would need to step out of the formation and wait for him in the next room. After the doctor had finished his group exam he came into the room and looked me over some more. He said he was concerned about my curved spine and the pressures that would be put on it from carrying a back pack, ruck sack in Army lingo. He wanted to have me re-evaluated by another doctor the following week.

At this point I thought my military career had come to an abrupt end. I went home feeling rejected. After getting back home I decided to go visit my Grandpap and Grandma Churilla who lived about 10 minutes from the Semler Farm in neighboring Hampton. I had visited them on a regular basis while attending school and thought they may be able to give me some advice. My Grandma said that she had a chiropractor that she saw on a regular basis and recommended that I see him and get a back adjustment. I had always thought of chiropractors as quacks and didn't know what this guy could offer me. My Grandma reassured me and sweetened the deal by offering to pay for the visit. Being a cash-strapped young teenager that was an offer I could not refuse.

So we drove over to the chiropractor and he assured me he could get my back into alignment. He said the adjustment should last about 30 days or so and I should see him for regular adjustment to keep it straight. To accomplish the adjustment he got me on his table and did the usual cracking, pulling, stretching, and low and behold I was as good as new and felt great. I felt very optimistic about my upcoming meeting with the MEPS doctor. As scheduled, I went to MEPS the following week, checked in with Aunt Betty, and was examined by the second MEPS doctor. He said he couldn't find anything the matter with my back and marked me fit for duty in the Army!

On my last night before shipping out to basic training my Uncle Mike and Cousin Dave threw me a party at the farm. We had a mini keg of Iron City Light beer and some pot so we got drunk and stoned. Beer and pot were our two major food groups and we totally over-consumed that night. I remember Dave leaving the barn we were partying in and heading back to the house. A few hours later Mike and I decided to turn in and we found Dave passed out in the driveway, halfway between the barn and the house. It was a warm July evening so we just left him there. I'm sure we were too messed up to be carrying him anyway. Needless to say the next morning was rough. I was hung over when SGT Roland arrived to take me to MEPS.

On the way down the lane I was still pretty drunk from the night before. SGT Roland began telling me that he knew he had said a lot of great things about the Army, but boot camp was going to be tough, tougher

5

then he may have let on. I told him I kind of knew that and not to worry, I would be fine. My only thought at the moment was that I just wanted to take a nap.

At MEPS we finishing up paperwork, swore our allegiance to the United States of America and then headed to the airport for our flight to St. Louis, Missouri. It was the 21st of July1982 and I was headed to Fort Leonard Wood, Missouri for basic training, also known as "boot camp."

UNITED STATES ARMY
FORT LEONARD WOOD, MISSOURI

2nd PLATOON, B COMPANY, 1ST BATTALION,

2nd TRAINING BRIGADE

21 July 1982 – 3 November 1982

The plane touched down in St. Louis late in the day on Wednesday the 21st of July without me noticing. I was awakened by a stewardess who nicely said it was time for me to get off the plane. As I lifted my head I could feel the bad crick in my neck and noticed I had drool trickling from my mouth onto my lap. I felt like crap. I remembered Dave passed out in the driveway and believe it or not wished I was him right about then. At least he wasn't heading off to the Army. I got off the plane and headed to the mustering point for catching the bus to Fort Leonard Wood. I could tell I was getting closer by the number of people I saw carrying large manila envelopes. We were given these envelopes to carry our records to boot camp in, a dead giveaway you were a recruit.

We were headed into the middle of Missouri about two and half hours from St. Louis. Fort Leonard Wood was out by itself with nothing much around it. I think the military likes it that way so if you decide to run away you really don't have any place close to run to!

The fort was named in honor of Major General Leonard Wood who was awarded the United States Army Medal of Honor for his actions fighting against Geronimo. He also saw action in the Spanish American war, Philippine American war, and World War I. He was a physician by train-ing and as a neat historical fact he is buried in Arlington National Ceme-tery, but his brain is held at Yale University. Of course I knew none of that at the time and it probably would not have made much of an impres-sion on my 18-year old mind in any case!

The bus ride was uneventful and I dozed on and off until we rolled into the base late in the evening. When the bus came to a stop some average

7

looking Army folks mustered us all off the bus and into an old wooden building for a quick briefing, basically stating that we were in fact at Ft. Leonard Wood. In the building, which was one large room, there was a wooden box with a small opening on the top near the door, and we were told that if we had anything we shouldn't have on us that this was our chance for amnesty and to put it in the box as we left. I had nothing to put in the box and moved on with the rest of the group to the next old WWII style two story building where we were provided a bed and were told to turn in.

Initially I was surprised at how relaxed things were here. I had heard that basic training was tough but that didn't seem to be the case at the moment. No one had told me all the details about boot camp. My dad just said, "It was no picnic" and SGT Rowland said, "It may be tougher then I have let on." The only traumatic event to happen the first week was that first night.

The sergeant that had tucked us all in for the night had assigned several of us to stand what he called a "fire watch." He assigned different hours of watch throughout the night to different people and departed with one final order, "Do not under any circumstances let anyone in until I get here in the morning." I was assigned to a bunk bed on the second floor. Finally sober from the night before I fell fast asleep.

At some point in the night I was awakened by the sound of heavy pounding on the wooden barracks door and the commotion of people arguing. As I sprang out of my bunk and came down the stairs I encountered about 10 guys huddled by the front wooden door. They looked scared out of their wits and were arguing the point of letting this guy pounding on the door in. The guy at the door was pounding and yelling to let him in or he would throw all of us out of the Army, or worse! Meanwhile the group of now about 20 of us were huddled inside and having a delirious debate on whether or not to let this guy in. There was screaming and crying and all sorts of carrying on and eventually the unknown person at the door was let in.

Needless to say it was a no-win situation. The unknown guy came barging in with a female on his side and a couple of male sidekicks in tow, all of whom were in uniform. They seemed to be about our young age of 18 and more than likely just got here a few weeks before us! The female seemed to be the ring leader's date and she had hickeys all around her neck. The ring leader gave us an ass chewing for letting him in and triumphantly strolled out the door with his girl and sidekicks in tow, leaving us all petrified!

All the commotion had everyone worked up and we all thought we were in big trouble and were going to be sent back home. But the next day came and went without a mention of the evening event. Nothing was ever said about it. I think someone just got their jollies by whipping the new recruits into a hysterical frenzy!

I later found out that we were just at a holding and processing center, and not boot camp. Although there were female recruits and cadre at Fort Leonard Wood, I was in an all-male forming company. Our days were filled with getting issued uniforms, gear, dog tags, pictures, haircuts and equipment. This always entailed about 30-40 of us marching to a different WWII era building and spending hours awaiting important items such as underwear, which was the only thing I had a choice in; boxers or briefs!

It was a sort of casual routine. We got up when revile was announced and made our way to the mess hall which was a huge tent structure that seemed sort of temporary. It had a wooden floor with wooden walls that went up about three feet and stopped. The rest was canvas tenting material. The side walls rolled up and you had a nice view of the processing area while you ate. After breakfast we would form up and go through the day of in-processing.

Getting our patriotic picture taken in uniform was another interesting event in this finely tuned process. At this point, we were all still wearing the civilian clothes we had arrived in. You entered the building and there was a rack of Army dress shirts and a pile of dress hats on a table. You picked an Army shirt and hat that fit you and put it on. You sat very officially in front of the camera and got your picture taken. Upon completion of the picture you removed your Army shirt and hat, placed it on the rack and table where you found it, and exited to wait for everyone else to finish.

My basic training picture

A few days later we were issued our real uniforms and our civilian clothes were boxed up and shipped back home. There would be no need for them in the next few months! My group was one of the first to be issued the Army's new battle dress uniform (BDU) which was a camouflage pattern. The older uniform was just plain green. I was really happy with the new BDUs because in my mind we looked more like soldiers.

After spending five days at the in-processing center we started packing up our gear and on Monday the 26th of July we were thrown to the wolves!

Transfer day started out early in the morning with us loading everything we had into our rucksack and duffle bag. We had been told that we should only have what was issued to us at the processing center, nothing else. I don't think a lot of guys got the message because some guys had a hard time getting everything to fit.

We were mustered in front of our old wooden barracks with all of our gear. We looked like we were shipping out to the front lines, wearing our BDUs with metal helmets. We were told that we would be picked up by cattle cars that would transit us to our new living quarters. Now these cattle cars were just that, real looking cattle cars towed by a semi-looking truck. There were no seats, just hand rails to grab on to. No windows, just slits in the metal walls. The only way in or out was through a set of double school bus style doors in the middle of the cattle car on one side. We all loaded up as tight as sardines into the arriving cattle cars. As I got on I noticed there were several guys wearing the older plain green uniforms and wide brimmed, brown, "Smokey the Bear" type hats. These guys didn't say a word and they didn't look happy. I could sense that bad things were about to happen.

As we started to pull away a small amount of chatter started up. As soon as the chatter started the guys in the Smokey Bear hats yelled "Shut your fucking mouths!" Well there was a deathly silence as we drove around for what seemed like an hour. I guess they didn't want us to know where we were going or how to get back to where we had come from. Finally our cattle car pulled up to this long and wide concrete driveway leading up to sets of newer style brick buildings, each being three stories high. As soon as the cattle car stopped, the school bus doors sprang open, and those guys with the Smokey Bear hats just started yelling and screaming and pushing guys off the cattle car. I mean they were just grabbing whoever was close and throwing them right out the door to even more guys wearing those Smokey Bear hats.

I was toward the back of the cattle car, which seemed to be a good place for the moment, as the Smokey Bears were busy with everyone at the front. As the car emptied and I made my way to the doors I hit the ground a-running and headed up the long grade of the concrete path. I had my rucksack on my back and my duffle bag in front of me in a bear hug. It was like running a gauntlet. There were guys on the ground crying and screaming, their gear strewn about creating obstacles in my path. It was like what you see in the war movies, when the landing craft reaches the beach and the front ramp drops down, and there is a full blown war going on right there in front of you. And the Smokey Bears yelling and screaming sounded like incoming artillery. I didn't really know what they wanted me to do but the trail of destruction seemed to be leading up the hill, about 100 yards and in front of one of the three story buildings. I made it to the front of the building and fell into formation with those who had survived the gauntlet ahead of me.

We were standing at attention in two rows facing each other about 10 feet apart. There was about five feet in between each man and in the middle of the two rows of men there were trash cans. The Smokey Bears informed us that they were to be addressed as "drill sergeant" and we were "maggots."

They then began to dump out everything we had packed in our duffle bag and rucksack onto the hot July concrete. As they dumped my gear and clothes on the concrete, the drill sergeant started to kick it all around looking for anything he didn't think I should have. He used his feet to sift through my gear giving me the impression he was above actually touching it with his hands. Once he was satisfied I didn't have anything interesting I was told to "Pick up my shit." As I was scrambling to get all my belongings back into some sort of pile I was thankful I wasn't like the guy next to me who had magazines and candy, an obvious no- no! The drill sergeant was throwing this guy's stuff all over the place and making him do push-ups for all his contraband. Another guy had pantyhose. I thought, what in the heck was this guy thinking! His rant to the screaming drill sergeant was that they are the best way to put a shine on his boots. The drill sergeant was not impressed, threw the panty hose in the garbage can, and made the guy feel miserable for a while!

There were also these two Hispanic kids that looked like "deer caught in headlights." They drew the attention of the head drill instructor who appeared Hispanic himself. He was yelling at them, asking them if they understood English. They really didn't seem to understand and like the rest of us seemed too afraid to talk. They were pulled aside and I asked myself, how the hell did these guys get this far in this process not knowing how to speak English?

The drill sergeants, now content with our total humiliation, had us run up to the 3rd floor of the building which would become our new home for the next three plus months.

I was in a room with about 20 other guys. It was an open room with metal lockers against the walls and two rows of metal bunk beds in the center. I was on a top bunk and would be here for the next 14 weeks, from the 26th of July to the 3rd of November.

The barracks

We must have been one of the first waves to arrive because over the next several days we watched as other cattle cars pulled up to the concrete welcoming mat just down the hill and the same scenario played itself out with newly arriving maggots.

I was on a working detail the next day and we were told to take a break out of the heat under a tree in front of the building. After sitting there for

13

a few minutes a group of cattle cars pulled up below us and I had a front row seat for the main event. It played out just like our arrival the day before. But once the drill sergeants had all the maggots up on the main concrete pad, a few of them passed out. One of the drill sergeants yelled at us to "Get your butts over here right now!" So we sprang up and ran over to him. Once there we were instructed to pour our canteens of water over the dazed maggots laying there on the concrete and drag them under the tree we had been sitting under. It seemed to revive them. Once back on their feet the process of dumping their gear out and so on continued.

The next few weeks were jam packed with events from 0330 until 1000. That's military time for 3:30am-10pm. Each day began with all of us springing out of our bunks and trying to cram into the bathroom to shit, shower, and shave. I had nothing to shave but they said I had to anyway! Also, our bunks had to be made and everything cleaned up within 30 minutes after waking up. Then it was down to our mustering spot in front of our barracks and morning physical training (PT) consisting of jumping jacks, push-ups, stretches, and a good mile or so run. Once back from PT we headed to the mess hall for breakfast and on with our day.

There were about 211 of us in Bravo Company when we started. I would have to say we lost about 25, who were discharged or reverted back to another company by the time we finished. I was in second platoon which consisted of about 72 when we started. My friends were the guys in my immediate platoon who I spent every minute of every day with. Guys like Knuckles, Vaughan, Kyle, and Sann. Everyone was known and addressed by their last names, mimicking how the drill sergeants addressed us. You never got really personally close with anyone because you never knew how long they would be around, and you were concerned foremost with getting yourself through this mess. If you didn't get kicked out you would be reverted back to another company behind us, and your boot camp experience would drag on.

It seemed like every week we would lose one or two guys for one reason or another. A few that stand out were our recruit company commander and a fellow in my own platoon. We were into our second or third week

14

when we lost our recruit company commander. He was an older guy that I heard had been in the Army before. The drill sergeant came out one day and told him to go pack his gear because he was leaving.

2nd Platoon, Bravo Company, 1st Battalion, just after we formed up. SFC Castaneda is holding the flag. I'm the 7th from the left on the top row.

Word was he falsified something on his enlistment papers and they had finally caught it. This was before computers and everything was hand generated, so it took time to verify your paperwork. At about that point I was wishing they would come and give me my walking papers. I remember standing there in formation about mid-way through our seven week basic training and thinking, there is no way I will be able to maintain this pace for my three year enlistment!

The other guy I remember leaving was a fella by the name of Taylor. He was a nice reserved guy who had hygiene problems. We were always getting in trouble and having to do push-ups or put in pain inducing positions because Taylor would not bathe or his gear was dirty.

One of the drill sergeant's favorite pain inducing positions was for you to stand up against the wall, bend your knees, and hold your arms out. It didn't take long before you started to shake and it was everything you could do to keep your arms up. If you couldn't hold it for long, the drill sergeant would come over and poke you or give you his boot. You didn't want the attention of the drill sergeant.

We tried all the usual things to get Taylor to clean up his act, such as hazing him and throwing him in the shower. None of it seemed to work and he really didn't seem to care. Well one day we were at the gun range shooting our M16 rifles. We were all sitting Indian style in this gravel parking lot waiting our turn to fire when we noticed that Taylor was shoving pebbles from the parking lot down the barrel of his rifle. One of the guys notified our drill sergeant and Taylor was whisked away, and we never saw Taylor again.

Besides a pulled tendon and a bad rash around my neck from my dog tags I made it through without a scratch. No one wanted to pull up lame for fear of being reverted back to another company or discharged. We ran and did all of our physical training in boots, BDU pants, and t-shirts. The boots were your typical black military boot that had no support, and were about 13 inches tall. After several weeks my Achilles tendon gave out on me. I tried to keep up the pace, but the drill sergeants picked me out limping along and sent me to the aid station to have it looked at. At the aid station they gave me some pads and put me on light activity for a few days. Of course that got the drill sergeants all over me, accusing me of being a slacker!

The guys that were sick, lame, or lazy, were like a leper colony. Whenever we formed up to march some place they always formed up behind the company and walked in a group trailing along behind so they didn't infect the rest of the company. They were easy pickings for the drill sergeants and usually didn't last long before being reverted back to another company or discharged. I spent a day or two back with them with my tendon issue and was very happy to get out of their ranks and back up with the company.

In letters home I was proud to report that I had quit smoking, was up to 44 push-ups, 49 sit-ups, and that I could run the mile in 7.48 minutes. The requirements were 40 push-ups and sit–ups within two minutes, and to make the run in less than 8 minutes, so I was passing. I earned sharp-shooter with the M16 rifle by hitting 34 out of 40 and marksman with the grenade. I'm not sure why they have an award level for grenade. You would think it would be simple, like pass or fail. Either you got the grenade close enough to inflict damage or not! No matter what the scoring was based on, the grenade course and fire and maneuver ranges were cool and I felt like I was learning something important.

Before completing the grenade course we had to complete the grenade range. This involved throwing a bunch of training grenades to get the hang of having the explosive in your hand. The training grenade was a blue colored grenade with a blasting cap in it to make the sound of a real grenade. It really gave you the feel for the weight of it and the time delay before the explosive went off.

Next it was on to the actual grenade course. This was about the length of two football fields and had a series of bunkers, foxholes, and vehicles that you had to sneak up on and then throw your training grenade at. It seems easy until you crawl about as close as you can get to the obstacle wearing all your combat gear and then try and lob a grenade into the small opening of your target. On some of the obstacles you had to make sure the grenade exploded just after landing. This was to make sure the enemy didn't have time to pick it up and throw it back at you. You did this by popping the pin on the grenade, waiting a few seconds and then throwing it. Once you popped the pin, the grenade was supposed to ex-plode in eight seconds, so you had to calculate the wait time according to the distance to your target. After about halfway through the course I was beat! My adrenalin was pumping and it felt like a real accomplishment to finish. I was scored on how many times I got my grenade on or in the target. I thought I did pretty well, but ended up earning a marksman medal which was the minimum standard for qualifying.

Finally, it was on to the last part of the grenade training which was to throw a real grenade! We were mustered up in the usual parking lot sized holding area and called up to the grenade range bunker in groups of five.

When I walked into the bunker I was given a flak jacket to wear along with instructions on how I would handle and throw the grenade. When it was my group's turn we were each handed a grenade and proceeded to five small individual bunkers. I was in the third bunker. The back side of the bunker was open to provide entry and the front and sides were piled five feet high with sandbags and wooden beams. There was a drill instructor there and he instructed me to crouch down and he once again went over the instruction for throwing the grenade.

As I heard the first position throw his grenade I started to get nervous. When the second position threw his I was even more on edge. It was my turn now!

The drill instructor gave me the order to stand, pull the pin on the grenade, and hand the pin to him, which I did. I now had a live grenade in my hand. I'm not sure who was more concerned, me or the drill instructor!

Following his orders I yelled, "Fire in the hole!" and threw the grenade down range and dropped to my knees. A few seconds later there was a loud explosion! What a relief!

It was the fourth position's turn and after waiting several minutes for an explosion there was nothing but silence. It was a dud. I was told to stay put and I waited there in the bunker with the drill instructor crouched down against the sandbags. After about 45 minutes an explosive ordinance team was called in to dispose of the dud grenade. They calmly walked down range and looked around for the dud. Once they found it they wired it with explosives. Then they walked back to the bunker area and detonated it, exploding the dud.

The fifth position threw his grenade without a hitch and I was glad to get out of that bunker and back out to the safe holding area!

The fire and maneuver course was pretty much the same as the grenade course only I used my M16 rifle instead of the training grenades. I had blank rounds in my weapon along with a partner who went through the course with me. Our objective was to advance on a target while giving each other covering fire. You would lose points if you moved before you had covering fire or did not provide covering fire when your partner moved. No medal for this, just a pass or fail.

There were several other ranges such as the M203 grenade launcher and the M72 Light Anti-Tank Weapon (LAW) rocket launcher. These ranges were fun but we never fired the real thing. At the M203 grenade launcher range we fired these dummy rounds that were filled with paint. The M203 attaches to the underside of the M16 rifle and we would line up and get one shot at firing the thing down range at a window sized opening in a wooden panel.

At the M72 LAW range we fired a dummy round that was similar to a bottle rocket! I'm sure it was to save money and I know that if I was a drill sergeant I would sure prefer teaching us on weapons that would cause little damage if we made a mistake!

The company drill sergeants and drill assistants were an eclectic lot of Hispanics, African Americans, and Caucasians. Our platoon's lead drill sergeant was Sergeant First Class (SFC) Castaneda. He was our primary drill sergeant, but any one of the company drill sergeants or assistants could be in charge of us at any given time.

SFC Castaneda was serious and stern. I remember always having a feeling of trust with him, knowing that he would not let anything bad actually happen to us. I saw his compassionate side that first day with the Hispanic guys that could barely speak English. Although he didn't let them off the hook with going through the first day welcoming party, you could tell that he was not giving them the full treatment once he ascertained that they didn't get it.

Speaking of those Hispanic recruits, the last time I saw them was at the gas chamber. As we were being prepared to enter the gas chamber these guys didn't comprehend what was going to happen. The gas chamber was a sealed room filled with some sort of tear gas. We were told that we would enter the gas chamber in small groups of 10 with our gas masks and chemical suits on. When we were all in side we would be told to remove our masks. Once we yelled out our full name and social security number we would be allowed to leave.

When you removed your mask it didn't take but a split second to be overcome with tear gas, your eyes burning and gushing with water. The instructions must have been lost in translation with these two Hispanic fellas. They came out of that gas chamber running and screaming as if someone were truly trying to kill them. They had no idea they were going to get gassed. By the time the drill sergeants got them under control, by tackling them, they were still freaked out. They were in such bad shape an ambulance was called to take them away. I think after that they were reverted back to another company a few weeks behind us to be retrained, and most likely enrolled in English classes.

The other drill sergeants in the company that assisted SFC Castaneda interacted with us daily. Very seldom did we do things as just a platoon. Just about every day we functioned as a company and any one of these drill sergeant could be in charge of us. The drill sergeants were SGT Abraham, Staff Sergeant (SSG) Miller, SSG Strickland, SFC Chatter, and SFC Wiley. There were usually two or three of them around during the day but it was very unusual to have them all together on one given day, but make no mistake, one was always around. Most of the daily barracks routine such as cleanups, watch, and getting formed up was left up to our recruit leaders. The drill sergeants and their assistants would patrol through at various times of the day and night and crank us up, just to keep our heads on a swivel.

Once we were formed outside we fell in to the hands of the drill sergeants and their assistants. The drill sergeant assistants were a sort of rotating lot of drill sergeants in training. The daily barometer of how hard the day would be seemed to be measured by how many drill sergeants walked through the door in the morning to get us cranked up and on with our daily routine. They all had us under total control and could break us at any given moment. Some just rode us hard for a while and backed off once we got going, while others gave it to us nonstop the whole day.

After a few weeks we were marched down to the mini Post Exchange (PX) that was in our training area. The large main PX is a store similar to a department store. The mini PX was like a convenience store. We had been issued an advance of $90.00 when we began training and told to budget this out for haircuts and toiletries. I was thinking what the heck else are we going to spend it on?

When we arrived at the mini PX the drill sergeant told us "You have 30 minutes to get in there and get a haircut, toiletries, and get back out here in formation!" Most of us double timed it in there, got our head shaved, got our toiletries, and got back out. Of course there were a couple of guys that came out with a standard haircut, which did not impress the drill sergeant who promptly called them pretty boys and sent them back in to get it shaved off!

Some other memorable moments were the first time we received a pass, the "unlocked locker" fears, the mess hall routine and the "sticky bun" matter, mail call, and my mattress turn in.

We received our first pass after the first few weeks of basic training known as "total control." It's called total control because the drill sergeants demonstrate they have total control over you by breaking you down and maintaining total control of your every movement. After they were satisfied that they had us scared to breathe, they let us go on pass for a few hours. We were only allowed to go a couple of blocks away from our barracks but it was freedom!

A bunch of us went over to the Davis Club, which was a huge building especially made to accommodate a large number of recruits at one time for drinking and socializing while on pass. I had two beers. I wanted more but knew better. The two hit me pretty hard as it was. Watching my peers it's amazing how many beers a guy can put away in a few hours on pass. Over doing it on pass was obviously expected by our drill sergeants and at the end of our pass they mustered us all out in front of the barracks and walked the ranks looking for anyone intoxicated. When they found one, they had them get out on the grass and had them doing push-ups, running in place, drop and rolling, and a wide variety of sobering exercises. They usually were not satisfied with your sobriety until you vomited all you had consumed out onto the grass. Lesson learned; don't drink too much while on pass!

The fear of leaving your locker unlocked was totally ingrained within a day or two of arriving at our new third story home. We were instructed to never, ever leave our lockers unlocked. After the second day we came marching down the maze of road sized concrete paths through endless barracks right up to the concrete pad in front of our barracks. As we did so there was a pile of someone's belongings; clothes, gear, and personal items strewn all over the concrete pad. We marched right through it as if it was not even there. Some poor guy's stuff had been thrown out the third story barracks window onto the ground below.

The drill sergeant stated that the owner of this gear had better get it picked up and fast! So we broke formation and ran upstairs fearing for the worst. Luckily it was not my gear. However this incident initiated my bad habit of checking and rechecking my locker about 20 times before I could turn my back and leave it! I unfortunately still have that habit to this day! It worked with the other guys as well because it was very rare that anyone's stuff was lying out on the concrete when we returned.

Eating meals at the mess hall was the highlight of the day because we basically got a chance to eat. I mean you got to eat at breakfast, lunch, and dinner and that was it. There is no snacking and this was the only time you came into contact with food. The routine was simple and as usual with the Army there were no wasted minutes or steps.

The process started with us marching down to the mess hall singing our cadence. SGT Abraham was an excellent cadence caller and my favorite. A good cadence caller picked just the right peppy tune to keep us in step and lift our spirits. It instilled a lot of pride in us when we had the tune down and managed to stay in step. Some of my favorites were, "nine to the front and six to the rear, that's the way we do it here," which told us how far our arms should move forward and backwards when marching. And, "ain't no use in looking down, ain't no discharge on the ground," which told us to march with our heads up high.

Once we arrived at the mess hall we would form two rows and have to go through a set of monkey bars about 20feet long and 10feet high. When you cleared the monkey bars you had to do 10 push-ups and 10 sit-ups followed by getting in line to enter the mess hall. If for some reason you fell from the monkey bars you got back in line to go through them again. Once in the mess hall your meal became a timed event. There was no choice in the matter, just take what was piled on your tray and get to a table as fast as you could and eat. Of course it was milk, water, or juice for a beverage. That's not to say there were no soda machines. There were, but only for the drill sergeants. When the last man entered the mess hall the first man was to be heading out the door. The drill sergeants had a keen eye for how long you had been in there and you always had just enough time to get your food down before the cattle prod of the drill sergeants eye had you up and moving.

On one occasion after leaving the mess hall we came marching up to the barracks and we did our usual facing movement towards the barracks. Our drill sergeant stated that he knew someone had taken a sticky bun from the mess hall and they were going to have an inspection to see who had it. All of a sudden a sticky bun appeared from nowhere on the ground, in the middle of the formation.

Everyone wanted away from that sticky bun as if it were a live grenade! But of course we were at the position of attention and could not move. The drill sergeants were not happy with this total disrespect for their authority. It was a long evening out there on the concrete pad getting drilled for someone taking that sticky bun. They wanted the sticky bun thief to come forward. But, the thief never came forward that I can remember. And no one was going to tell on him. Because the infraction worse than getting caught with a sticky bun would have been snitching someone out for having the sticky bun!

Punishment always trickled down our recruit chain of command; from our company commander to the platoon leaders to the section leaders and so on. I was in no leadership position while in boot camp and maintained a very low profile in the back row of our formation. The higher you were in the recruit chain of command the harsher the punishment was from the drill sergeants. It was obvious after day one that you didn't want a position of authority or any type of visibility in boot camp! These drill sergeants had no problem putting their hands on you. They would grab you, throw you around, and call you every profanity they could think of. They did not want any misunderstanding about who was in charge!

Ranked right up there with chow was mail call. Nothing boosts a soldier's morale like letters from home. During mail call we would be in formation on our beloved concrete pad. If you had mail the drill sergeant would call your name, you would have to break formation properly, run up, and get your letter. For me this was done by taking a step backwards, coming to the position of attention, pivoting to my right, marching to the end of the formation, pivoting left, sprinting to the drill sergeant at the head of the formation, stopping in front of him at the position of attention and stating, "Private Semler reporting for mail."

Nothing is free in boot camp and to receive your mail you had to pay for it with 10 push-ups. No need for the drill sergeant to wonder if you did all ten because you had to scream, "one drill sergeant, two drill sergeant," and so on at the top of your lungs while making your payment. And you didn't want to get a package! You had to open it up there in front of the drill sergeant so he could inspect it for contraband. And if you had contraband you just lost it and gained push-ups!

Well, one day SSG Strickland was holding mail call and called "Semler." It was my first letter and I came running up to get it. SSG Strickland stopped me before I dropped to pay for it in push-ups. With his smoke-glazed glasses that obscured his eyes he said, "Semler, I don't remember you, have you been hiding from me?" I said, "No drill sergeant, I have been here in the back row since the beginning." SSG Strickland said, "Semler you have been hiding from me, so give me 20." I snapped off with a loud, "Yes drill sergeant" and commenced my push-ups as my letter was tossed on the ground for me to collect when payment was made in full.

Two weeks before the end of basic training, over the Labor Day weekend of the 4th through the 6th of September, the drill sergeants solicited for 40 volunteers who still had money left over from our initial advance of $90.00 when we entered boot camp. I was a little hesitant to volunteer because I was warned by my dad to never volunteer for anything in the Army. Up to this point I had followed this rule, but for some reason decided to give in since I had plenty of my initial advancement of pay. Turns out it was a great move because they took us on a two-day pass to the Lake of the Ozarks state park. We loaded up on buses and made the hour drive to a beautiful retreat area that we had all to ourselves. Even though we were under the watchful eyes of our drill sergeant it was a really relaxing weekend in which we stayed in log cabins and water skied on the Ozark Lake.

The break was just what I needed to get me ready for the jam packed final two weeks of basic training. I had to pass the basic training test, confidence course, road march, and last but not least our final three days in the field known as "Bivouac."

The final basic training test was a series of stations consisting of first aid, general orders, saluting, addressing an officer, weapons, and so on. At each station you would be tested and had to pass that station in order to proceed. For example in the case of the general orders station I had to enter and state my general orders, in the case of the weapons station I had to tear apart the M16 rifle and reassemble it in a certain amount of time. Of the 190 left in the company only 50 passed it the first time, me being one of them. There was one more chance and all but four passed. The four failures were reverted back to another company.

The confidence course was a series of huge wooden obstacles that had to be overcome one by one. Some were small and others huge structures that got harder and harder as you went on. As you climbed up and down these barriers you would progressively get worn out, making the next one even that much harder. Some of these were low to the ground but others towered 30 feet in the air and you had to have confidence in yourself to get through it.

You're always told to never leave a comrade behind, and that seemed to be the point of the road march. We loaded up with all of our equipment in our rucksacks along with our helmet, gas mask, and weapon for the 20 or so mile march. It was fast paced, almost like run walking, which caught a lot of us off guard. As we went along in two columns spread out along the road, it wasn't long before there were injuries such as pulled muscles. These guys were loaded up into the medical vehicles that trailed the march. Those guys who were simply fatigued started to fall behind and were quickly picked off by the drill sergeants who were stalking behind the formation like a pack of malevolent wolves.

As guys started to fall back, we started to take some of their gear off of them to make it easier for them to keep up. No one wanted to fall back and into the jaws of the drill sergeants. That would assure being reverted. Toward the end of the march we were more of a collection of guys carrying and helping each other along rather than a structured formation on a road march. Although there were losses we made it pretty much as a group. That appeared to be the goal as the drill sergeants seemed content.

Bivouac was the last event in boot camp. It was three days out in the woods pretending like we were at war. The weather was getting pretty mild in late September so being outside wasn't so bad. Our days were spent pitching tents and pretending we were hiding in the woods from the enemy. Our nights were spent standing guard and protecting our weapons from being taken by a drill sergeant. It was drilled into us that "you will always have control over your weapon!" If you were to lose it you were done. And the drill sergeants were always on the prowl for an unsecure weapon.

One night there was a ruckus and it turns out one of the drill sergeants had tried to sneak into one of the two-man tents and take a weapon from a sleeping recruit. The recruit woke up and kicked the drill sergeant in the face! Nothing was done over the incident, just a scared recruit and an embarrassed drill sergeant!

On Friday the 17th of September we finished boot camp and would start advanced individual training (AIT) on Monday after a pass over the weekend. I spent those days on pass lying around watching TV and drinking beer in a Rolla, Missouri motel room with four of my buddies. Rolla was about 40 minutes away and the small and dated motel seemed like paradise away from the rigors of basic training.

Monday the 20th of September was our first day of AIT and I remember the day very vividly. We were all standing out in formation on the concrete pad in front of our barracks for the usual 15-20 minutes waiting for the drill sergeants to come out and direct us in our daily routine. The famous SSG Strickland came out and stood on the elevated landing that led up to his office, lit his trademark long cigarette, and said in his unique robotic drawl, "You are no longer in basic training, you are in AIT." He then turned and walked back inside.

Our routine stayed pretty much the same throughout our basic and AIT training, just the type of training changed. I really would have never known the difference if not for SSG Strickland's proclamation. Instead of non-stop training on shooting, marching, and basic soldiering, we moved on to bridge building, knot tying, explosives, and land mines!

Learning how to tie knots in AIT

As we neared graduation from AIT some things like going to the PX were lightened up and we were allowed to go by ourselves instead of marching as a company or platoon. I really didn't like this and preferred transiting with my company and drill sergeant. If we passed a drill sergeant or an officer as a company, the drill sergeant leading us would handle all the formalities like saluting. When out on my own I had to handle the formality and that scared me, especially if I ran into an officer! Would I salute correctly and at the correct time or get my ass chewed. What if I ran into another drill sergeant! Would I be able to stop fast enough and come to the position of parade rest and let him pass?

It was like running another gauntlet whenever I had to go someplace. It didn't take long for my fear to materialize. I was standing outside of the big main PX with a friend and an officer walked out toward us. I got scared and turned away like I had not seen him. It must have been pretty obvious because he walked up to me and chewed my ass for turning my back and not saluting or addressing him!

All of us in boot camp and AIT were in the military occupational specialty (MOS) 12 series and had to learn the basics of that series. After graduation about 90% of the company would go on to be MOS 12Bs which specialize in handling the explosives and land mine duties. I was a MOS 12C and would go on to specialize in building combat bridges. There were actually two guys in my company who were also MOS 12Cs and would transfer on to Korea with me, Mike Guertin and Terry Baer.

On the 28th of October we had our graduation ceremony and officially completed AIT. I was now a combat bridge crewman MOS 12C, making $541.40 a month, and a private in the United States Army. All I had to do now was out-process and await my travel orders. Part of out-processing was turning in my non-personal gear that was assigned to me such as my tent half, rucksack, canteen, helmet, locker, mattress and other things I had no memory of ever having signed for. I guess on the first day I arrived I had signed for my mattress and locker. Now if you remember how I detailed the first day of boot camp you will understand I would have signed anything for any reason.

Well the drill sergeant came to inspect my mattress and locker to make sure it was in the same condition in which I had received it. He flipped my mattress over and there was a stain on it about the size of a small pizza. It looked like someone had either soiled it or spilt metal cleaner on it. The drill sergeant in an annoyed tone of voice asked something to the effect of, "How did this get here Semler?" I'm thinking; how the heck do I know, I didn't put it there! Of course I don't even remember signing for a mattress in the fog of the first day and I couldn't see myself having any reason or desire to flip it over to inspect it. The drill sergeant was not happy and told me I needed to carry that mattress down to the supply room, which was about a mile away, and show them the mattress.

So I cart this twin-sized mattress all the way down to the supply room and explained to the supply clerk that the drill sergeant had sent me down to show them the mattress. They frankly told me to get my ass and my mattress out of their supply room! So I carted that mattress all the way back up to the barracks and up three flights of stairs to my awaiting drill sergeant, who proclaimed that I had just bought a mattress! I never did see it come out of my pay so I'm not sure how I ever paid for it except in embarrassment carrying it around the base.

After out-processing and receiving my travel orders I boarded a Greyhound bus and departed Fort Leonard Wood on the 3rd of November. After taking 15 days of leave at home in Pennsylvania I departed for Korea on the 17th of November 1982.

CAMP PELHAM KOREA

1st PLATOON, E COMPANY, 2ND ENGINEER BATTALION,

2nd INFANTRY DIVISION

18 November 1982 – 18 November 1983

I arrived in Osan, Korea on the 18th of November 1982 after a long 18 hour commercial flight from Pittsburgh, Pennsylvania. The flight made stops in St. Louis, Los Angeles, and Tokyo, Japan for refueling. The sight of snowcapped Mt. Fuji as we circled for our landing in Japan is still vivid to this day. After arriving in Korea I was taken to the 2nd Infantry Division in-processing center at Camp Casey in the city of Tongduchon.

The processing center was known as the "Turtle Farm." They called it that because the in-processing and out-processing buildings were right next door to each other and it took your year-long tour to get from one building to the other. Hence, you were referred to as a "turtle." This nickname would stick with you for about the next six months where ever you went in country. It was also slang for doing something stupid. The phrase, "You dumb fucking turtle," was a commonly used good example. After your first six months you morphed from a "turtle" to a "short timer," known as just plain being "short." Unlike "turtle," guys were very proud of this designation and would walk around holding up their thumb and index finger almost touching saying, "short!"

31

The Turtle Farm was a relaxing place in itself and I don't remember going off-base, or if I was even allowed to venture off into the economy. We did spend our free time going to the bowling alley on base and that's where I first encountered human pin setters. As you rolled your ball down the alley there were these young Korean kids who sat up above the pins out of sight. After your ball hit the pins, these kids would hop down and reset your pins and roll the ball back up the alley to you. At the end of bowling we would throw money down the alley as their tip.

Most of our day was spent in-processing, which entailed lectures on the country, shots, and everything else needed for our new unit before we were shipped out. During one of these lectures they discussed the two Army divisions stationed in Korea, the 2nd Infantry Division and the 8th Army. I was so amazed at how cool the 2nd Infantry patch looked over the plain 8th Army patch. I wasn't really sure where I was at and hoped I was heading to the 2nd Infantry Division, because they had a better looking patch. An obvious priority of an 18 year old! As luck would have it, and since I was already at the 2nd Infantry Division in-processing center, that's where I was headed!

The departure day arrived and I loaded up into a two and half ton truck, known as a "duce-and-a-half" with a bunch of other turtles. The back of the truck had a long wooden bench seat on each side with a canvas cover. This was in December and there was no heat in the back so we were freezing. The truck, loaded up with turtles and our belongings, headed out the gate of Camp Casey on its way to various destinations within the 2nd Infantry division's area of operation.

The 2nd Infantry Division operated in the western corridor of South Korea around the Demilitarized Zone (DMZ). The DMZ is what separates South and North Korea and is a heavily fortified area. The DMZ cuts from one side of the country to the other. The United States 2nd Infantry Division guards the western half of the DMZ and the South Korean Army covers the eastern section. The section of the DMZ guarded by the 2nd Infantry Division is considered the most strategic. This is because of the location of Seoul, which is the capital of South Korea. The 2nd Infantry Division acts as a buffer between North Korea and strategically important Seoul.

This was a combat infantry division and no women were assigned to the units up on the DMZ. The area was also known as a hardship tour and you were not authorized to bring any family members. Some of the guys, mostly NCO's and officers, who were married to Koreans, had their wives and families meet them and settled near the camp. There was no family support network, so if you brought a spouse and family you were on your own finding a place for them to live.

View of the DMZ and North Korean guard post

Since the cease fire in 1953, 29 years prior to my arrival, there have been numerous incidents and deaths of United States and Korean soldiers who patrol this area. The DMZ, when I arrived, was pretty much where it was when the cease fire was established in 1953. This area is also known as the 38th parallel because of the DMZ's proximity to it. Toward the end of the war, when both sides seemed to be in a stalemate around the 38th parallel, some of the fiercest fighting occurred at places such as Pork Chop Hill, Bloody Ridge, Old Baldy, The Punchbowl, Heart Break Ridge, and

Outpost Harry. The area Camp Pelham occupied had been held by North Korean and Chinese forces several times as the war waged back and forth. The battles previously mentioned straddled the current DMZ and some occurred on the South side and some on the North side.

The 2nd Infantry Division had about 20 camps strewn out amongst the countryside north of Seoul up to the DMZ. These little camps had two or more combat company's assigned to them. It was my understanding that where ever a company was dug in during the cease fire was where they pretty much remained. I was headed to a place five miles from the DMZ by the name of Camp Pelham. Camp Pelham was about a mile and a half east of a major town named Munsan in a little town called Sunyu Ri. The Korean spelling was Seonyuri but for some reason it was spelled Sunyu Ri by U.S. forces. I would soon find out my movement in this area would be regulated by passes and curfews, and I would be held to rationing protocols.

As the deuce-and-a-half rumbled out of Camp Casey we turtles were huddled in the back trying to keep warm from the freezing temperatures outside. Every now and then we would pull back the tarp covering the back and see where we were. The countryside was made up of semi paved roads, dirt roads and small shacks. The little towns we passed were just a grouping of more dirt roads and shacks.

As we rumbled on we lost more and more guys as the driver made stops at various outposts on the way to Camp Pelham. It began to get dark and a peek out the back flap revealed total darkness and I thought to myself, where in the heck am I going? Finally, at the very end of his route, our driver pulled into Camp Pelham and dropped me off along with the only other passenger still on the truck, at what would be our new home for the next year.

The Camp was named in honor of John C. Pelham, a young Confederate artillery officer who served under J.E.B. Stuart during the Civil War. He was very popular and known as the "Gallant" Pelham for his bravery.

Unfortunately, he was mortally wounded at Kelly's Ford, Virginia in 1863, dying the next day at the age of 24.

Camp Pelham Korea 1983

The camp was situated in the middle of a huge rice patty with a bridge connecting it to the little road that ran through the little village of Sunyu Ri. There wasn't a lot to Sunyu Ri, just a lot of low level structures. Vehicles were limited in this farming community and most of the time when you saw a car it was a taxi. The locals all drove a sort of rototiller on two wheels that were connected to a cart. The man would drive and the family would be in the cart.

Downtown Sonyu Ri with the typical rototiller vehicle

Sunyu Ri was a very friendly town and community. I never felt fearful of the civilian population there and they always seemed to be appreciative of our presence. We provided an economy for them with jobs at the camp and patronage of the village bars. And any time we could offer humanitarian assistance, we did.

Like on the 21st of August 1983 when a local village boy was hunting the poisonous Salmosa viper valued for its health and medicinal value. The boy was hoping to cash in on the 30,000 won, $50.00 USD, the snake would bring. He unfortunately was bitten on his hand. Because the camp was the closest medical facility he was taken there for treatment. When he arrived the U.S. medical personnel realized he was in bad shape and he was medevac'd by helicopter to the 121st Evacuation Hospital at Yongsan, near Seoul. The fast action by the Camp Pelham aid station saved his hand and maybe his life.

The buildings on camp were very basic, single-story structures, spread out over the compound which held Echo Company, 2nd Engineers and Bravo Battery, 2/17th Field Artillery. I was assigned to the "River Rats"

36

of the 2nd Engineers which consisted of four officers and 117 enlisted men. The 2/17th field artillery had similar manning and maintained a fire base known as 4-Papa-1, which was the only active firebase in the Army at the time. Their mission was to shell invading North Korean forces with their 105mm and 155mm howitzers.

Living conditions were very basic. All the barracks were one story structures of simple wood and metal construction and heated by oil furnaces. We had open bay style living with metal bunk beds and metal stand up lockers, which acted as walls between each set of bunk beds. The showers, toilets and sinks were in an adjacent building known as the latrine. The latrine was always interesting to get to in cold weather, which seemed to be year round. The normal mode of operation was to get naked with your towel rapped around you, shower flip flops on, and bath kit in hand. You would brace yourself for the cold, then swing open the barracks door and bolt out the door as fast as you could to the latrine. Once there you would find a row of sinks, row of toilets, and a huge open bay shower. Check your modesty at the door!

South Korea has mandatory service which requires all males to serve in the military. Those that were highly educated and attending college were the most likely to become Korean Augmentation to the United States Army (KATUSAs). This was because only those that score very high on the Korean Service exam are assigned as KATUSAs. KATUSAs were assigned to U.S. military units to assist in translation and help in the day to day activities of getting around the country. Like every unit we had KATUSAs all throughout our company, with several assigned to our platoon and one to our squad. The KATUSAs worked alongside us, slept in our barracks, ate in the chow hall and shared in most all of the privileges we had, with the exception of PX goods. Although they did the exact same work as us a KATUSA sergeant only made 4,500 won, or $5.90 USD a month, compared to $760.80 USD a month made by a U.S. military sergeant!

The KATUSA assigned to my squad, and who I shared a bunk bed with, was Joo Myung Ho. He was a corporal for most of my tour and was promoted to sergeant before I left. Like all the KATUSAs he had a great sense of humor and always maintained the highest standards of Korean honor and tradition.

Corporal Joo Myung Hoo

Their English was good enough to get them by and our language barrier was the only thing that kept us from really long and detailed conversations. For the most part the KATUSAs didn't share a lot of personal information and kept to a more professional relationship. They didn't go into the village with us drinking or whoring around. They had their own little building on the camp where they met and drank. We would always say they reeked of kimchee and Jinro, a favorite food and liquor, when they came back at night from their hangout!

Those of a lower education, and usually of a lower standing in Korean society, are entered into the Republic of Korea (ROK) forces. The ROK service was very tough and there was no tolerance for disobedience.

I was riding in a bus from one camp to another when we got stuck behind a group of ROK soldiers road-marching down this road with all their gear on. One of the soldiers was trailing behind and he was followed by a senior soldier beating him in the back with his weapon every time the straggler tried to slow down. I don't mean beating him lightly; I mean he was beating him to hurt him. This went on for quite a while until they turned off the road. I can't image what happened when they were out of sight.

On another occasion while I was standing guard duty on a drill bit stuck in the ground (more on that later), I walked over to watch the neighboring ROK soldiers training with mortars. They were doing an exercise of putting the mortar together and disassembling it. Whenever they messed up they had to take a piece of this very heavy mortar and do pushups with it. After watching for a few minutes I had to walk away because I felt sorry for the poor guys.

The camp had primarily semi-paved roads and a few sidewalks. When it rained or snowed everything turned to mud. On the edge of the roads on both sides were these two-feet deep by two-foot wide concrete square ditches that lined the roads and were for catching water run-off. They were actually quite treacherous if you miss-stepped. We called them, "turtle traps" because the new guys always seemed to take a tumble into these at least once.

There was a small chapel, mess hall, club, barber shop, tailor shop, and associated military buildings such as armory, and orderly room which had the only TV around. The TV was black and white and only brought in the single Armed Forces Network (AFN) channel. The orderly room was the hub of all activity for the company. It's where we picked up and turned in our passes when leaving the base and hung around on the cherished sofas waiting for friends to get changed to go out on pass. It's also where we got paid every month and collected our mail. The company clerk and staff were located there and right next to the orderly room was the armory, where we checked in and out our weapon and gas mask.

On the camp there was also a photo shop ran by a Korean guy named "Snap." Snap would patrol the camp, village, and motor pool, taking pictures of anything, or anyone, he thought he could get money out of. Once a week you would swing by and see if Snap had any pictures of you and purchase them. He also made custom albums made of laminated wood and mother of pearl inlay. I bought one customized for me before I left.

There was an annex on the other end of the village named RC4, which housed the PX and several other U.S military units. Because of the extensive black marketing of American goods everything American made was rationed. I was issued a ration card and was limited on the amount of cigarettes, alcohol, and just about everything else I could purchase in a month. This was serious business to us because we all smoked like freight trains and drank like fish.

We had a nice club on the camp with Korean employees. It was mostly used as a backup watering hole if you couldn't go into the village because you couldn't get a pass or were on restriction. It wasn't that bad as clubs go and they always had something going on; they even had a pole dancing stripper as entertainment! It was also a gathering spot around the holidays as they always had a tree up and the place decorated for the season. Soon after I arrived the Dallas Cowboy Cheerleaders visited the club on a Christmas U.S.O tour. What a surprise that was. I was detailed to put up a huge, 32 feet long by 16 feet wide, tent known as a GP Medium to accommodate the over flow of food and drink for the event. As you can imagine they drew a huge crowd!

Our sole mission there at Camp Pelham was to build an escape bridge over the Imjin River, which was about a mile away. The purpose of the bridge was to evacuate civilian personnel on the other side of the river and military personnel in the Joint Security Area at Panmunjom, Camp Greaves, and Camp Liberty Bell.

Bridge constructed across the Imjin River

There were only two permanent bridges going over the Imjin River and they were both wired for demolition should an attack from the North occur. The United States Army controlled Freedom Bridge and the ROK Army controlled Liberty Bridge. Our sister engineering company at

41

Camp Edwards East, a few miles away, maintained the explosives on Freedom Bridge that would be used to blow it if needed. The ROK Army maintained the explosives at Liberty Bridge. With these two bridges blown up it would be up to us to erect our pontoon bridge and evacuate anyone left on the other side. The reason for destroying the fixed bridges was to prevent North Korea from crossing them, hence slowing their advance.

I had the opportunity to go over Freedom Bridge once. Our deuce-and-a-half driver had broken his arm and they needed a replacement driver to shuttle some guys from another unit over to the live fire range on the other side of the Injim River up around the DMZ. This sounded like something different so I volunteered.

The task was to take these guys over Freedom Bridge to the firing ranges, let them do their thing, and bring them back. Going over Freedom Bridge was exciting in itself. As I mentioned earlier, the bridge is kept wired for demolition 24/7 by our sister engineering company of MOS 12Bs. There is nothing like the feeling of driving over a bridge wired with tons of explosives!

We loaded up and headed out on a nice sunny day and made our way over Freedom Bridge and down along the DMZ. The first stop was at the M72 LAW rocket launcher range. These guys shot a bunch of these LAW rockets at a tank downrange while I took a cat nap in the truck. When they were about done they called me over and asked if I wanted to shoot one. I had never fired a real one before and said "Sure." It was a really cool experience to have that rocket shoot out of the shoulder fired launcher and wiz down range to the awaiting tank and explode. Nothing like the bottle rocket in boot camp!

The next stop was the M203 grenade launcher range. This is mounted to the underside of the M16 and fires a grenade. Now that my adrenaline was pumping from the LAW rocket launcher experience I asked if I could fire a few grenades down range. It was another great experience.

And these weren't filled with paint like boot camp; they were the real thing and exploded!

On our way back we got close to the DMZ and I could see the barbed wire fencing and observation towers going on for as far as the eye could see. This was it, the actual DMZ. It gave me an eerie feeling knowing North Korea was just on the other side and could take a shot at me or anyone else at any moment. It was the only time I ventured across the river and had no desire to go back.

Alert sirens were sounded whenever there was a threat of North Korean aggression. We were right up on the DMZ so alerts were always taken very seriously. When an alert was sounded you would hear the alert siren wailing away and we would go into battle mode. The whole area went into an immediate lockdown and we would scramble to get our weapon, gas mask, head to the motor pool, and roll out to the Imjin River. These could be anything from infiltrators to a plane flying into South Korean airspace.

This happened a lot, and each time we never knew what was going on. But the urgency to get to the motor pool and get rolling to our combat position, the Imjin River, was high. Every alert was an adrenaline rush and every unit was rushing to their combat position. The 2/17th called them "speed balls" and rushed to 4-Papa-1, our sister engineering company of 12Bs rushed to Freedom Bridge, and so on. There wasn't a shortage of adrenaline rushes in 1983.

On Friday the 25th of February we went on alert when there was a report of a North Korean fighter jet flying over the DMZ and headed for the capital of Seoul. It turns out it was a defection and not an attack. A 28 year old North Korean Air Force captain assigned to the 1st North Korean Combat Air Division flew his Chinese built MIG-19 fighter jet across the Yellow Sea. He said he took off at 10:30 am from Kaechon Air Base, which is about 160 miles north of Seoul. He was flying with another MIG-19 fighter on a rocket firing practice mission. A few minutes after taking off he said that he broke away from his partner and sped south at about 3,000 feet going 531 mph. As he raced south he was hailed via radio calling him to turn back. This caused him to dive to only a few hundred feet above the ground maintaining an air speed of around 575 mph. When he crossed the DMZ at around 10:45, near Haeju, he was 80 miles northwest of Seoul. He was then intercepted by ROK fighter jets who escorted him to the ground. This was only the 5th such defection since 1950.

He said he defected to warn South Korea that the North Korean Communists were pushing war preparations in a frenzied manner, claiming war was the only way to unify the divided Korea. He said things escalated as the South started preparing for the huge military exercise known as Team Spirit 1983.

On May 5th the highly unusual hijacking of a Chinese jetliner with 105 people on board placed us again on high alert. The civilian plane was hijacked by six Chinese defectors while on a flight inside China from Shenyang to Shanghai. The hijackers stormed the plane's cabin and shot and wounded two crewmembers and forced the captain to divert and fly over North Korean airspace in route to Taiwan. The pilot tried to trick the hijackers and land at Pyongyang, the capital of North Korea, but the hijackers caught on and derailed the attempt.

As they flew over the Korean DMZ the plane was intercepted by South Korean fighter jets and escorted to the U.S. military base at Camp Page Korea near the mountain resort city of Chuncheon. This would be about 40 miles west of Camp Pelham and 45 miles northeast of Seoul. The Chinese immediately demanded their plane and people be returned. This was a little problematic since there are no political ties between China and South Korea since they fought each other during the Korean War. The Chinese were currently supporting the North Koreans as they did during the war.

Taiwan was urging the South Korean government to retain the hijackers as they would be immediately executed if returned to China, which had happened to the last hijackers of a Chinese plane. The hijackers were

44

eventually tried in South Korea, receiving sentences ranging from four to six years and the 99 passengers and crew returned to China.

A North Korean Army captain, Captain Shin Chung Chol, walked across the DMZ near Yanggu about 60 miles northeast of Soul on the 7th of May sending us on alert. A South Korean Army patrol spotted him and he indicated he wanted to defect, and was led to a nearby guard post. The captain was from the 13th North Korean Army Division and said that life was hard in North Korea. Later on that year on the 1st of August Captain Shin was commissioned as a major in the South Korean Army.

On the 19th of June we were once again on alert. Just a mile away from Camp Pelham, in Munsan, three North Korean infiltrators were killed crossing the Imjin River which we bridged. They were carrying Russian made pistols, Czech made submachine guns, sophisticated silencer pistols, daggers, knapsacks, maps, radios, binoculars, 500,000 won ($680.00 USD), and South Korean Army uniforms. In a hail of rifle fire and grenades they were killed by ROK soldiers.

In August three incidents occurred within eight days of each other placing us on alert. The first involved the killing of four North Korean frogmen on August 5th. The North Koreans had disguised their 60 ton vessel to look like a Japanese fishing boat complete with a Japanese name. A South Korean patrol boat became suspicious and when it engaged the vessel a fire fight broke out and the North Korean vessel was sunk. It was thought that this vessel was a mother spy boat for other infiltrators because of the equipment on board and a secret gate type device on the stern to launch and recover smaller boats.

In a more dramatic defection on the 9th of August a Chinese Air Force colonel flying a MIG-21 crossed the Yellow Sea. He was seeking asylum in Taiwan which had a standing reward of 9,310 ounces of gold, worth about 3.85 million dollars at the time, for any Chinese pilot who defects with a MIG-21. It was originally thought that the plane was part of a North Korean invasion and South Korea issued the first air attack warning over Seoul since the cease fire with the North in 1953. It ordered all citizens of Seoul and surrounding areas to take shelter and turn off all electricity. Obviously this caused wide spread panic as all cars on the streets were stopped, sending passengers fleeing. It was only the third Chinese Air Force defection since 1953.

The pilot Colonel Sun Tien-ching later said that he defected because his father was tortured to death while in prison in 1968. He said he left behind his mother, wife, son and daughter. The pilot, who earned $60 a month in China, was given a promotion to colonel in the Taiwan Air Force and received his reward of 9,310 ounces of gold, making him an instant millionaire. South Korea ended up keeping the Mig-21 but Taiwan decided to give him the money for his heroic defection.

The third incident involved the killing of at least three North Korean boat crewmen on a spy boat on the 13th of August. Like on the 5th of August this vessel was disguised as a Japanese vessel and refused orders to heave to and began to flee at 40 knots from South Korean forces. Three intact bodies recovered, parts of bodies, communist weapons including machine guns, dive suits, and notebooks with pictures of the North Korean leader Kim IL Sung and his son.

On the 2nd of September Korean Air Lines (KAL) flight 007, a Boeing 747, carrying 265 passengers from New York to Seoul was missing and reportedly intercepted by Soviet fighters and forced to land. One of the 61 American passengers was United States Congressman Larry P. McDonald, a democrat from Georgia. He was heading to the 30th anniversary ceremony of the signing of a defense pact between South Korea and the United States. He had missed an earlier flight with several other congressmen and ended up on KAL 007. The next day the KAL plane was found to have been shot down by a Soviet SU-15 fighter jet as the 747 strayed over the Soviet island of Sakhalin, killing all 265 on board. It was the fifth worst aviation disaster in history.

South Korea did not have diplomatic relations with the Soviets. Since the plane was shot down near Japan, and there were numerous Japanese nationals on board, the Soviet ambassador to Japan was immediately called in to explain what happened. He explained that the plane had crashed and reports of it being shot down were propaganda. The Japanese however had overheard radio transmissions between two Soviet fighter jets that intercepted flight 007 and one had radioed to ground control that he had fired a missile, and the target was destroyed. It was determined that one of the Soviet fighter jets was trailing behind the KAL airliner. It fired one heat seeking Anab rocket, which brought the 747 down.

The Soviets would later admit that they mistook KAL 007 for an American RC-135 reconnaissance aircraft. The RC-135 was operating within 75 miles of the 747 when the passenger jet mistakenly crossed into Soviet airspace.

The whole world condemned the attack and was outraged. The unprovoked downing of flight 007 hit hard with us at Camp Pelham as we had all arrived in Korea via commercial planes. Possibly on KAL flight 007. It scared me because I was getting short and would be heading home in a few months via a commercial carrier.

This downing was eerily similar to KAL flight 707 a few years earlier. It was traveling from Paris to Seoul and carrying 110 passengers on April 20th 1978 when it was shot down by a Soviet Mig fighter jet. It luckily was able to crash land on a frozen lake in Murmansk, a port city in the USSR, killing only two passengers. The Soviets claimed the KAL jet had strayed over its airspace and was shot down after refusing to acknowledge the Mig fighter's demands to land.

With both KAL flight 007 and 707 the airliners had strayed off course and inadvertently were flying over very sensitive Soviet military installations. The Soviets made accusations that the planes were spying and this is thought to be the reason why they were shot down. South Korea did not have diplomatic relations with the Soviets and relied on other nations such as Japan and the United States to step in and to negotiate on their behalf.

On the 9th of October all of South Korea was placed on high alert when the President of South Korea, Chun Doo-hwan, narrowly escaped an assassination attempt while visiting Burma. The blast killed 21 people including 17 South Korean dignitaries while 48 people were wounded. Four of the 17 South Korean dignitaries killed were cabinet members. The only reason President Chun was unhurt was the fact that his motorcade was stuck in traffic and arrived five minutes late to the event. The three captured suspects were later identified as North Korean commandos sent to assassinate the South Korean President.

Leaflet showing North Korean assassins attacking
South Korean President Chun

I found the above leaflet around Camp Pelham, delivered by a North Korean balloon. On the right it says, "The ghost that follows you" and the words on the two North Korean assassins say "Anti-Chun Doo-hwan power." The scared lady and gentleman in the center are South Korean President Chun Doo-hwan and his wife.

The tension on the DMZ was very high after the assassination attempt and the North Koreans fired over 2,000 rounds from two of their guard posts on the 14th of October. The North had claimed that 10 South Korean soldiers crossed into the North firing 500 rounds. President Chun accused the North of plotting to invade the South.

Luckily no one was hurt in the one sided firefight. I know the guys up at outpost Ouellette and Collier, the two northern most American guard post on the DMZ, must have thought WWIII had started!

Every now and then we would wake up to find North Korean propaganda spread all over the ground at either the barracks or motor pool. The North Koreans would send balloons filled with the small leaflets over the DMZ into South Korea that would burst at some predetermined time in flight. The KATUSAs assigned to us would scurry around and scoop them all up and tell us not to look at them, of course that made us want to see them!

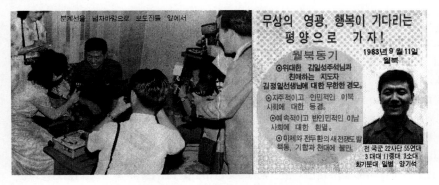

North Korean propaganda leaflet

This is a typical one that I found one morning down in the motor pool. It shows a South Korean ROK soldier who defected to the North on the 11th of September 1983. On the right it says, "The highest supreme honor, let's go to Pyongyang, where happiness is waiting!" In the center it reads "Motive for Defection: Boundless joy and admiration for the glorious President Kim Il-sung and for the beloved leader Kim Jong-il. He fantasized about the Socialist life to the North and became disillusioned with the anti-citizen ways of the South. He is against the Americans and

49

the war-mongering regime of Chun Doo-hwan, who actively seeks to restart a war."

I'm sure that's what they want us to think. And by the looks of their not-so-state-of-the-art camera's and recording equipment, even for 1983 standards, I'm sure things were not all that great in North Korea!

The defection that was talked about the most in my circle was not from the North, but from the South, and involved an American. PFC Joseph T. White, with the 2nd Infantry Division, shot the gate door padlock off with his M-16 rifle at guard post Ouellette in the Joint Security Area of the DMZ on the 28th of August 1982. Although he made it into North Korea, he left behind a duffle bag with a camera containing undeveloped sensitive film of the bunker and tower system of his post and information about American radar sites in the area.

He was apparently distraught about not being granted leave to visit his sick South Korean girlfriend who was hospitalized in South Korea. The 21 year old was reported to have brushed up on his Korean language skills before defecting. His defection was the first by an American in 17 years and the fifth since the Korean War fighting stopped in 1953. In 1985 his parents received a letter from a North Korean friend of PFC White's stating that he had drowned in August of that year in the Ch'ongch'on River in North Korea. The requested body was never returned to White's parents and was reported to never have been recovered from the river.

There was also the stress of being up on the DMZ that just drove guys nuts. In June of 1983 Private Mark A. Burford, who was assigned a few miles away at Camp Greaves, checked out his M-16 rifle along with ammunition and took several hostages. Like PFC White it seems he was distraught about not being able to see his South Korean girlfriend. After an eight hour standoff he surrendered to authorities at the camp. PVT Burford had only been in country six months, since the 6th of December 1982. Heck he was probably only a week behind me at the Turtle Farm!

Our daily routine while we were at the camp was up at 0500 for physical training (PT) and a two mile or so run out into the village and surrounding countryside. This was always a colorful event. The camp was too small to run in so we would always run out the gate, through the town, and into the countryside. We didn't wear our military uniforms but instead we wore tailored PT outfits made by the local Korean tailor. Everyone had their own style and color. Think 80's disco!

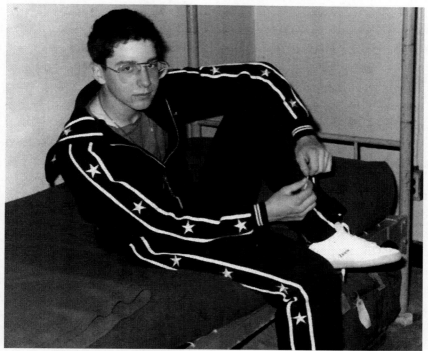

Getting ready for PT in my custom made PT outfit!

And when you run in the Army you sing cadence like in boot camp to keep everyone in step. We sang your typical military authorized cadence like, "Airborne Ranger" which was one of my favorites. It went sort of like this:

C-130 rolling down the strip,
Airborne Ranger going to take a little trip.

Hop up, buckle up, shuffle to the door,
jump right out on the count of four.

If my chute don't open wide,
I have another one by my side.

If that one don't open either,
I have a date with ole Saint Peter.

If I die in a combat zone,
box me up and ship me home!

Along with a nice tune like that we mixed in local raunchy cadences
about the prostitutes and bars that were just vulgar. I guess it really didn't
matter because the locals didn't understand English.

When I first arrived at Camp Pelham I was put in a break-in PT detail.
We would run in the evenings so that we would build up our running
endurance and be able to hang with the company's longer runs in the
morning. The running wasn't bad but what really worried me a bit was
running out along the country roads in a small group of four or five. I
was new to Korea and it just seemed odd to be running along these dirt
roads between these huge hills so close to the DMZ. Especially in neon
sweat suits!

Once back from a run the first thing I did was smoke a cigarette. It
sounds weird but that smoke after a long run tasted so good and gave me
a slight burning sensation that was actually pleasant. After our morning
PT run and cigarette it was a shower, breakfast, and then formation down
at the motor pool for work.

Meals at the mess hall were about our only daily interaction with the
2/17th field artillery. We shared a common mess hall and that was about
the only time you wanted to engage them. The threat was from North

Korea but the 2nd engineer's nemesis' was the 2/17th. I'll get more into that later.

Then it was down to the motor pool, which was just outside the camp to the right at a little annex. Once there we would inspect our trucks, start them up, and then sit in them while smoking and telling stories about back home. Guys that didn't have a truck assigned to them would hang out with someone that did. At some point the snack truck from RC4 would come rolling through and we would all pile out of our trucks and get a snack. After our snack we performed maintenance on our truck and bridge equipment.

When I was assigned my own truck, a few months after arriving, it didn't run and it didn't have a roof on the cab. It was truck number E-109 and everyone referred to it as "109 dead on line." I referred to it as "109 best on line," sort of as a joke.

My truck, E-109 "Best on Line"

After a few weeks E-109 finally made it into the motor pool garage to be worked on; and it spent a lot of time in the motor pool garage getting worked on! The first time it made it out of the garage it only made it a few feet. The mechanics had parked it just outside the garage facing the huge 30 feet high by 20 feet wide garage doors.

That night the alert siren went off. Now when the alert siren went off there were always a few guys detailed to run to the motor pool and start all the vehicles while the rest of us drew our equipment. One of the guys on this detail was a great guy from Boston named John Sodek. Sodek had never driven before he came to Korea. He grew up in the city of Boston and said he never needed a car or had the desire to drive.

Of course when he got to Korea the Army decided to teach him to drive. One of his first lessons was on the main road, outside the motor pool, which was mostly dirt and lined with rice patties. He was driving our typical five ton bridge truck with a huge bridge bay section on the back. The bridge bay had these huge round prongs which stuck out on either side of the bridge section and were used to lock the bridge sections together. Sodek was driving along and a bus was coming down this narrow dirt road right at him. He didn't get over far enough for the bus to clear those metal prongs and he opened up the side of that bus like a can opener! Luckily no one got hurt. He finally did get the hang of driving and turned out to be good driver. But when E-109 was pulled out of the garage and the alert siren went off, Sodek was still in the early stages of learning how to drive.

So Sodek hopped into my truck and in a rush turned the ignition key to start it. The truck was still in gear and it lunged forward and slammed into the huge garage door. Startled, he just sat there with a death grip on the steering wheel as the truck continued to lunge forward and into the garage door. After several lunges E-109 finally conked out and came to rest against the garage door, as a slow stream of antifreeze drained onto the motor pool ground. Needless to say it was back into the garage for E-109! That wouldn't be the last time it was laid up.

We had been doing day and night bridge building training on the Injim River. It had been raining for the past several days and everything was muddy and the rice paddies were full of water. My truck held a bridge bay section and after the bridge bay was dropped into the water it was parked up along the dirt road lined by rice patties. I was working on the actual bridge construction so the evolution of driving and parking my truck was done by someone else. We worked all day and late into the night in the cold fall rain. Late into the night we started to wrap things up and head back to camp. I walked up the road through the rock road block, known as a tank trap, to my parked truck.

Tank traps are these huge areas cut out of the river bank and lined with rocks and explosives. If the North were ever to attack, these rock formations would be detonated and the road way would be covered in the falling rocks.

Tank trap in the background while assembling a bridge on the Injim River

After reaching my truck late that evening with my buddy Tim Bailey we fell asleep awaiting the order to move out. At some point after falling asleep someone came by and banged on the truck door and yelled to get ready, we were moving out. I opened my eyes and saw the small slits of light coming from the blackout lights of the company commander's jeep as it pulled up to the truck in front of me. At night we operated in black-out conditions and all you could see of the truck in front of you was the small sliver of light coming from its blackout lighting. I started the truck and when I saw the truck in front of me pull away onto the road I put my truck in gear and started to move forward.

After only going several feet the truck started to lean over toward the passenger side and slipped off the road and down into a rice patty. I was pretty confused about what had just happened along with my now wide awake passenger, Tim. We quickly got our wits about us, climbed out the driver's side window, and onto the road. We could then see, through the pouring rain, that the truck was indeed lying on its side in a rice patty. One of the sergeants bringing up the rear told us to sit tight until morning and they would send someone back to get us. Tim and I got back in the truck and slept until morning.

When morning came we awoke to the sound of this huge M88 wrecker tank and a military tow truck coming down the muddy road. The M88 was basically a M1 tank with the turret and gun removed and a towing crane in their place. The M88 with its huge treads maneuvered around in the mud with ease and just got a hold of us and yanked us right out of there. Once out we were towed back to the motor pool.

The next day I was hounded with heckles from my peers and SSG Garrett, my platoon sergeant, wasn't happy at all! After lecturing me on how pissed the farmer was that his rice patty was munched up by an M88 tank, he said he was presenting me with his first ever "dog bone" award. The "dog bone" was actually the piece that held the bridge bay section together so I don't know why he was giving it out as an idiot award. I think he just liked the name of it!

After our work day we would scamper back to our barracks and start to drink. We liked to "get our drunk on" before hitting the village where mama-san had the prices jacked up. It was common for us to get a case of beer and a bottle of liquor and polish them off before changing into our civilian clothes and heading into the village of Sunyu Ri. That was of course if you didn't have duty, were not restricted to camp, and you had a pass.

Passes were limited and they were only good until midnight. There was a curfew in effect up where we were and no one was allowed on the streets during curfew, military or civilian. The normal pass had a red stripe at one end and the overnight pass had a yellow stripe. You would go pick your pass up from the person on duty at the orderly room who had a list of people eligible to leave for that given day. When on pass we never strayed too far from the camp's main gate in the event of an alert.

As you went through the camp gate on pass you checked out the sign on which was posted the top five venereal disease (VD) clubs, and made a mental note to stay clear of them!

Top VD clubs in Sunyu Ri and the nearby towns

Outside of most military instillations no matter where you are in the world you'll find seedy bars and illegal activity. Korea was no different, only here prostitution was legal and accepted by the military and civilian community. And where there is prostitution there are sexually transmitted diseases.

Once out the camp gate and in the village there was no shortage of bars and whore houses. The larger bars, like the Paradise and Blue Angel, were considered neutral ground and open to anyone. They were loud and usually had a lot of scuffles between engineers and gun bunnies, our name for the 2/17th field artillery guys. Most of the smaller bars were claimed exclusively by us, the engineers, or the gun bunnies.

You didn't want to make a turtle mistake and walk into the wrong bar or you could get your ass kicked. These bars were operated by an older lady known as a mama-san and she usually had three or four girls working as prostitutes. Their job was to make money for mama-san and themselves.

The whole prostitution thing, out in the rural behind–the-times Korean countryside, seemed weird to me but the Koreans seemed to behave like it was all very normal.

There were a couple of things you learned real fast when in the village. First, don't flash your money around. As soon as mama-san or the prostitutes saw you had some they were on you like a bad smell on a hog. Second, don't waste all your money buying the prostitutes drinks. They hounded you to do it because they made money for mama-san. You paid top dollar for a drink for them but it was really just water. It was better to just fork over the $10.00 or $20.00 USD and have them for a short time (quickie) or long time (overnight). Third, never drink from an open bottle. Mama-san would always try and put an open bottle of beer on the bar for you. You never accepted it unless you see her open it, or better yet open it yourself. Mama-san was a money maker and she was famous for pouring left over beer into a bottle and serving it up as a new fresh bottle. Her odds of pulling this trick off increased as you got drunker. Mastering these things would hopefully move you out of dumb turtle status to just turtle.

Mama-san had no problem running a tab for her patrons and that usually kept a loyal group of guys in the bar all the time. At the end of each month we would get paid in cash in the unit's orderly room. I made an extra $8 a month in overseas pay and had $250.00 sent directly to a savings account, leaving me with about $280.00 a month for spending. That was enough to get me into plenty of trouble!

Once I had received my pay from the pay officer, mama-san, Snap, and a whole list of characters would be waiting right there in the orderly room to collect their debts. Mama-san would usually ask in broken English, "You see Smith?" or Jones or whoever. Usually my answer was, "He go to land of big PX" and mama-san knew that he had transferred back to the states and stiffed her.

The prostitutes were in all the bars and we got to know the ones in the bars we frequented pretty well. We spent most of our evenings drinking, shooting pool, and hanging out with them. They were our age and at the time filling a legal profession. They had to be documented and checked for health issues on a regular basis. Sexually transmitted diseases were an accepted consequence of hanging around prostitutes. We were young, full of testosterone, and felt that nothing was going to hurt us, even VD.

If you did contract VD or any other sexually transmitted disease it was something you couldn't ignore. The pain and discomfort was unbearable and you would have to see the medic. First, in order to see if it's VD the medic would do a procedure called "rodding". We all knew about rodding but it was something you never wanted done. It starts with the medic taking a six inch long metal rod with a cotton swab at the end and inserting it about three inches up into your penis to get a culture. Now if you think that hurts, wait until you take a leak later! Oh my! After having that done you get marched down to the village and you are required to point out the prostitute you were last with so she can get tested and quarantined. Let's just say you're not welcome back in that club after you dime out one of mama-san's girls, took her out of commission for a few weeks, and probably put her club on the top five VD board at the camp gate!

Oh, and when you are out-processing to go back to the states, you are "rodded" again just to make sure you're not taking anything home.

VD was a huge heath problem in Korea at the time and there were articles in the American servicemen's paper called the "Stars and Stripes" that said there were untreatable strains of the disease floating around the country. In an effort to come up with a drug to prevent VD the local clinic was soliciting volunteers to participate in an experiment to test a new VD vaccine. Some would get the real vaccine and others would just get a water solution. But you would not know what you received until after the study. The whole idea of the Army testing a drug on me was not appealing, and I opted out. A few of my friends did participate, got the real vaccine, and their feelings were mixed on the results. As far as I know the vaccine was not a success.

Speaking of the clinic, I was over there one day waiting out in the tiny waiting room with another guy who was from the 2/17th. He seemed nervous and was sweating and visibly shaking. I asked him casually how he was doing and he said, "Not to good, I accidently injected myself with atropine." During this time, and through most of my military career, we were in the cold war with Russia. And one of the biggest threats we prepared for was their use of nerve agents against us. The antidote we carried for nerve agent was atropine and 2-PAM-CL auto injector shots. If you felt you were exposed to nerve agent you would administer these shots, or injectors, into your thigh. You would use your thigh because the needles on these things were pretty long! Once you were done you would bend the needle and hook it through the collar of your shirt so if you passed out someone coming along would know how many shots you had given yourself, and wouldn't over dose you with more.

You didn't want to take one of these injections unless you had to. The side effects are just about as bad as nerve agent without killing you! You get nervous, anxious, confused, hallucinate, shake, and vomit; get the picture?

Anyway, this poor guy had somehow shot himself with one of these injections by mistake, horsing around or trying to get a buzz. Medical just had him sitting there while they watched him until the effects wore off.

After a while in country some guys would find themselves a Korean girlfriend and rent a room, known as a "hooch," in the village. These girls were usually prostitutes still working for mama-san or ex-prostitutes who had gone out on their own. Some of these relationships blossomed and it wasn't unusual for guys to get married to a local Korean.

The normalcy of having a relationship drove me to seek out a girlfriend. I ended up meeting a girl who was waiting for her previous GI boyfriend, who had transferred to the states. She was waiting for him to send for her and she would be moving to the states when he did. That worked for me.

She already had a hooch which was a typical one room simple structure that led into a courtyard surrounded by other hooches. The hooches all shared a common hole in the ground toilet that you squatted over and it stunk. There was no running water and all your washing and bathing was done down at the bath house. I never ventured down to the bath house, choosing to use the facilities on camp instead.

The hooch was heated by placing coal blocks in a heater outside known as an ondol, which heated the hooch floor. The older man who rented my girlfriend the hooch took care of that. I asked him what he wanted in payment for tending the ondol and he requested razors for shaving. So whenever I would see him I would give him a bunch of razors, and boy would that put a huge smile on his face!

My girlfriend didn't last long. Overnight passes were limited and I only got one every couple of days. The first time I had one I over slept my alarm and was late getting back on camp for morning muster. SSG Garrett placed me on a week's restriction and extra duty. In those days there was no paperwork for minor infractions, your platoon sergeant took care of you. Extra duty consisted of breaking down semi-truck tires in the motor pool after work. There was never a shortage of tires because SSG Garrett would have them stacked up for just this type of situation. It took hours to break them down using a sledge hammer and wedges.

The next time I had an overnight pass the same thing happened. I was late for muster because my alarm didn't go off. SSG Garrett gave me more of the same punishment. While I was breaking down tires SSG Garrett came down to see me. He was a rough and tough older sergeant who always seemed to be chewing tobacco, the type in the pouch that produces that big spit. I knew he was married to a Korean and this was his second or third tour over here. He was a good, fair man and gave me some fatherly advice; get rid of the girl! He told me, "You know that girl is playing you. She is messing with your alarm so you over-sleep and get restriction. She knows how the system works. With you on restriction she has the place to herself and does what she wants while you pay the rent."

Good advice from the old sergeant to a naive 19 year old. When I was off of restriction I went and got what little I had in the hooch and was done with that!

In early March we headed south for a huge war game known as Team Spirit. This was a joint exercise with the U.S. and ROK military and would be the largest joint exercise in the free world. It initially kicked off around the 1st of February and would last until the end of March, involving more than 191,000 Korean and American military personnel. It would involve every aspect of warfare to include the Navy's 7th fleet, two carrier battle groups, marine amphibious tasks force, Air Force Strategic Air Lift and Tactical commands, and several Army divisions to include the arrival of the 7th Infantry Division from California and the 25th Infantry Division from Hawaii.

Of course the exercise gets North Korea all worked up. They go on a proactive heightened state of tension and look at Team Spirit as an act of aggression. The North announced it would be in a semi-war state of alert for this year's event, the first time they had reacted so strongly in the eight year history of the exercise. Remember earlier when I mentioned the North Korean Mig-19 pilot who defected in February? He claimed he defected because the North Korean Communists were pushing war preparations in a frenzied manner, claiming war was the only way to unify the divided Korea. He said things escalated as the South started preparing for Team Spirit this year. The atmosphere was so tense at Camp Pelham I was actually happy to be deploying south for the war games and away from the DMZ.

I would be driving my truck to the operating area and my passenger on the trip would be Terry Bear who had been in boot camp with me. Terry was a happy-go-lucky guy who always had a cigarette in his mouth and would mumble when he talked. He was a good guy to make the trip with. We would be driving over eight hours south of Seoul to where the war games would take place. This would not be an easy drive with our huge equipment on the twisting old Korean roads which were used by outdated Korean farm equipment. On the way down one of our vehicles got into an accident with a Korean pedestrian and there was a fatality. The incident had us stopped for hours waiting to clear the matter up. It was sad that someone had to die. You knew it was bound to happen with our huge vehicles on the tight confined country roads. Thankfully the rest of the trip was smooth and punctuated only by several stops to camp overnight.

Once down in the Team Spirit operating area we became part of the blue forces that would be fighting the orange forces. We were identified by blue bands around our helmets and blue triangles on our vehicles. We initially dug into a huge sandy field and covered all of our gear with camouflaged netting in preparation for the upcoming battle.

This was March and wouldn't you know it, it snowed! It was actually forecasted to be a colder than usual winter and if it wasn't snowing it was freezing rain. This was camping at its best with below freezing temperatures, outdoor shitters, tents, and canned food officially known as Meal Combat Individual (MCI), known to us as "C" rations. There were no showers and you washed and shaved out of your helmet. Our sleeping quarters were the usual huge green GP medium tent.

We would all pile into that tent which was heated by a gas stove and hunker down for the night. Our biggest enemy was the cold. Our second concern was theft. Out here in the scrub you always kept your gear away from the tent edge because there may be sticky fingered locals about known as "slicky boys" looking for their opportunity to swipe our gear.

Our portable toilets were made of a wooden board with holes cut out of it which sat on 55 gallon drums cut in half. The only thing that kept you from being seen sitting there doing your business was the camouflage netting draped over the thing. Once a day, in the morning, someone would get detailed to burn the waste in the 55 gallon drums, never a good detail.

Even at this remote location the locals eventually found out where we were. They would drift in to see what we were up to and "ahjussi," a Korean older male, or mama-san, would be selling cooked noodles or soda out of his or her makeshift kitchen that they carried on their back. Even in the rural country side there are entrepreneurs!

The battle started out in the early morning hours around the 23rd of March with orange forces crossing the Hwachon River into blue force territory on a major offensive. The battle picked up from there as we waited in reserve until a river crossing was needed by our blue forces. While waiting we found a nice sized lake and commenced ferry, or what we called rafting, exercises to hone our skills. The lake was really different from our usual Imjin River site. The lake was bordered by stones, which were harder to drive on, and easier to get stuck in while backing up to the water to drop a bridge section or boat. The training kept us busy and we were eager to get the call to head to the front.

Dropping a bridge bay section during Team Spirit 1983

After about a week we packed up and moved out to the battle front. The blue forces were on the move and counterattacking the orange forces. On the second day of the counterattack we were called up to build a bridge to facilitate a river crossing of the Han River, at Ipo near Ipo-ri, about 75 miles south of Seoul. The only noticeable landmark on the way was the OB beer factory along the way near Icheon.

When we made it to the Han River, about the 1st of April, a huge smoke screen was set to cover us from enemy forces. This was created by a unit with huge smoke generating machines that belched smoke at just the right concentration to allow us to do our work and yet remain invisible to enemy forces. Under the smoke screen we deployed our bridge sections and boats into the water and started ferrying elements of the spearhead attack force across the river. The ferry was made by connecting several sections of the floating ribbon bridge and securing one of our 27' boats to each side. The ferry, or raft, commander would then stand at the front of the ferry and direct the boats with hand signals to guide the ferry across the river.

Once we had the advance force across and we had secured the beachhead and buffer zone, we commenced to build a full crossing bridge from one side of the Han River to the other. This was in place long enough to cross major tank and armored personnel carrier (APC) elements of the blue force onward to engage the orange forces. It was pretty cool once the blue forces were rolling across because a trio of B-52 bombers from the Strategic Air Command came roaring overhead in a simulated bombing support run of our advancing forces. What a sight that was.

When the bridge was no longer needed we packed it up and commenced following the blue force column in case they needed to cross another river. We were getting into April and the weather was turning to cold rain and mud. The mud roads were getting especially bad after following the tracked tanks and APCs that made a mess of everything. Soon after packing the bridge up our long convoy had come to a halt along a dirt road near a dried river bed. As we sat there waiting to move out I could hear this low thumping noise in the distance. The noise kept getting louder and louder until I could see about 20 or 30 Huey helicopters coming straight for us. I was sitting there in my truck with a front row seat to this spectacle thinking, wow this is pretty cool, never thinking it could be the orange forces attacking us!

View from my truck window of the blue team air assault landing in the wrong LZ. You can see our command "gama-goat" vehicle giving directions.

The helicopters came in fast and low and landed in the river bed next to our line of parked trucks. They came in to land in waves of about five and as soon as the helicopters hit the ground, soldiers loaded down with gear piled out of them and started setting up defensive positions along the dried river bed. The helicopters relieved of their cargo took off to allow the next wave to come swooping in. After the first wave hit the ground I noticed our commanding officer's vehicle, an ugly half jeep and half trailer known as a "gama-goat", pulling down to what appeared to be the helicopter air assault force leader. There was some discussion and a few minutes later the empty helicopters came swooping back down to pick up their cargo of troops. It later filtered down the grapevine that the air assault guys in the helicopters were blue forces. They had landed in the wrong landing zone (LZ) and needed to be a few miles ahead attacking orange forces.

At one point toward the end of the war games my platoon had the unusual opportunity of harassing the orange force. I guess, since we had finished our bridge duties and had nothing really left to do, we seemed like a logical choice. We were sent up toward the orange teams lines for a few days and pitched our GP medium tent. It was cold out and the ground was frozen solid. Unlike our strict code of military dress, such as helmet on at all times and uniforms worn per regulations, we would be dressed on this mission anyway we wanted. Since all we really had was our uniforms the only thing we really changed was swapping out our helmet for a black ski mask cap. It was an unbelievable relief not to have that damn helmet on for a few days!

While conducting this operation we would be using a shooting system that sent a laser beam out the barrel of your weapon every time you fired a blank shell. The system was fairly new and known as Multiple Integrated Laser Engagement System (MILES). Everyone had vests on that had sensors on the front and back. If you were hit by the laser shot from someone's weapon your vest emitted a constant beeping that sound like a smoke alarm, indicating you had been shot. If it only beeped once it meant someone had taken a shot at you and it was a near miss. The only way to stop the constant beeping was to take the key out of the laser box on your weapon and put it in the box on your vest. Doing this disabled you from firing your weapon and took you out of the game.

To me, the most memorable event of the operation had us going out at night to ambush an orange force patrol. We made our way up a hillside overlooking a road that was about 25 yards away. We had a perfect view of the road below us and we set up about five yards apart from each other. We would wait until we had the bulk of the patrol right between us before opening up on them. Shortly after we set up the orange patrol began to slowly and quietly come walking down the road in a typical staggered formation of two lines. We waited as planned until the bulk of them were right in front of us and we opened up with M16 fire. All you could hear was the pop-pop of the M16s and the beeping of laser gear going off! When we stopped firing and turned to get out of there the sweet sound of about 20 lasers beeping let us know we had accomplished our mission. We headed back to our GP medium, slipping and sliding all the way down the frozen road, laughing and telling tales reliving the skirmish!

As the war games wound down we started to free-lance and the company drifted off into the countryside to do separate bridge training. We had come to this river lined with rocks and it was decided that this would be a good area to try and do some ferry training. A scout jeep was sent out to see how fast the river flowed, how deep it was, and the best possible place to cross. After sitting around waiting for a bit I walked down to the river's edge and asked a guy standing there where the scout jeep was. He pointed out to a sand bar in the middle of the river with a yellow flashing light just below the water and said nonchalantly, "It's under that flashing yellow light." After that it was decided we would camp in the nearby field until they figured how to get the jeep out of the river.

As we set up camp a young Korean had come down from the nearby village and was talking to one of our KATUSAs. The young Korean was studying English and wanted to hone his skills. He told the KATUSA he wanted to invite one of the Americans up to his family's restaurant for dinner and to speak English. The KATUSA asked me if I was interested and I said yes. After clearing this with my sergeant I walked up into the village in my field gear with the young Korean. We arrived at his family's restaurant and had a seat at a large table with a traditional gas grill built into the middle of the table. The young Korean and I talked in English as his family joined us around the table for the family style Korean meal. As the propane gas grill heated up, food was placed on it and once done was picked off for consumption.

After about 30 minutes of sitting there I started to feel really dizzy and my vision started to blur. All I could think of was that these Koreans were trying to drug me and get my weapon or kidnap me! I started to get up and stumbled. I made it to the door as the young Korean and his family were yelling and getting excited. This just fueled my concern for my safety and I ran out the door and stumbled back to the camp in a daze. Once there I explained what had happen to the KATUSA. Soon after my arrival the younger Korean followed and he and the KATUSA discussed what had happened. It turns out that there was a gas leak on the stove and I was starting to be overcome by the gas fumes! I was embarrassed and apologized to the young Korean. The KATUSA affirmed my apology to the young Korean just in case something I said was lost in translation.

Team Spirit ended and we returned to Camp Pelham. A few weeks later we were standing in formation and the company commander presented us with "Team Spirit 83" key rings. That would be our reward for over a month in the mud, rain, snow, and freezing temperatures conducting war games.

Not long after we returned from Team Spirit I ran in my one and only half marathon, which was 13 miles. It was a huge event held on Friday the 27th of May and involved the whole battalion. The 2nd engineer battalion was headquartered out of Camp Red Cloud which was located in Uijongbu, about 20 miles south east of Camp Pelham. The battalion had just started this tradition the previous year and it involved the five subordinate companies consisting of the Stallions, Beasts, River Rats, Village Rats, and the Renegades. These companies were spread out over the DMZ area and this was the only time we ever got together as a battalion.

The half marathon, which finished at nearby Camp Casey in Tongduchon, was slow and painful. Because we ran in such a large group the pace was more like a fast walk than a run and I just couldn't get into a running groove. And of course it rained! The only upside was at the end of the run, there was a picnic complete with beer! Oh, and there was a commemorative t-shirt that read "CRC in 83." I had only been in Korea for six months and had been awarded a key ring and a t-shirt!

Soon after the half marathon our company's leading sergeant, known as the first sergeant (1SG), began soliciting for volunteers to attend the week long ROK 9th Infantry Division Ranger Training Program. The 1SG was a "no bullshit" type of guy by the name of Sauceda, but we always addressed him as "first sergeant."

This was an elite branch of the ROK Army and similar to the U.S. Army's Rangers. I had seen the ROK Army in action plenty of times and knew I didn't want anything to do with them! And yet, for some reason, I ended up volunteering along with 10 other guys like PVT Mike Johnson, PVT Neil Swanson, PFC Mike Geurtin, SP4 Jeff Hanks, and several KATUSAs like CPL Kwon. Maybe I thought it was like back in boot camp and we would spend the week sitting around a lake water skiing! Well 1SG Sauceda was one tough guy and he knew we were not going to be water skiing! And he was not about to have himself or his men shown up by these ROK Army Rangers. For nearly a month before we left for the training 1SG had us running and doing exercises twice a day. We would do our normal PT in the morning and do our ROK Ranger training in the evening. This evening training was nothing like our normal PT. 1SG had us doing long runs in the back alleys and along the narrow rice patty paths, so we had to pay attention while we ran. It was good preparation but it soon became apparent that it wasn't nearly enough!

We left Camp Pelham in late June. We headed out into the deep countryside about 20 miles away in our company's deuce-and-a-half to the Kamaksan Training Compound near Uijeongbu. After winding through the hills and into the middle of nowhere we arrived at the ranger school. There was really nothing there except for a simple concrete building which was their main office and mess hall. We would be sleeping in our own two man tents, eating our own "C" rations, but sharing their bath house. The bath house wasn't a house at all; it was open and consisted of a couple of pipes sticking out of a natural rock wall about head high with spring water flowing out of them. The water was as ice cold as ice cold could be! The toilets were the traditional hole in the ground; you just straddled the hole and did your business.

We got our gear together and started up the hillside to our camp site on the side of a good sized Korean hill. Once at the camp site we merged with several other American units participating in the same week long training. The first couple of days were filled with non-stop obstacle courses and running.

You would be running through the woods and come to a huge obstacle. You had to clear it or keep trying before you could proceed. It was only the first day and 1SG was getting upset at the ROK cadre because he thought that they were going a little too far with their discipline. It seemed to come to a head when we were trying to clear this one obstacle, which entailed swinging from rope to rope over a huge mud puddle. Some guys were beat-tired and could not get out of the mud once they fell in. The red shirted ROK cadre had no tolerance for failure. When someone would fall into the mud they wouldn't let them out and kept pushing them back into the mud as a sort of punishment. 1SG had one of the KATUSAs reluctantly translate that enough was enough. After some testosterone positioning on both sides the cadre seemed to give us a little slack, for that obstacle only.

Needless to say there was no getting out of the spring water shower at the end of the day. We would be covered head to toe with dirt and mud and just wanted it off. The initial shock of the ice cold water never did subside so you got wet, soaped up, and rinsed in a hurry. I would then eat my "C" ration and fall fast asleep.

After the initial obstacle course we advanced to riskier and riskier obstacles like rappelling down the hill's rock face, crossing valley gorges on single strands of rope, pulling ourselves up 50 foot towers and then rappelling down them, just to name a few. Rappelling down the hillside's steep rock face seemed the most dangerous to me. Partially because we had to pull ourselves up 100 or so feet of almost vertical hillside by rope and partially because we were jumping off of it holding onto nothing but a rope. But It seemed the most dangerous because once we were at the top of this steep hillside, the cadre had us shimmy out on this long narrow rock ledge where we waited in line to be hooked up to rappel back down. There were no safety lines or anything else to prevent us from falling as we waited in line. We were all clutching the side of the hillside in fear of falling to our deaths! Meanwhile the cadre casually maneuvered around our frozen bodies, hooking us up and sending us on our way.

Toward the end the young ROK Ranger cadre softened up and we took the time to take group photos and share some laughs with the KATUSAs translating for us.

ROK cadre in red shirts and Echo company trainee's

I was very proud to receive my ROK Ranger patch and certificate after completing the course on the 2nd of July. Unfortunately the patch was not authorized to wear on my uniform. I have kept it in a safe place and have it proudly displayed in my Army shadow box of medals and ribbons.

In late July, 1st platoon was detailed to support the 2nd Battalion, 61st Air Defense Artillery (ADA) in an exercise. They were stationed right on the other side of Sunyu Ri at RC4. The live fire exercise was going to be held at Chulmae Range near Daechon Beach, which was southwest of Seoul and on the Yellow Sea. This was over 150 miles away and most of the trip would be by train. The members of the platoon going were SGT Groceman, PFC Lewis Blankenship, PFC Tim Bailey, PFC John Fisher, PFC Milo VanAuken, PVT Mike Johnson, PVT Jerry Paul, PVT John Cotton, PVT Brian Houston, me, and our KATUSA CPL Joo.

We drove the truck to the nearby Munsan train station and had it loaded onto a flatbed car along with the air defense vehicles. Of course we had to be different and added a red "River Rats" flag to the front of our truck.

Loading up for ADA duty. Left to right; PFC Semler, PFC Bailey, SGT Groceman, PFC Cotton, PFC VanAuken, CPL Joo, PVT Houston, PVT Johnson, PFC Fisher, PVT Paul

After making sure the truck was safe and sound we took our passage in one of the regular train cars.

The train ride was slow and rambled through the small villages and countryside. At one point we stopped at a large station and got off to use the bathroom. It was at a major train hub and there seemed to be a lot going on. The bathroom was a huge room with stalls but no toilets or urinals, just holes in the ground for you to relieve yourself in. Oh the smell!

At Daechon Beach we off loaded our truck and drove over to the live fire location at Chulmae Range, which was a U.S. military complex. Once there we set up our gear in another huge GP medium tent, only this one had metal bunk beds in it. That was all that was in the tent, rows of metal bunk beds. It was warm so we had the flaps of the tent on either end tied open to catch the breeze. We thought since we were on a military installation we could leave our gear lying about. Wrong! Even though it was a military complex slicky boy got my cassette player radio one evening while I was asleep. Slicky boy was everywhere!

Over the next few days we could tell that other things were turning up missing and that someone was getting into the tent during the night and stealing. Private Houston also had a cassette player and he was worried it was going to be next. He devised a plan of placing empty beer cans all over the inside of the tent, as a sort of booby trap. When slicky boy came into the tent in the middle of the night he would be bound to kick one of them over and wake us up.

Sure enough that night I awoke to a pitch black tent and all hell breaking loose! Houston and several others had been awakened by the kicking over of a beer can and they had wrestled down a Korean there in our tent. As soon as the Korean saw Corporal Joo he kept saying he was a friend of his and he was just coming to visit. Corporal Joo however said he didn't know him! We turned the intruder over to the camp military police who were Korean.

The next day those of us who were missing items were called to the camp's police station to identify and pick up our missing belongings. My cassette player was there and I regained possession of it. I also felt bad for the slicky boy who I knew was probably getting the shit kicked out of him somewhere. The Koreans are a very honorable society and they were shamed by the event. And I was sure slicky boy was paying the price for embarrassing his fellow countrymen.

In the evenings we would put on our civilian clothes and walk into the sleepy seaside village for a few beers and walk the beach watching the villagers fishing or hunting for clams. Daechon Beach was a seaside resort and very relaxing compared to the constant tension up on the DMZ.

Chaparral missile APC

We would spend a week here as the ADA guys fired Chaparral, 20mm Vulcan cannons, and Redeye missiles at unmanned drones. Now the drone part is where we came in. We had a rubber commando style boat with an outboard motor on it and we sat on the beach and waited until the ADA folks shot down one of the drones. When they shot one down, we would hop into our boat and speed out to the drone and retrieve it. If they missed the drone, it would be directed close to us by remote control and the engine killed. A parachute would then deploy and it would float to the water for us to retrieve. Not bad duty!

Our small boat and a drone that didn't get past the live fire

It was pretty interesting watching the ADA process unfold. The small APCs that the chaparrals and 20mm Vulcan cannons were mounted on would line up at the beaches edge on an elevated platform overlooking the Yellow Sea. The 10 foot long red drone was pulled by a remote control plane that was launched from a huge catapult. When they were ready to fire, the plane was catapulted off into the air and the drone was pulled off the ground behind it. The ADA guys would then track it and fire their weapons.

This wasn't a cheap event. The Chaparral missiles went for around $70,000 per round and the Redeye missiles were around $25,000 each. At those prices you want to get the best training with a limited amount of misses.

After they fired we would do our thing and go get the drone or wait for it to float down to the water. The ADA guys fired day and night, which kept us pretty busy. During this exercise they made history and conducted the first night firing of a Redeye shoulder fired missile in Korea.

When we finished up at the end of our week-long tour we loaded our truck back on the train and headed back to Camp Pelham.

In the fall the company geared up for another exercise up around Camp Pelham. We wouldn't be taking our bridge equipment this time as this training would be to hone our infantry skills. Conducting infantry training meant long days and short nights with little sleep, basically pretending we were at war. So we loaded up and headed out into the countryside. We set our company perimeter up and dug foxholes per our normal procedure. When we set up a perimeter in the field there are two guys to a fox hole. At night one of the two was awake and on watch while the other slept. We usually rotated one hour on and one hour off.

I was getting ready to fall asleep one night and the sergeant came around and said I had been detailed to go out to a forward listening post about 150 yards out from our perimeter. Great, I'm tired as hell and now I have to go pull some duty. John Fisher and John Cotton would be sent out with me. The three of us walked over to the command tent, picked up our radio, and were briefed by the lieutenant. He told us that if we see or hear anything we needed to radio it back to him. With a smart "Yes sir!" we headed out to the listening post area.

Now this was a little unsettling to me because up here on the DMZ the ROK guys did not mess around. They carried live ammunition and shot first and asked questions later. I mean these ROK boys were on war time standby 24/7, and as I said before, they routinely ran into North Korean infiltrators.

During this exercise we didn't carry live ammunition. I could never understand that. It was almost like the command was afraid we would hurt ourselves with it! That's probably why the last place I wanted to be was here, hiding out on this hillside and those ROK boys thinking I was an infiltrator. Cotton and Fisher felt the same way.

Nevertheless the three of us made our way out to the listening post area and sort of just hid on the ground in the high weeds together side by side. We were in a ravine with steep hills all around us. We had a radio and were to contact the company command tent if we heard anything. It was getting dark and we didn't really have good bearings but knew that our company was behind us.

As we sat there, Cotton decided it would be a good idea if we had some sort of booby trap set up so that if anyone came up to us we would know. Well crazy ass Cotton, who was already famous for getting stoned drunk one night and tearing up the gun bunnies' bath house, slipped out into the dusk of evening to find booby trap material. About 15 minutes later he came back with all this wire, which we thought was strange. Where would he find wire way out here? He said let's tie it to the trees around us and it would act as trip wire. It sounded pretty good to Fisher and me so we did it. Heck we caught the slicky boy there at ADA live fire with beer cans!

We settled in laying there side by side in the tall grass and decided we would rotate watch and set up a schedule with Cotton leading off. At some point in the middle of the night I woke up to the sound of what I assumed were ROK soldiers voices and someone sneaking around. I looked over at Cotton and Fisher and they were both asleep! I looked to my side without moving a muscle and could see by the light of the moon; Koreans in uniform walking very slowly by us. I didn't make a sound and I'm not sure if they noticed us or not. I couldn't be sure if they were South Koreans or North Koreans! I lay there still as could be until I guess I fell back asleep because I was awakened by the light of morning.

I relayed the story to Fisher and Cotton about the Koreans walking by us in the night and asked them if they had seen or heard them. Neither one did and said they must have fallen asleep.

We worked our way back into the perimeter and checked in with the command tent. After we turned in the radio we briefed the lieutenant in charge that we had not seen or heard anything. He looked at us skeptically and asked "Are you sure you didn't see anything?" We said "No, we hadn't seen a thing." If we told him we had, we would have had our asses handed to us for not calling it in. The lieutenant said, "That's strange, because the ROKs are all upset because someone cut a bunch of their communication wire last night and they had to run new stuff all around us in the middle of the night!" After that statement he told us to get back to our platoon.

The next several days were filled with sleepless nights standing guard in our foxhole and maneuvers during the day. One of these maneuvers was a 20 mile road march with all our gear. Road marches were not unusual as we did them about once a month. But being out here in the field with no shower and already being tired made this one worse to begin with.

Road marches were a good paced walk. We walked on the sides of the dirt road, guys on either side, staggered, with about thirty feet between each other. As we walked along in silence we passed around the heavy machine gun, known as the M60, taking turns lugging it. Every now and then the guys in front of me would stop or kneel down and I would do the same. After a few minutes we would be up and walking again. That's how it was done for 20 miles.

As we marched through the countryside we crossed this field of solid white feathers. I couldn't figure out what they were doing there until we got to the other side and there was this huge chicken processing building. We had just walked through the remains of millions of chickens!

As we made our way through a small village we encountered a couple of men under a bridge burning the skin off of a couple of dead dogs. They had these two dead dogs strung up under this bridge by their hind legs and were burning the skin off in preparation for a Korean meal of dog meat, which is a delicacy I'm told. At about this point into the march I could have helped them eat that dog I was so hungry.

The march drug on for most of the day with almost no stops. Toward the end of the march we cut through a potato patch. I was so hungry I scooped one up and started to eat it. What an awful taste! I will never forget the taste of that dirty raw potato! Soon after getting back from the road march someone took a picture of me next to my camouflaged fox-hole. You can see I was not happy!

Taking a break in front of my foxhole after returning from the road march

The maneuvers were coming to an end just in the nick of time. We were all very tired and getting on each other's nerves. It didn't end fast enough for Cotton. He had some sort of medical breakdown and had to be mede-vac'd out by a helicopter, which they called a "dust off." After popping a smoke grenade this Huey medevac helicopter came swooping down in a cloud of dust and took Cotton away.

Apparently Cotton had been taking these pep pills known as "skoshy yellows" and had over done it. Tim Bailey said he was riding in the back of a duce-and-a-half with Cotton when he started to go into almost a seizure type convulsion and was choking on his tongue. Tim said he tried to cut off the bandana around Cotton's neck with his knife, thinking that was causing him to choke, but Tim made things worse by cutting Cotton's lip! Eventually they got him out of the truck and the medevac helicopter was called in.

Cotton was always into something. He was such a good natured guy and he loved to tie one on. Like I mentioned earlier, Cotton had gotten all messed up and ended up tearing up the gun bunnies' latrine. Story was that he went into the village, tied one on, tore up a club, and must have had a bad run-in with the gun bunnies. When he got back to camp he decided to get back at them and took it out on their latrine. It caused a big ruckus and both commands got involved, which is never a good thing.

This snowballed the next day when Tim Bailey and I went into the village to do some drinking. We didn't know it but we were heading into the club that Cotton had just trashed the night before. As we headed toward the club, which was down an alley off the main street, I told Bailey I was going down to RC4 to pick something up from the PX and would be back in about 30 minutes.

By the time I got back to the club Bailey was about ready to pass out. I shook him and asked him what was going on, but he could hardly speak. Just 30 minutes before he was sober as could be. I knew something was wrong so I picked him up, put his arm over my shoulder, and out the club we went, with me pretty much dragging him down the alley. We ran into a few other guys I knew and we got him back to camp and into his bunk. Later, we figured that mama-san must have recognized Bailey as being a friend of Cotton's and slipped something in his drink. Perhaps they were waiting for him to pass out so they could kick the shit out of him. It wouldn't have been the first time something like that had happened. Obviously they thought he was alone and didn't expect me to come walking in. When Tim finally came to all he could remember was walking into the club. That was it!

During the winter of 1983 there was a plan to put a guide wire across the Injim River to help us build an ice dam which would make a natural ice bridge. But this entailed drilling a hole in the cliffs above the river to run the guide wire through. At some point during the drilling process the expensive drill bit got stuck in the ground. Because the Koreans were known to be very slick with recovering anything for money, it was decided that a guard would need to be placed on this bit until the ground thawed and they could get the bit out. You had to respect the slicky boy!

I thought it was a bit much to think they could get the bit out of the frozen ground, but they did almost get a whole jeep out of one of the camps. Turns out they pulled a jeep into the back of a garbage truck, filled the truck with garbage covering the jeep, and tried to drive out of the camp gate. Luckily the guard was on the ball and probed the pile of garbage with a stick and kept hitting something hard. When they removed the garbage they found the jeep.

Reminds me of a story my dad would tell when we were living on the Philippine Islands in the mid-1960s. We were living on Clark Air Force base and he said the locals stole the base fire truck. They just turned on the sirens like they were heading to a fire and drove right out the main gate with the gate guards holding the gates open for them. Guess slicky boy really was everywhere!

Getting back to the drill bit stuck in the ground, I was detailed to go out and guard this thing with another soldier. The truck dropped us off in the middle of nowhere on the cliffs of the Injim River to an awaiting GP medium tent. There was a long metal shaft sticking out through the top of the tent about 20 feet in the air. Yep, this thing was that long.

The guards we relieved passed the usual guard duty log to us and were happy to get into the truck to take them back to camp. I stepped into the tent and there was the rest of the metal shaft going straight into the frozen ground. There were also two cots and a gas burning stove. My partner and I spent the day keeping the gas stove running and staying warm in the tent. The stove ran off of gasoline cans positioned outside the tent and we would just switch the suction line whenever a can ran dry. At some point in the middle of the night I woke up freezing cold and went out to switch the gas suction line only to find out our gas cans had been stolen! Slicky boy had struck again! Needless to say it was not a good night for me and my frozen partner. Waiting for the relief truck until the morning seemed like an eternity!

During my tour I did make it into Seoul on my only three day pass. We caught the train in Munsan and took it into the heart of Seoul. The train was packed with locals and we stood out like sore thumbs. We did some sightseeing but always managed to end up at some point in the bars in Yongsan, which is a suburb of Seoul. Seoul was the 8th Army's territory and they were not under the same curfew and control restriction that we were up at Camp Pelham. Blowing off steam and staying up until the wee hours seemed like such an indulgence.

My last duty at Camp Pelham was guard duty when President Ronald Reagan visited the DMZ on the 13th of November. He would be the first American President to visit the DMZ. That was a tremendously bold statement given the current environment. Within the past few months the Soviets had shot down a Korean jetliner killing 269 passengers, 241 service members were killed when the Marine barracks in Beirut, Lebanon was bombed, Marines had just invaded the Caribbean Island of Grenada held by Cuban forces, and there was the assassination attempt on the South Korean President.

I was so short, only a few days from heading to the Turtle Farm. I was so short my fingers were touching! It didn't matter. The President of the United States was at the DMZ and needless to say the whole area was extremely tense. For weeks the area had been abuzz with military vehicles massing in case of a problem.

To make matters worse, two South Korean soldiers had deserted their guard post outside of Seoul on the 7th of November and had shot and killed another guard. They were at large with M16 rifles, four grenades, and 600 rounds of ammunition. After killing two more people they finally committed suicide the next day when they were surrounded while holed up in a building.

The normal guards that patrolled around Camp Pelham were civilian contractors. They patrolled the perimeter and manned the guard towers strategically placed around the camp. They were not a slack bunch and you didn't want to try and sneak into the camp after curfew because they would shoot you. This was definitely a "shoot first and ask questions later" type of place. But on this occasion they wanted Americans standing guard until the president had cleared the area.

I was assigned guard duty at night and stationed in one of the guard towers. It was the middle of November and freezing cold. I was issued live ammunition and told to climb up the tower and radio if I saw anything unusual. It was cold as hell and I was totally bundled up in all my cold weather gear. The tower was 30-40 feet high, open to the elements, and was made for one person. The ladder up to it was narrow and straight up. It was a tough climb up with my bulky clothing, radio, and weapon. Once up there, for the first time since I had been at Camp Pelham, I had a bird's eye view of the sleepy little village of Sunyu Ri. It was late at night, after curfew, and the village was at peace. It was a nice final impression of my neighbors for the past year.

President Chun of South Korea said he had ordered forces to be ready to fire an artillery barrage in between President Reagan and the North Koreans in case he was attacked and said President Reagan was the only leader that had the courage, fortitude, and leadership to make such a visit. President Reagan came to the most hostile place in the communist world and from guard post Collier stared over the 1,100 yards of barbed wire and mine fields that separated him from North Korea.

President Reagan later gave a speech in the mortar bunker at Camp Liberty Bell, which is located near guard post Collier. In his speech he said, "Somebody asked me if I'd be safe up here so close to North Korean troops, and I said, I'll be with the 2d Infantry Division!" Such a statement from such a great man made us all very proud.

I received my orders to Fort Polk, Louisiana and was to leave Korea on the 18th of November, exactly one year from my arrival. I had been waiting for my orders like a kid waits for Santa on Christmas morning. I was out in the village and it was getting late and my buddies and I decided to head back to camp before it got close to curfew. We stopped at one of the street venders selling fried potatoes. The way they served them was by taking a piece of paper, making a cone out of it, and serving your fries in the cone. The paper was always recycled, and I don't mean recycled like now-a-days. It was always trash paper from the camp. As I was eating my fries I noticed the paper had type-written English on it so I gave it a look. It was a copy of my orders! Now what were the odds of that happening? Not my actual correct orders but obviously a draft copy with errors that had been thrown in the trash. I couldn't believe it. The next day I went to the company clerk and asked him if he had my orders, and he did. I told him that I found a copy in town wrapped around my fries and he calmly said "It happens."

Before leaving Camp Pelham I was awarded the Army Achievement medal for "exceptionally commendable service." It was a total surprise. I totally credit our young 2nd Lieutenant, Paul W. Kelly, who saw enough in me to put me in for the award. After checking out of Camp Pelham I headed back to the Turtle Farm to out-process.

My Grandfather, Ben Churilla, and Cousin, Tim Semler, passed away while I was in Korea. I didn't find out until weeks later in both cases. Phone calls were very hard to arrange at that time and the only means of communicating back home was via letter. My folks were still living in

Australia and that made it even harder. I never made a phone call while in Korea and my only communication with my family had been via letter.

Once finished with the Turtle Farm I boarded a civilian plane that would take me home on leave and then to Fort Polk, Louisiana. As I made myself comfortable for the long flight home I never thought of KAL 007 or anything else that happened over the past year. My only thoughts were for the moment and leaving Korea. I was sitting back in the smoking section and after taking off I lit a cigarette and took a nice long drag on it. As the stewardess walked past me she asked if I would like something to drink and I said "Yes, a beer please." The stewardess asked me if I was 21 and I replied, "No I'm 19." She flatly told me I wasn't old enough to drink!

FORT POLK LOUISIANA

1st PLATOON, E COMPANY, 7th ENGINEER BATTALION,

5th INFANTRY DIVISION (MECHANIZED)

18 December 1983 – 16 June 1985

I spent most of my 30 days of leave between the Semler farm in Pennsylvania and my parents' house in Manassas, Virginia where they had recently relocated after leaving Australia. When it was time to leave I caught a flight from Virginia to New Orleans, Louisiana. After spending a few days visiting with Steve Williamson, a buddy from Korea who lived in New Orleans, I caught a Greyhound bus up to Fort Polk. It was my first time in the South and the five hour bus trip gave me a chance to see the southern countryside while stopping in numerous small towns to transfer passengers and mail.

Fort Polk is in the center of the state toward the western border with Texas. The fort was named in honor of Leonidas Polk, the first Episcopal Bishop of the Diocese of Louisiana, and a general for the Confederacy during the Civil War. He was killed in action on June 14th 1864 while scouting enemy positions near Marietta, Georgia.

Now this is the second Confederate named installation in a row I had been assigned to. I had nothing against the Confederacy except for that fact that my great-great grandfather, John Gunsallus, had fought for the Union during the entire civil war with the 51st Pennsylvania Infantry. He entered as a private in 1861 and was mustered out as a first lieutenant in 1865. He saw action at Roanoke Island, Newbern, Camden, 2nd Bull Run, Chantilly, South Mountain, Antietam, Fredericksburg, Campaign of the Mississippi, and Spotsylvania Court House just to name a few. Two of his brothers, Zachery and Samuel, also fought for the Union. Zachery was with the 13th Pennsylvania Calvary and Samuel was with the 148th Pennsylvania Infantry. Ironically all three brothers were fighting around the same location in Spotsylvania, Virginia when Samuel, who had survived the battle of the Wheat Field at Gettysburg, was killed at the battle of the Spotsylvania Court House on May 16th 1864.

Now at Leonidas Polk's namesake I was assigned to another in-processing center. Fort Polk was an old fort and I was once again assigned in a WWII era barrack. These buildings were typical two story buildings made of wood, with no apparent insulation, and a white paint exterior which seemed to be peeling away from exposure to the hot southern summers. I was assigned to the second floor and in a room with one other guy.

My stay at the in-processing center was only a few days and then I was transferred to my new unit Echo Company, who were also known as the "River Rats." Echo Company belonged to the 7th Engineering Brigade of the "Red Diamond" 5th Infantry Division consisting of five officers and 146 enlisted men. It was almost a mirror image of personnel and equipment that I had left in Korea.

My new accommodations were a night and day difference from what I had experienced in the Army to this point. I arrived to new state of the art digs. The barracks and surrounding buildings such as the mess hall, barbershop, and orderly room were all new, modern, and made of solid brick. The barracks were three stories high and had four rooms on each floor with a recreational area in the middle which had a sofa, table, and several lounge chairs. Each room accommodated three people. Each person had their individual wooden bed with a nice large wooden wall locker and desk. There was also a shower, sink, and toilet in each room. This was like five star living compared to Camp Pelham!

I should probably only have given it four stars just because of the huge cockroaches that were all over the place. It was typical for Louisiana, but not for this Northern boy. These things were everywhere and there was no use killing one because five more would take its place. It was a shame to be lying in such a nice bed in such a nice room and have these two inch long things crawling over your blanket and up the wall!

I moved around several times in the barracks but spent most of my time on the second floor of the building that housed our platoon. My room-mates were McDonald from Philadelphia and Tate from Chicago. That's the way it was in the service, you always addressed a guy by his last name and you always knew where he came from because that's all they ever talked about. Tate and I had actually been in Korea together but in different platoons so we didn't run in the same circle of friends over there.

I was joined by other guys I had served with in Korea like Lewis Blankenship, John Fisher, Terry Bear, Avery McGee, James Tate, Steve Williamson, and Milo Van Auken. It was good to be around friends again. I arrived just before Christmas like I did in Korea and would spend my second year in a row away from home for the holidays. It wasn't too bad because the fort was pretty much shut down for the holidays. Most of the company was on leave and it gave me time to get acclimated to my surroundings. The Army always took care of you and I got a knock on the door on Christmas day with people bringing us care packages and making sure we were doing okay over the holidays.

Our daily routine at the fort was similar to that of Camp Pelham. Up at 0500 for PT and a several mile run, followed by chow and muster down at the motor pool. We ran in government issued banana yellow sweat suits here and the fort was so big we could run for miles and miles and never even get close to running out of room. The day at the motor pool consisted of maintenance on truck, boat, and bridge equipment. This was another ribbon bridge company like in Korea, so it only took a few weeks for me to come up to speed with their routine.

It seemed like we were always going out to the field at Fort Polk compared to Korea. Going "out to the field" was our term for what the Army called field training exercises (FTX). These usually consisted of a week of training and roughing it out in the Louisiana scrub and swamps. Fort Polk covered over 100,000 acres so there was plenty of room to roam. Being out in the field was nasty. You never changed your clothes, didn't wash, did your business in holes you dug, and stunk. We were so nasty after an FTX that we had a rule that when we came back to the barracks no one was allowed in the room with their clothes or gear until they had been washed!

The back woods and swamps of Louisiana are a nasty place to be roughing it. The state bird was jokingly called the mosquito, and there were all sorts of spiders and snakes that could really put you in a bad way. When we got to our field location we camouflaged our trucks with netting and then dug our foxholes. The foxholes were always filling with water because the water table was so high there in Louisiana. Once you got one dug you seemed to spend the rest of the day bailing it out.

After we got all that done it was time to pitch our little two man tent for shelter. Now this is when you had to really trust who was assigned to be your foxhole buddy because each of us had half the tent, or was supposed to. When you are issued your field gear you get one half of the tent canvas, four tent stakes, one piece of rope, and one tent post which comes in three pieces. Now to put the tent together your foxhole buddy is supposed to have the same items you do so that together you have the makings for one tent.

Going to the bathroom was always an adventure. There were no portable toilets and you had to go dig a hole if you needed to go. The deal was you dug it, used it, and most importantly filled it. Going really wasn't an issue because the "C" ration meals we would eat would bind you up for a week, just about how long we were in the field. The "C" rations were canned food meals nicely packed into a small brown cardboard box.

Getting your meal was the luck of the draw. Breakfast was usually trucked out to us in these huge stay warm containers which didn't keep things warm. You would go through the chow line, get your breakfast, fill your helmet with hot water for shaving and washing up from a huge drum of hot water, and pick out your two "C" ration meals for your lunch and dinner. There were only about six varieties of "C" rations that I ever saw and the best ones went fast. Once back at the foxhole you ate your cold breakfast and washed your face and shaved in your helmet of water. After that you commenced to trade for better "C" rations.

The worst one was ham and eggs, followed closely by chicken loaf. It really didn't get too much better but I was fond of the classic beans and franks. These "C" rations had a shelf-life of at least 20 years so you can imagine what ham and eggs looked and smelled like when you opened the can. Every meal had the entre in a can, a dessert such as canned fruit cocktail, a can of a bread item such as crackers or cookies with a cocoa powder packet, salt, pepper, matches, toilet paper, a spoon, sugar, instant coffee and gum. Some of the older ones even had cigarettes. These last items came in paper packets and were tough to keep dry in the ever damp bayous of Louisiana. Socks, underwear, and toilet paper were the items you always tried to keep dry no matter what.

Everyone carried a small can opener known as a P-38 to gain entry into their canned "C" ration cuisine. Most of the time these were eaten cold, but every now and then I would build a little fire at the bottom of the foxhole, so the flames could not be seen, and heat them up. It didn't make them taste any better, but eating them warm made them go down a little easier. I also really enjoyed the cocoa powder and always tried to trade for it. By just adding a little water to it you could make a thick chocolate paste just like pudding.

On one FTX we left Fort Polk via convoy to an area in Louisiana on the Red River. This was unusual and one of the only times we left Fort Polk on maneuvers. Our FTXs were usually in the vicinity of this little lake, appropriately named Engineer Lake, which we used for bridge ferry training. Driving out on the highways and byways of Louisiana was exciting and I felt liberated from the fort.

After a good day of driving we wheeled into a huge cow pasture that bordered a part of the Red River. It was a typical pasture with knee high grass and cows. Like always when out on a FTX, we conducted ourselves as if we were in the middle of an active war zone. That meant full field dress, 24 hour watches, foxholes, "C" rations, and everything was camouflaged. So as we came into the cow pasture we set up toward the river and commenced to camouflage everything. We pitched our two man tents and would have dug foxholes if it were not for the fact the cow pasture owner was not keen on the idea. That night when the sun set, the cows were grazing way over on the other side of the pasture, about 400 yards away. When the sun rose, they were grazing all mingled in with our equipment and tents. It was actually pretty cool to herd them along their way and back out into open pasture.

That first night also revealed our first casualty. One of the guys was bitten by a spider, or something, and had broken out with a rash from head to toe. I mean he looked like hell. This was no small skin irritation, it was full blown head to toe red bumps. No one wanted anything to do with what had gotten hold of him! He was transported back to the hospital on the fort. It wasn't the first time that had happened. On another FTX a guy was bitten on the face and half his head swelled up.

I don't really remember conducting any bridging operations on the Red River, but I do remember crossing the river. I was assigned with a couple other guys to take one of the inflatable boats and paddle over to the other side and scout for the enemy. We were not actively in a war game scenario with anyone else so there wasn't any real enemy, just us doing our normal and annoying pretending. So the four of us climb into this black reconnaissance raft with our M16s slung over our bodies, loaded down with field gear, and paddled about 100 yards over to the other side of the river.

The river was moving pretty fast and it took everything we had to paddle over to the other side. Once there we scouted around and as expected, found no enemy. We had gathered at a point just on the edge of the river bank behind a huge log. While lying there in the weeds, we discussed if we had spent enough time messing around to satisfy the command. One of the guys pulled out a joint and suggested it was a good time to get high, so we did. Mistake!

On the way back we were about midway across the river when we somehow flipped over. I think we started to get turned around, the current was moving too fast, and the raft just flipped on us. We all went into the muddy water along with our gear. It sure as heck scared any buzz I had out of me and I was relieved to reach the shore. Luckily we all made it to shore, which was amazing since we were all stoned and the water was moving so fast. Once there it was discovered that one of the guys had lost his M16 in the river.

Now this was a major problem because the only thing worse than getting bitten by something out in the field and breaking out into some disfiguring rash, was losing your weapon. You never wanted to lose your weapon and you never wanted your command to have to write a report on it. When a weapon is lost in the field everyone goes into lock down and your every action is all about finding the missing weapon. A mound of paperwork has to be filled out and you're the center of attention, exactly what you don't want.

So the whole company spent the next day or so trying to retrieve the M16 via grappling hooks and anything else we could think of to no avail. At some point it was given up as lost and, with no M16 found, we finished our FTX and headed back to the fort. Although I'm sure the guy that was missing the M-16 still had plenty of long days dealing with the consequences of losing his weapon.

We usually smoked pot while out in the field. At that time in the Army there really wasn't a big penalty for smoking pot, usually extra duty. Harder drugs would get you discharged, and I never encountered them.

We were all young, single, didn't have anything to lose, and the Army seldom conducted drug testing, so we never worried about it.

On another notable FTX we headed out into the scrub of Fort Polk. On this particular occasion we would be playing war games with other units in the area. We set up our perimeter in our normal location near Engineer Lake and dug in. On this FTX we were using the same MILES laser gun technology I had used during Team Spirit in Korea. My foxhole buddy and I had dug a nice sized hole and started to go out into the firing zone, out in front of our foxhole, to set up some trip wires. These were pretty cool. It was a wire that you strung across a path, or clearing, and the wire was attached to something similar to a bottle rocket. If someone tried to sneak up on us they would hopefully set one off and alert us.

It was cool and rainy out in the scrub and it didn't take long for all of our stuff to get damp and wet. As usual our foxhole kept filling with water and needed constant bailing out. I remember one night sitting at the edge of my foxhole, against a tree, trying to stay dry with my rain gear on and poncho covering me. I was tired, cold, hungry, and I stunk. The only joy sitting out there was getting a good drag on a dry cigarette. The next good feeling was getting my turn to sleep and crawling into my nasty sleeping bag with all my clothes on for 55 minutes of sleep before I had to watch the foxhole for another hour.

On the second or third night we had heard that we might be attacked so we were all up and in our foxholes. Every now and again our squad leader would come crawling by to check on us and pass any information. At some point in the night a trip flare went off and it was on! The pitch black night was broken by the flashes of bottle rockets and there was the sound of MI6's firing and laser gear buzzing. Your adrenalin just about makes your head pop off at times like that. I can't imagine how it would be if it was actually life or death. As the battle heated up you could hear the platoon's M60 machine gun buzzing away and hear breaches in our perimeter. As quick as it had started, it ended with the assaulting force drifting back into the pitch black woods. After that we were all on pins and needles for the rest of the night.

The next night would be our turn. We started out in the afternoon and headed through the woods in a long sweeping motion toward the enemy. We wanted to take it very slow and get into position before dark. That way we wouldn't have to make a lot of noise stumbling through the woods at night. As usual, it was raining and the dampness seemed to penetrate every layer I had on. We walked very slowly for several hours without talking. Every now and then we would get the motion to stop and we would crouch down by a tree and cover ourselves with our poncho and have a smoke. That smoke always seemed to give me such a moment of relaxation and enjoyment in what seemed to be a miserable environment.

Eventually we made it to the location where we would hold up until night. As night fell we waited a few hours hoping the enemy was getting tired and thinking we were not coming. Eventually we started to move forward and someone sent up a trip flare and it was on again! Just like the night before the adrenaline started pumping and there was an escalation of gun fire, flashes of light, and the sound of laser gear beeping. I started running up this grade and toward a foxhole in front of me. I could see pretty clearly because the trip flares had really lit the place up. When I reached the foxhole no one was there and I hopped in and kept firing. I soon thought it best to get back to our regrouping location so I headed back. On the way I ran into my fellow squad mates and we started howling and laughing about the whole event. I wondered, what happened to the guys in the foxhole I had hopped into? Had they been that scared that they took off, or was there never anyone there? Anyway, that was a memorable FTX and we swapped war stories for days after that!

In early summer of 1984 I was wondering why I had not been promoted with my peers to specialist four (SP4). When I asked my chain of command, they gave me the usual spiel that it should be coming down soon. After several weeks of no promotion I began pestering my command again and they eventually sent me up to headquarters to see what was going on. Headquarters was a huge building in the center of Fort Polk that housed the clerks I needed to see along with the fort commander, a general. I had never seen anyone of a higher rank than a captain before, so I was a little more than hesitant to go up to headquarters where the general hung out.

There was just so much protocol with saluting, and what if the general's car drove by? I knew you were supposed to stop and salute the car, I think? I was having flash backs of getting my ass chewed out in front of the PX back in basic training. All of this was racing through my mind as I walked to the center of Fort Polk.

As I approached the building, low and behold there was the general's car parked out front with his red flags with white stars sticking up from the front bumper. That meant, in my mind, I could pass him at any moment! I treaded softly into the building and found my way to the administration section housing the clerks. Once there my clerk sat me down and opened up my very thin personnel record. He calmly said that the reason I had not been promoted was because the only entry in my record was that I had arrived at Fort Leonard Wood for boot camp. Now this was in the days before computers and everything was hand written into your record. The clerk said he would update it and I should be promoted soon. True to his word I was promoted on the 1st of August to SP4. Oh, and I never did run into the general!

One of the duties I had to stand was charge of quarters (CQ) watch. This was a 24 hour watch stood at the company's orderly room. The responsibilities included answering phone calls and checking guys in and out of leave. One of the unusual responsibilities was administering medication to guys not responsible enough to be in possession of their own medications. One of those medications was Antabuse, which was a treatment for alcoholism.

While in Korea I had served with a legend of a staff sergeant by the name of Manis. He was a John Wayne type of guy and a legend for being a great platoon leader and a heavy drinker. He was my platoon leader before SSG Garrett in Korea, but here at Fort Polk he was in charge of another platoon. Over in Korea and here at Fort Polk he was highly admired. He was so admired that he was simply known as "Warrior."

He was already old and beat up when I first got to work for him in Korea. Army life had taken its toll on Warrior. He wasn't alone, very few of the older sergeants were in good shape. When we would form up for PT in the mornings they would be there to check in when their name was called for muster. After muster all those with medical profiles would be released and they would head back to the barracks before we would start to exercise. The rest of us would assume the front-leaning rest position and start doing push-ups! No one held it against them. Most of them were Vietnam veterans and had our respect.

So on one of my CQ duty days I was told that SSG Manis would be coming in to take his Antabuse. I was to watch him take his pill and log in the logbook that he indeed took his Antabuse. Warrior came in as expected and I handed him his pill which he balled up in his weathered bear paw of a hand. He turned away, and started to walk out of the orderly room. I called to him, "SSG Manis I was told that I needed to see you take your pill." His reply was, "You did." And he walked on out the door. I should have never questioned him. I simply wrote in the log that SSG Manis reported as directed and had taken his Antabuse pill.

In the late summer of 1984 we were told that we would be heading to Germany for almost two months to participate in the European war games known as Return of Forces to Germany (REFORGER). We would be taking part in Operation Certain Fury while elements of the 2nd Armored Division and British troops would be participating in Operation Spearpoint. We were all excited about getting out of the backwoods of Louisiana and going to Germany! A lot of the guys in the company had done tours in Germany, so the stories of beer houses and Oktoberfest started to season the excitement of deploying. In preparation we took classes on the German culture, had to pass European driving tests, and were briefed on the possibility of espionage that came along with the REFORGER event.

The Russians were highly interested in REFORGER and had intelligence gatherers out trying to gather information on NATO equipment and movements. This was during the Cold War when Germany was still divided between a communist East Germany and democratic West Germany. The Berlin Wall which separated East and West Berlin would not come down for another five years, in November of 1989, and Germany would not reunite until 1990.

We were told to report any suspicious activities we saw and disrupt the efforts of suspected intelligence gatherers if we could. The theory of disruption would go down something like this; we see a car full of seedy looking guys pull up next to the convoy as we are driving down the road and they start taking a lot of pictures. We were supposed to maneuver our vehicles to box in the suspect vehicle and trap them until authorities could get there. Sounded like a James Bond movie to me!

The plan for going to REFORGER was to leave all of our bridge equipment in Louisiana and pick up bridge equipment when we arrived in Germany. Other units of the 5th Infantry division shipped about 800 vehicles from Fort Polk. They would begin rolling off of ships in Antwerp, Belgium around the 11th of September. On the 8th of September we loaded up in Air Force C-141 troop carrying aircraft and flew out of Barksdale AFB, located in northern Louisiana, to Rhine-Main airport in Frankfurt, Germany. We boarded the C-141 aircraft wearing our military BDUs and carrying our weapons. Our duffle bag with all of our other gear was loaded as checked baggage. In preparation for the huge amount of duffle bags to sort through we each painted our unit and the last four numbers of our social security number on the bottom of our bags. That way when they were all stacked up like cord-wood we could easily identify our bag.

From Frankfurt we boarded buses and drove about 100 miles south west to the town of Pirmasens, which is about 5 miles from the French boarder. The drive was beautiful and so pristine. We drove on the autobahn and through little villages that had been there for thousands of years. We arrived at the U.S. military instillation named Husterhoeh Kaserne on the northern edge of the city of Pirmasens and would spend the next week there drawing our bridge equipment out of storage.

Husterhoeh Kaserne was part of a huge network of storage facilities in Germany known as Prepositioning of Material Configured in Unit Sets (POMCUS). The facilities housed equipment staged in the event of a war with the Soviet Union. Everything was there except the soldiers who would be flown over to Germany to man it.

The U.S. storage facility at Husterhoeh Kaserne was unbelievable. There were these huge aircraft hangar sized buildings that stored all the bridge trucks, boats, and equipment we needed. They also housed tanks and APCs being drawn out by other units. The process took about a week because this equipment was in what they called long term storage. Everything needed to be mechanically readied, such as having oil and fluids added, tires checked, engines started, and vehicles inspected. The military facility there was enormous and had all the amenities we needed, along with German merchants selling food. I was astonished at how many different varieties of bratwurst you could get from the guy at the bratwurst cart!

Once we had drawn all of our equipment and had it inspected for release we were ready to roll. The plan was to convoy further south east about 150 miles to a place 50 miles east of Stuttgart. From that location we would wait for the REFORGER war games to start. Traveling 150 miles in the states doesn't seem like a big deal, but in Germany it would take us about a week! We had to convoy our five ton bridge trucks, which are huge, through country roads and towns only meant for small car traffic. The height of our equipment would also make it very hard to go through the small villages and towns, so we would need to by-pass them.

It was a stop, wait, and go process of driving a few miles then stopping to wait for the scout jeep to see if we could make it down a road or through a village. Instead of trying to drive a whole convoy through the countryside at once we were broken up into smaller groups of about five vehicles and would stagger our groups by several miles. This would ease the disruption to the locals.

Our biggest obstacle turned out to be the weather and not the roads. This would turn out to be the wettest September in southern Germany in 40 years. Not only was it damp but this was the start of winter in Germany and it was cold. I put on my long underwear, field uniform, and rain gear complete with rain boots in early September and did not take it off until we finished in late October.

The rainy weather made driving more difficult. The roads were so narrow that if you got off them you had a good chance of getting stuck in the mud of the fields that came right to the road's edge. We would transit during the day and then regroup at night at a predetermined location and make camp, usually in some field or in the woods. This was like being back on an FTX in Louisiana, and for the most part there were no showers, or hot meals, just "C" rations.

It actually turned out to be a great way to really see the countryside and interact with the German citizens. As we would be stopped along some road or in a village we would get out and stretch our legs and mingle with the locals. Like I said some of the guys had been stationed here before and knew some basic German which always broke the ice.

On one occasion we had stopped just inside a small village and were told to wait. We knew there was a bigger town ahead and it would be the usual hour or so before the scout jeep had figured out a way through or around it, so we got out stretching our legs. Apparently we had stopped right next to a restaurant and hotel known as a guest house. At the urging of those guys who had been to Germany before, we decided to go into the guest house and get something to eat. The Germans were very friendly and sat us in a nice big corner table. We had all of our field gear, along with our weapons, and must have been quite a sight. The locals made us feel right at home and we shed our winter jackets and piled our M16s in the corner. After eating a great meal we thanked our wonderful hosts and went back to our trucks to await the order to move ahead. From that point on we always took advantage of any opportunity to eat and mingle with our very hospitable Germans hosts.

It wasn't unusual to get lost and detached from the main company while transiting through these cities and towns. It seemed like we were always passing broken down vehicles from the guys that were pushing ahead of us. Since we were way back in the reserve, as a bridge company, we saw a lot of them and the destruction they caused on the roads and fields. I remember one of our small groups getting lost for several days. There were also the mishaps, such as hitting houses and tearing up pastures with our vehicles. The locals took it in stride and we were only held up long enough for the details to get worked out before moving on.

Sometimes we would stop off at remote U.S. military bases, which were very small, and seemed to just blend in with the countryside. They were usually perched on some hill or other strategic location. These were always welcomed stops because we could shower and eat in their mess hall.

Once we did get down to our operating area for the war games we primarily stayed in a field near a small village. There was a dirt road that led from the small town back into the field and like everything else in Germany at the time, it was water logged. About the only duty we had was to stand guard up in the town overlooking the road entrance. When I had the duty I would always take up a position crouched down under a store front doorway, safe from the rain, watching the traffic coming either up or down the road. The locals would walk right by me as if nothing was going on, even though I was dressed in field gear with my helmet and an M16.

In the field during REFORGER. 1st platoon, 2nd section. Front left to right; PFC Melvin, PFC Gonzales, PFC Allen. Back left to right; Sgt Lee, SP4 Lagman, PFC Mcdowell, SP4 Semler, SGT Magee.

When the war games started we were in the rear, north of the Danube River, which was the border between us, the blue forces, and the enemy orange forces. The orange forces were supposed to try and put in their own ribbon bridge on the 17th of September for an attack, but the wet weather made the river too dangerous for the heavy M1 and M60 tanks to cross. Instead, they used the existing bridges near the town of Dillingen to kick off their offensive. Eventually, on the 19th the river slowed up a bit and the 10th Engineers of the 3rd Infantry Division and the 385th Engineers of the Army Reserves put in their ribbon bridges at Dillingen and Petersworth.

As the orange forces poured over the Danube River the M-1 Abrams and older M60 tanks battled it out over the German terrain until around the 24th of September when blue forces started to counter attack.

We were called up from the rear to assist in crossing the Danube in the counterattack. As we were conducting rafting crossings with blue forces, several orange team Cobra attack helicopters swooped down on us and attacked. After an initial pass, it was ruled by the war game umpires that we had sustained damage to two of our bridge bay sections and they had to be removed. We changed them out and carried on with our mission.

By the 26th, the 3rd Battalion, 77th Armor of the 5th Infantry Division was leading the charge and driving deep into orange forces territory. By the 29th, the orange forces had been driven back well across the Danube and Certain Fury was over.

The training we conducted in Germany was exciting because at Fort Polk all we had to work on was Engineer Lake, in the middle of the fort. Here we had actual rivers again like in Korea. The equipment was also newer. We had the older style 27' propeller boats back home and here in Germany we were issued the new MKII twin jet boats.

When the war games finished we convoyed back up to Pirmasens to turn in our equipment at Husterhoeh Kaerne. This was another lengthy process which took about a week. All the equipment had to be power washed clean, parked, all the fluids drained, inspected, and stored for the next REFORGER or actual war. After passing our equipment turn-in inspections we were sent to a temporary holding camp to await transport back to Louisiana.

The holding camp was at Heidenheim, about 20 miles east of Stuttgart, and was a mass of these huge green circus sized tents, with row after row of green cots in them. No walls or lockers, just cots. The toilets were a bank of port-a-potties that were set up outside and adjacent to the rows of tents. At one end of the camp was the bath house, which was made of converted mobile homes, filled with showers and sinks and covered with a huge tent. So you didn't lose your wallet or valuables you were handed a plastic bag to take your valuables in the shower with you.

The mess hall was under another huge tent by the bath house. There was everything you needed here at tent city, a post office, library, barbers, venders, phones, arcade, theatre, and finance center to cash checks.

Probably the biggest entertainment was watching all the field mice running around. There must have been thousands of them, granted we were in their field.

Because of all the rain it was one huge mud puddle and all the tents were joined by a maze of wooden pallets acting as sidewalks. You did not want to get off of those pallets as it was solid mud! I don't think I saw a sunny day in Germany; it was all rain and fog.

We would be here for about a week before we flew out. One day we were lying around on our cots and I heard a gunshot outside. I ran out to see some guys huddled around the row of port-a-potties lined up in front of our tent. Apparently, a guy in another tent had blown his head off in one of the port-a-potties. His body was removed and you could see the blood splattered around inside. Word was the guys in the company he was in were harassing him and it got to be too much for him. I was told he had been to the firing range recently and they suspected he had pocketed a few rounds waiting for just such an opportunity.

The suicide, surprisingly, had little effect on me. I know that sounds cold, but since the guy was not in my nucleus of friends, my platoon or company, I was able to move on from the incident pretty quickly.

There were also lighter moments at the holding camp. Our hosts wanted to keep us busy, since idle minds are the devils workshop, and offered day tours which I took advantage of. We had been told to pack a set of civilian clothes and this would be the first chance I had to put them on since arriving. I took a tour bus to Nurnberg and did some sightseeing around the city, and on another trip I took a Rhine River cruise which was very scenic. The boat had a nice eating area and the views of the castles perched up on the hills were breath taking.

Enjoying some sightseeing while in Germany for
REFORGER 1984

In the last week of October we were bused back to Frankfurt and boarded another plane for the ride back to Louisiana.

Once in Louisiana it was back to the humdrum life of the fort and guard duty. I was recognized as the outstanding soldier of the guard on 30 December 1984 and then the outstanding soldier of the month for the 7th Engineer Battalion for the month of January 1985. The outstanding guard award got me out of standing post duty, which was very nice! We had been detailed to pull guard duty over the Christmas holidays at various outposts on base. We would muster up for inspection and the soldier with the best looking uniform and gear would be relieved from duty for that day. The rest would be transported out to the middle of nowhere to stand guard duty.

And I mean the middle of nowhere! I was carted out to ranges all over the base, and had to sit out there alone for four hours at a time in the freezing cold, until I was relieved. You wouldn't think Louisiana gets cold, but it does! It all seemed pointless to me. Once out at the guard post there was no way to contact anyone if something did happen and I didn't even have live ammunition to stop anyone! Every now and then a jeep with the guard duty supervisor would come out and check on me. And I don't mean to see if I was ok, I mean to check and make sure I was awake and offered the correct challenge.

The correct challenge was for me to yell, "Halt who goes there?" After the answer of let's say, "Lieutenant Smith," I was to say, "Advance to be recognized." At which point the lieutenant would approach and show me his identification card. He would then question me on my general orders. If I did it correctly I didn't get an ass chewing.

After several days of freezing my butt off out at these deserted ranges I decided I was going to be selected as the "outstanding guard." So I spit polished my boots, creased my uniform, and folded my poncho perfectly. The effort paid off and I was selected! My reward was that I didn't having to go out to the range that day.

The outstanding soldier for the battalion was a little tougher. For that I had to compete with other soldiers at formal interview boards, as well as present a good military appearance. I reported to a board of non-commissioned officers (NCOs) in my dress uniform. They asked me questions while I was at the position of attention and they were seated at a table in front of me. The board asked me questions about general military knowledge such as; what were my guard duty standing order, who was the general of the fort, who was the commander and chief, and so on. They would also get into some pretty strange stuff, such as what was the ball on top of the flag pole called, and what was in it. They asked other intellectually deep questions such as; if you walked halfway into the woods, how far would you have to go to get out! Oh, and the answer they wanted to hear about the flagpole was that the ball is called a "truck" and it contained a bullet. The bullet was to be used by the fort's commanding officer to shoot himself if the base was ever captured. How he was supposed to get up there and get it, I have no idea!

My appearance and answers were good enough for me to win, and advance to the subsequent outstanding soldier of the 5th Infantry Division. The competition was tough and I didn't make it. That was fine with me. It was fun up until that point but the higher I went in the process the more nervous I became, and that just put me out of my comfort zone.

On the 25th of January 1985 I was appointed to the rank of acting sergeant. This meant I could wear the E-5 rank of a sergeant, but would not get paid for it. I had been to the E-5 promotion board, which was similar to the outstanding soldier board. I did okay, but the waiting list for advancement was long. I had 400 and some odd points and needed over 500 to guarantee me advancement.

The appointment was a huge jump in the pecking order of the platoon and in the Army in general. An E-5 was considered an NCO and as moving into the leadership ranks. You were looked upon differently, given special privileges, and a whole lot more responsibility. Of course, at my age, I was more interested in the privilege than the responsibility.

With this unofficial promotion I was moved into the barracks housing the NCOs. My roommate would be one of the sergeants in my platoon. I don't think he was too happy to give up his space in a double room to a roommate. Having no choice, he put up with me and we just gave each other space.

Even though I didn't own a vehicle the entire time I was in the Army I was stopped twice by the police, both times driving my buddy John Fisher's 1979 Ford Mustang.

The first time we were at a party at some off base housing complex. It was late afternoon and a buddy and I were hungry and wanted to get some food. So we decided to go to this fast food restaurant which was a few miles away on the main drag leading into Fort Polk. Now we were pretty lit up at the time we decided to go, and I don't know why John even gave us the keys. But, John and I had been friends a long time and I'm sure he didn't even think anything of it. In any case, neither of us could have been thinking too clearly at the time.

We got into the car, which was parked under an open sided carport supported by four posts. My buddy got into the driver's seat, but left his door open for some reason. As he started to back out, the open driver side door got caught on one of the car port posts and started to bend the door. I told my buddy that he was too drunk to drive and to let me drive, although I'm sure I was no better off than he was. We made it over to the restaurant without an incident, but I misjudged the entrance, and accidently pulled into the bank parking lot right next to the restaurant. That didn't seem to be a big deal because they were only separated by a grass divider with a curb. I thought I could drive right over the divider, curb and all, and into the restaurant parking lot. Mistake!

The curb was a lot higher than I thought and the grass divider was on a downward grade. I subsequently got the Mustang stuck on the curb. My buddy and I got out of the Mustang and tried to get it off the curb by rocking it back and forth to no avail. By this time we had the attention of the restaurant's manager, who must have called the police because the sheriff showed up.

The sheriff reminded me of the character Jackie Gleason played in "Smokey and the Bandit," with the Smokey-the-Bear hat, tan uniform, southern drawl, and big attitude. My buddy had walked over to the restaurant and called back to John to let him know we had his car stuck on the curb and needed help. I was standing there next to the Mustang when the sheriff sauntered up with his mirrored sunglasses. In a somewhat sarcastic tone he drawled, "Now what do we have here?"

I explained that I had missed the turn into the restaurant and I was trying to cut across the divider. The sheriff said "I can see that, now give me

110

your driver's license." When I provided him with my Pennsylvania driver's license he commented more than asked, "You're not from around here now are ya?" I thought to myself, this is going to be a long night!

At about this time a vehicle full of guys from the party, including John, arrived on scene. I told the sheriff that my buddies and I could lift up the car and get it off the curb, and we would be on our way. The sheriff told me that I was going to have to pay $50.00 to have a tow truck lift it off. Now $50.00 was a huge amount of money to me back then, about a quarter of my take home pay, and I thought about arguing the point. But fortunately, I had sobered up a bit by now and realized that he was actually giving me a break by not hauling my drunken ass off to jail! So $50.00 later, and a small amount of work by the tow truck driver, and the car was off the curb. John took possession of his Mustang and we were on our way back to Fort Polk and calling it a night!

The second time I was pulled over, I was leaving the town of Lake Charles, Louisiana. John, Cecil Cooper, and I had driven over to Lake Charles to hit the bars. This was after we had taken Cecil to get a tattoo in Leesville. We had done some damage and were heading back home. I was driving, John was in the passenger seat and Cecil was in the back seat. It was past midnight, the streets were empty, and I was on the outskirts of town when I saw the blue lights flashing in the rear view mirror.

As the policeman walked up to the Mustang, John and Cecil were sleeping. The policeman told me to get out of the vehicle. At about this time Cecil pushed open the back door on the passenger side and just started puking all over the place. The policeman, unfazed by Cecil puking, asked "Let me see your driver's license." I complied, also handing him my military identification, and he asked me "Do you know why I pulled you over?" I replied "No" and he said "I pulled you over for running a red light" I was thinking to myself; I didn't remember seeing a signal light! I know I had been drinking, but I didn't feel like I was intoxicated.

As the policeman was looking at my license, another police car came racing up and suddenly stopped right next us. It startled me, and I was

111

thinking I was in big trouble. The newly arrived officer yelled from his car to his associate that there was a code something or other going on back in town. The officer that had pulled me over tossed my license and ID card back at me and ordered, "Wait here, I'll be back."

After sitting in the car for several long, tense, minutes I thought; really? Should I wait? John was still sleeping and Cecil had resumed his passed out position in the back seat. I was thinking; that policeman had to have gotten my name for sure. I saw him write something down. Oh, screw it! And I took off! I sweated it out for weeks afterward, but never heard a thing about it.

My last major evolution in the Army was a trip back to Fort Leonard Wood, Missouri for training in the spring of 1985. I was excited to be going back wearing sergeant stripes. Our company had been tasked with going to Fort Leonard Wood for two weeks of refresher Bailey bridge training. Since I had predominately built the pontoon type bridge my whole career, this would be fun and different.

A Bailey bridge is the steel beam bridge most recognizable in a lot of old World War II movies. It comes in sections and to build it you basically keep joining sections together and pushing the bridge out on rollers across whatever it is you're crossing. As long as you have more bridge weight on land, the bridge won't fall into the gap your crossing. It was originally made to be assembled, disassembled, and moved. They were used by a lot of small town municipalities across America to cross creeks and small rivers and can still be seen in small towns like Urbana, Maryland and Rattigan, Pennsylvania.

The bus trip up to Fort Leonard Wood was really scenic and relaxing. We stopped at civilian restaurants, like the Ponderosa, for dinner and the tabs were covered by the Army. It was the first time I had eaten at a civilian restaurant on the military's dime. It was actually pretty interesting. We were issued government vouchers for a certain dollar amount and we could go in and order whatever we wanted, up to that dollar amount. It felt good to have some control and freedom of choice for a change!

Once at Fort Leonard Wood we were assigned to the good old fashioned WWII barracks again. These were the two story wooden barracks with a pot belly stove in the middle of the room and open bathrooms on the end. Very rustic compared to our nice barracks back at Fort Polk. The training was really fun as we built Bailey bridges for two weeks.

At one point we had a slow period and I decided to walk over to the recruit training area and see my boot camp barracks, Bravo 1-2. I was a sergeant now and not afraid of the drill sergeants wrath! As I neared the training barracks area, the memories of boot camp flooded back to me. As I passed recruits, they would stop suddenly and come to the position of parade rest as I passed, afraid I was a drill sergeant out on the prowl. I gave them a stern "Carry on," and kept on my way. The buildings and surrounding area were just as I had left them three years ago and it was like seeing an old friend. When I got close to my old barracks a rush of fear suddenly came over me. I was too afraid to actually go into the B-1-2 building! What if I ran into one of my old drill sergeants? What if SSG Strickland was still there and recognized me!? I did an abrupt about face and scurried back to the safety of my WWII barracks!

When we returned to Fort Polk, my three year enlistment was coming to an end and I needed to decide if I was staying in the Army or getting out. The Army wanted me to stay in and had set up a meeting for me with an Army re-enlistment counselor, who obviously tried to get me to re-enlist. He even guaranteed me promotion to a full paid sergeant!

But, I was ready to move on and wanted to give the civilian world a try. Everyone in my circle of friends was getting out and all we could talk about was getting back home. All my Dad's stories had come to life for me and I was homesick. I declined re-enlistment and waited to be discharged.

In my last days at Fort Polk I was assigned to supervise a trash detail that patrolled the fort. It was a week-long detail and was pretty easy. I rode around in this modified pickup truck that had steps on the back for two guys to stand on. I had a driver and two guys hanging on the back standing on those steps. As we slowly drove around the fort's main and back roads, the guys on the back would hop off and pick up trash.

Every now and then I would get a call on the radio that there was trash reported at some location and we would divert to that location and pick it up. These were usually high profile trash issues, like a soda can in front of the general's house! One such emergent call was to get to the PX because a skunk had been killed right in front of it and they needed the smelly thing removed ASAP! We diverted over there and scooped the smelly animal up, deposited it in a dumpster behind the PX, and continued on with our duty.

Before leaving the Army a friend of mine, Robert Beck, and I took a motorcycle trip over to Galveston, Texas. I must have been out of my mind riding on the back of that thing for over 500 miles there and back. It was probably the most dangerous thing I did in the Army! While in Galveston we got drunk and ended up sleeping on the beach. When we woke up in the morning, we dusted off the sand and started to look around for someplace to eat. We saw this GP-medium tent there on the beach and decided to see what was going on. GP-medium tent could mean Army guys, hey maybe they had food!

When we walked into the tent there were these guys in blue uniforms lounging around listening to short wave radios. I asked what unit they belonged to and they told me they were with the United States Coast Guard. I wondered; why didn't I join the Coast Guard? I could have been sitting here on the beach the past three years!

UNITED STATES COAST GUARD

US COAST GUARD TRAINING CENTER CAPE MAY

CAPE MAY, NEW JERSEY

18 November 1985 – 31 December 1985

After being discharged from the Army I went back home to Butler, Pennsylvania where my parents had settled down after my Dad retired from the CIA. My plan was to live with my folks for a few months until I could find a job, move out on my own, and resume civilian life. The town of Butler was reeling from the loss of one of its biggest employers, Pullman Standard. They made railroad cars and had recently shut down, flooding the area with the unemployed. The loss of Pullman also affected all the businesses that supported such a huge organization. Finding a full time job on my own was proving to be nearly impossible.

I remembered when I was being discharged from the Army I was told to register with my local unemployment office and that a veteran's representative would help me with finding a job. So I headed down to the local office in Butler to see my representative. When I arrived the place was packed with the unemployed. I waited my turn and filled out the required forms to enter me into the job pool. When it was my turn to see the veteran's representative he didn't have any good news for me. As he took my paperwork and moved it to the bottom of this foot high stack on his desk he said, "My best advice to you is to go back into the service."

After three months of job hunting, working odd jobs, and not finding a full time job, I was demoralizing. It was hard enough having to move back in with my parents who still had two of my school age siblings at home. I also found that in the civilian world I was on my own and it gave me an empty feeling. I missed the strong relationships I had with my Army buddies. That got me to thinking about going back into the military but I didn't want to go back into the Army. And then I remembered those Coast Guard guys on Galveston beach.

115

So while visiting my grandma and Uncle Mike on the farm I pulled out the phone book and looked up the Coast Guard. The nearest recruiter was in Monroeville, which was about 35 minutes away. I called them up and talked to a recruiter. After several questions about my discharge code from the Army it looked like I qualified and was asked to come on down to the recruiting office.

My recruiter was Marine Science Technician Chief (MSTC) Michael Condra. He showed me the usual recruiting material which depicted cool small boats and little picture perfect beach stations, along with helicopters swooping in and rescuing people. I asked if the Coast Guard was part of the military and he said "Yes, but the Coast Guard is under the Department of Transportation, not the Department of Defense like the Army, Navy, Air Force, and Marines." This sounded even better!

After reviewing my records Chief Condra determined that my Army job as a combat bridge crewman didn't equate to anything in the Coast Guard and I would have to come in as an E-3. Basically I would lose one pay grade but that was not a problem for me. I would have to pick another career field and go to school for that specialty before I could make E-4 again. This sounded good to me and I decided I would join the Coast Guard. I wanted to become an aviation survival man, the guy that jumps out of helicopters to save people, because the job rating looked so cool in the recruiting pamphlet. So I went back down to the MEPS station in Pittsburgh and took another physical and another ASVAB test. I scored a qualifying 71% on the ASVAB and passed my physical, but not without question.

I worried about my back during the physical and hoped it would not be an issue like when I joined the Army. The adjustment the chiropractor had given me before joining the Army had long since worn off. The curvature of my spine was back and I hoped the doctor wouldn't notice it. The doctor did notice it and pondered my back situation, finally concluded that since I already did three years in the Army it wouldn't be a problem.

Chief Condra told me I would have to go through boot camp again and I would be in what is known as a prior service company in boot camp. Its official name was Prior Service Indoctrination. He said I should expect the same boot camp experience I had in the Army, only this would be condensed to only four weeks. I hesitated, because in my mind I could see SSG Strickland! With his smoke-colored glasses, cigarette in his hand, smiling, and saying, "Four more weeks Semler! Drop and give me 20!" But I was determined to join, so I accepted my fate. And on the 18th of November 1985 I headed to Cape May, New Jersey for Coast Guard boot camp.

I arrived at the Philadelphia airport and just like in the Army I met up with the rest of the manila envelope carrying recruits at the bus pick up point. As the bus rolled into Cape May I felt my stomach tense as I dreaded the prospect of four more weeks of boot camp. When the bus came to a halt a guy in a blue uniform with a blue Smokey-the-Bear hat came storming aboard and started yelling for everyone to get off the bus, with the exception of the prior service guys. I thought to myself; we must be in for it, this is just like Army boot camp only the colors of the uniforms have changed.

As they marched the new recruits off yelling at them, the drill instructor came back on the bus and said in a very relaxed tone "All you prior service guys can get off and muster in front of the bus." Once we mustered he said, "If you got em', you can smoke em'" and called roll. I thought; okay, this isn't going to be so bad, and it wasn't.

Our drill instructors were relaxed and seemed to be pre-occupied with other things. They told us from the start that they knew we had all done tours in other branches of the service and they were not going to treat us like recruits for the most part, which turned out to be true.

After being issued our uniforms and gear, known as our sea bag, our days were filled with learning the Coast Guard way of doing things. Unlike the Army, there was no photo taking or issuing of dog tags.

We were berthed on the second deck of Munro Hall, which was a big three story brick building that sort of resembled an "X" if viewed from the air. Each wing of the "X" housed a recruit company on each floor. The berthing area had the typical boot camp, open bay style communal living area with metal bunk beds, now called racks in the Coast Guard, and an open bathroom, now called a head, at one end. We had metal wall lockers which lined the room and were just big enough to hold what was issued to us in our sea bag, which in the Army had been our duffle bag.

Our laundry was stowed in netted laundry bags secured to the end of our racks with a huge six inch metal safety pin. Once a week the netted bags were collected and taken to the laundry, washed, and returned. They washed everything while still in the bag. What you received was a wrinkled mess! But this is what it was like on the bigger cutters and they wanted you to get used to it here at boot camp.

We took classes on seamanship, customs and courtesies, and marksmanship with the 9mm pistol, shotgun, and M16 rifle. During our trip to the firing range I shot expert with the M16 and was issued my first Coast Guard medal. I guess I had an advantage after being in the Army. Usually we would get free time at the end of the day and were allowed to go to the club for a beer. It was common to run into our drill instructor there! That was always weird. This was quite different from the Army boot camp experience!

There were guys from all the branches of the military in this prior service company. It's funny because the only guys that didn't make it all the way through, except for the drug test, were Navy guys who could not pass the Coast Guard swim test! The swim test was probably the most difficult event for everyone. It was a make or break event. If you couldn't pass it, even after several tries, you were discharged. It sort of makes sense if you're going to be in the Coast Guard and save lives at sea you should know how to swim!

The test was conducted in a huge indoor swimming pool. It started off with jumping into the pool from a raised platform to simulate abandoning a sinking ship. From there you had to swim the length of the pool and back, which was about 100 meters, and then tread water or stay afloat for about five minutes.

About five of the Navy guys just could not pass the test and were discharged. They were mostly older guys, who were crossing over as E-5s and E-6s, and had obviously spent a lot of time in the Navy. I felt sorry for them because I could tell that the Coast Guard was a big opportunity for them. Like me, they faced a hard economy out in the civilian world and this was a good job opportunity.

On the 6th of December I had my four wisdom teeth extracted because I had received orders to a cutter as my first assignment. The Coast Guard liked to make sure if you were going to a cutter or isolated duty, that your risk of having a medical or dental incident was limited. When you're out bobbing around in the middle of the ocean it could take days to get to proper medical attention. Removing your wisdom teeth limited your risk of having a dental problem. The procedure went fine and I spent the night in the sick bay for observation. It was a painful night and all they would give me was Tylenol. And I don't mean Tylenol with Codeine, I mean regular old Tylenol. The next day I was sent back to my company feeling like crap and looking like a chipmunk!

A week later my company had chartered a tour bus through the morale office to take us to Atlantic City to visit the casinos. I hesitated to go because my mouth was still swollen and hurting. I wasn't making things any easier on myself. I was trying to quit smoking and had been using Copenhagen snuff as a replacement for cigarettes. The snuff was so fine that it was getting past my sutures and causing problems. What a mess, I basically was adding weeks to my healing process. I did finally heal but it took several weeks and a lot of self-induced pain. Oh, and I did make the trip to Atlantic City.

One of the usual formalities while processing through boot camp was a drug test. It's performed by providing a urine sample. In the few months between the Army and the Coast Guard I had been smoking a lot of pot. I really didn't think much of it. It wasn't a big deal in the Army and I thought once I was in the Coast Guard I would stop and that would be the end of that. A couple of weeks after I took the drug test, and about a month before we were to graduate, our drill instructor came walking into our classroom and said, "Some of you have failed your drug test!" I had a sinking feeling in my stomach. He read out a few names and told them to pack their sea bag; they had come up positive for cocaine and were being discharged. I thought, cool I'm safe. He then read out a few more names, mine being one, and said, "Come with me." The five or six of us went with the drill instructor who explained that we had come up positive for marijuana. He explained that we would be held there at Cape May until our drug tests showed that we were below a certain threshold of marijuana in our systems, and then sent on to our next unit. Wow, had I dodged a bullet!

So once a week I would go down and submit another urine sample and wait for the results. As long as the results were going down I could stay in the Coast Guard. If they went up it meant I was using marijuana and would be discharged. As the weeks went by my sample levels slowly dropped closer to my threshold level and the opportunity to move on. When our company graduated on the 12th of December I was still not below my threshold and stayed there at Cape May. I was assigned to the facility maintenance department to keep me busy. I wasn't alone, because all of us that got busted for pot were still above our threshold level!

We spent our days repairing the lockers in the barracks that were vacated by graduating boot camp classes and doing odd jobs in the metal shop. In the evenings we would head over to the club and have a few drinks. We stayed in the permanent party barracks, which for us consisted of a three man room with an attached head. Slowly, one by one we cleared our threshold and moved on. I was the last to go!

At the club one evening I had hooked up with a female seaman who was there at Cape May as a carryover like me. She wasn't being held over because of drugs, but to study and retake her ASVAB test. She was a really good looking, sandy blonde, southern girl. We had gone out a few times and one evening I arranged it with my roommates so I would have the barracks room all to myself for a few hours.

Well I'm in the rack, naked with my female companion, and the damn fire alarm goes off! It's a violation to have a member of the opposite sex in your barracks room, let alone having sex, so I convinced her that it was just a false alarm and we should just stay and ride it out. Wouldn't you know it but the fire department decided to check every room to make sure the barracks were empty! So here we are butt naked in the rack together and the fire department comes walking in. Needless to say it was a walk of shame as the two of us came walking out of the building, escorted by the fire department. We had to walk over to the muster point, where everyone else from the barracks stood watching us and waiting for the event to be over with. I ended up on the bad side of the master at arms who managed the barracks. He assigned me extra duty picking up trash around the barracks for my punishment. I would have to say it was worth it!

Just before Christmas I was detailed with mess cook duty at the galley. When I reported with the 10 or so other guys I was detailed to the scullery to wash dishes. I liked the assignment because I was out of the way and no one came into the hot, steamy scullery! As the recruits and permanent party folk would finish their meal they would bring their tray and dirty dishes up to the scullery window. I would take the tray of items, rinse them off, and place the items in containers to go through the huge steam dishwasher. I was working with a few other guys, and since it was Christmas time we started to sing Christmas carols to help perk the place up. It wasn't long before we were told to secure the festivities. Apparently, boot camp does not like a festive atmosphere!

Because I wanted to be in one of the aviation ratings I had to take a special physical at Cape May to make sure I met the physical qualifications for the rating. During this physical they found out that my eyesight was too bad to be in aviation and I would have to pick something else. That was a real blow to me. All my thoughts of jumping out of helicopters went down the drain. Nothing else else interested me. There were only

23 ratings in the Coast Guard and 5 of those were aviation ratings, which I now didn't qualify for.

The Coast Guard, unlike the other services, does not guarantee you a certain job field when you join. You normally come into boot camp as a recruit, which is pay grade E-1. When you graduate boot camp you are promoted to apprentice, which is pay grade E-2. At this time you elect to be either a fireman apprentice (FA) which covers the engineer ratings, seaman apprentice (SA) which covers the deck, operations, and supply ratings, or an airman apprentice (AA) which covers the aviation ratings. Once you leave boot camp you are sent to a unit to work as an apprentice in one of these fields until you are selected from a waiting list to go to your desired rating school. It's the Coast Guard's way of getting some manual labor out of you before you go to school and become rated in a job specialty. Once out in the fleet the wait list ranged from one week to over two years depending on which specialty you chose. But the normal wait time was about a year. While you wait you are referred to as a "non-rate."

I ended up choosing fireman apprentice because it sounded more exciting than seaman apprentice, and I couldn't be an airman apprentice. Because I was coming into the Coast Guard as an E-3 I was the rank of fireman. When you are promoted to E-3 the "apprentice" is dropped. You would then become a fireman, seaman, or airman. As a new fireman I was issued orders to the *USCGC Sumac (WLR-311)* out of St. Louis, Missouri.

USCGC SUMAC (WLR-311)

ST. LOUIS, MISSOURI

08 January 1986 – 11 October 1986

USCGC SUMAC (WLR-311)
On the Mississippi River

The *Sumac* was a 115 foot river tender built in 1944 that pushed a 136 foot barge. Together they were referred to as a cutter or river tender. The barge was loaded with red and green buoys, concrete sinkers, and steel wire used to mark the channel of the Mississippi River. Over the years she had been assigned several different homeports but spent the bulk of her life on the Mississippi River until she was decommissioned in 1999. She had an all-male crew of 21 and was commanded by Chief Warrant Officer (CWO) Maxson when I first arrived, followed by Master Chief Boatswain Mate (BMCM) Nadeau. They were referred to as the captain or commanding officer (CO) of the vessel.

My tour aboard the *Sumac* would be short, less than a year. But in that short period of time the Coast Guard and I would both go through changes. The Coast Guard would implement major policy changes and I would come to a cross road that would lead me to focus on a military career.

I arrived at CG Base St. Louis, Missouri which was located south of the city at the Foot of Iron Street. It was a cold January day and I pulled my 1985 Chevy Silverado pick-up truck through the unmanned gate and into the parking lot. The Silverado was brand new and I had purchased it with

$9000.00 I had saved up while in the Army. My truck along with my sea bag was all I had in the world.

The buildings on the small base surrounded the parking lot. There was the club and small exchange on the right, barracks in the middle facing the river, and the industrial building to the left. I couldn't see the *Sumac* but knew she was in port. I could tell that the river must be behind the barracks and made my way in that direction. As I rounded the barracks I could see a labyrinth of stairs dropping down, 20 to 30 feet, to a boat dock. The entire stair system and boat dock floated and moved up and down to accommodate the rise and fall of the river. At this time of the year the river was at a very low level.

Sumac was indeed in port and moored up to the boat dock. I slung my sea bag over my shoulder and headed on down to check in. It was regulation to check in wearing your dress uniform and present a smart appearance. The guy on watch met me at the gangway and welcomed me aboard. He walked me around to the bow of the *Sumac* to introduce me to my new boss, the Machinery Technician Chief (MKC) Trofhos. I was still using snuff trying to quit smoking. As I rounded the front of the *Sumac* I spit on the deck before entering the MKCs stateroom. The chief saw me spit from his stateroom window, and the first thing out of the chief's mouth when I entered was, "Son, get your ass out there and clean up your spit! And don't let me ever catch you spitting on my cutter again!" That would not be the last time Chief Trofhos yelled at me.

The engineering department consisted of a few fireman apprentices & firemen, an electricians mate third class (EM3), machinery technician third, second & first class (MK3, MK2, MK1), damage controlman first class (DC1) and the MKC. We maintained all the machinery aboard the *Sumac*; the main engines, generators, steering system, sewage system, water system, and so on.

Beside my daily engineering duties I had to qualify as an engineer of the watch (EOW) and in-port officer of the deck (OOD). These were watch-standing duties. To get qualified in these positions I had to stand what they called "port and starboard" duty until I finished the requirements for both qualifications. Port and starboard duty was one 24 hour day on duty and one day off duty. This meant I could only leave the cutter every other day.

124

I still had my normal work day from 0800 to 1600, so basically I could only leave the cutter every other day from 1600 until the following morning at 0800. Not a lot of free time! Finishing these qualifications would put me in the normal duty rotation of duty every fourth day in port and enable me to stand a four hour engine room watch underway.

It took me until the 1st of March, almost two months, to finish the watch requirements on a cutter this size. Bigger cutters took up to six months and longer. The engineering qualifications took the longest for my rating and centered around drawing out, on paper, every mechanical system on the cutter. Yes, there are blue prints of these on board, but someone decided long ago it would be better if you actually made your own copy. So my evenings after working hours were spent tracing out water, fuel, sewage, and numerous other piping systems. I equate it to looking for the water pipe coming into your house. Follow it from that point on to every fixture it goes to in your house like sinks, toilets, spigots, and so on. Draw it out to include every valve and denote when it passes from one room to the other. When you're finished sit back and enjoy the satisfaction of knowing where your water pipes are located!

Underway the four hour engine room watch required me to stand watch in the engine room, monitoring the main diesel engines and generators, checking every space on the hour, taking readings on machinery, and making log entries documenting any event. Communications with the bridge were via a brass tube that ran from the bridge to the engine room. If the bridge wanted to relay some bit of information down to me they would flick a switch that would activate a light in the engine room. I would remove the cover from the tube and we would yell our communications back and forth through the tube.

On the tender, watch rounds would be made of the steering gear room, known as the Lazarette or "Laz," reefer flats where the food refrigeration was located, sewage tank space, engine room, and storage and office space. On the barge we had the air compressor and crane to monitor and fore peak space to inspect.

After spending time around the machinery technician rating I found that I really enjoyed this type of work. And since my ASVAB score in mechanical aptitude qualified me for this rating specialty, I put my name on the machinery technician school waiting list. You could obtain a rating specialty in two ways, going to school or striking. Going to school was usually the preferred way to advance to a specialty because you got to transfer, go to school, and move on to a new unit. It was mandatory for some of the more technical ratings to go to school, but not all.

On the job training in your rating specialty was known as "striking." You formally applied to strike at your unit and you were then trained by the rated personnel in that rating there at your unit. Once you finished all the written and job performance qualifications you were advanced. Sometimes you remained at your unit, sometimes you were transferred. I could have applied to strike the MK rating there on Sumac, but I wanted a change of scenery and decided to go to the formal school.

Our normal operating schedule was to leave St. Louis on Monday and transit down the Mississippi River to the town of Cairo, Illinois. This took about a day, and on the way down the CO would document what work needed to be done on the way back. We would then work our way back up river replacing missing buoys, adjusting existing buoys, picking up buoys that had broken their chain or sinkers and washed ashore, repairing day boards, replacing day board batteries, and clearing day board sight paths. These were all used by river traffic to effectively navigate the river. The Coast Guard along with the Army Corps of Engineers, who managed the locks on the river and some navigation aids, guaranteed a navigable channel within the buoys at a depth of at least nine feet. And everyone using the river trusted us to make sure that depth was maintained.

Although my primary duties were in the engine room, I was called upon to help out on the buoy deck when needed. The buoy deck was operated by the boatswain mate rating and seamen. I didn't mind, working on the buoy deck was pretty exciting and it gave me a break from the engine room. The buoy deck had these big flat metal dump plates on both the port and starboard sides of the barge. The crane operator would set a 1000 pound concrete block, known as a sinker, on the deck plate. The deck hand would then attach a predetermined amount of wire cable to the concrete block and the eight foot tall buoy. The remaining wire was set in a roll on top of the sinker. The wire length was yelled down from the pilothouse depending on the river's depth.

126

Red buoys marked the right side of the channel and green ones marked the left, when viewed returning from sea or heading up river. As the tender was steaming along, the CO would yell, "Set it!" where he wanted the buoy, and the deck hand would pull the pin on the spring loaded deck plate holding the sinker. Away the 1000 pound sinker would go with a big splash, followed by the wiz of the remaining wire and the whoosh of the buoy getting pulled off the deck and into the water. As soon as the buoy was off the deck the deck hands commenced to get the next one ready. All this was done rain or shine.

One day I was assigned to work on the buoy deck. I was going to help out in one of the small boats we used to scout ahead of the cutter looking for dislodged buoys. We would travel ahead of the cutter and comb the river's edge looking for beached buoys that had broken their cable and washed ashore. Sometimes the buoys would wash up by themselves and just be laying there on the river bank. Others were tied to trees by folks looking to make money. Folks along the river would more or less find them and tie them to trees for safe keeping until we arrived. They would write their name and address on them and the Coast Guard would send them a finder's fee for securing them for us. We would collect the buoys with the small boat and tow them out to the cutter when she caught up.

It was a cold day and the Mississippi River, as always, was really moving. Its current moved between one to three miles an hour, which is pretty fast for water. I was in the small boat with one of the deck hands and our little outboard engine was struggling as we headed up river fighting the current. He wanted to cross from one side of the river to the other to pick up a buoy. As we were cutting across the river, a commercial tug was coming down river with a large load of barges. The commercial tug had the current behind her and was really moving. The deck hand was at the helm of the small boat and realized the commercial tug was going faster than he thought. He backed off the throttle to let the commercial tender clear us. What he had not anticipated was the huge wake of water the commercial tender was putting out and it hit us like a brick wall. I mean that water felt like someone had thrown a concrete block at me and I caught it in my chest. It knocked the wind out of us, soaked us, and swamped the little boat we were in.

So there we were in the middle of the fast moving and frigid Mississippi River, in a boat full of water, scared half to death! We needed help and I looked down river searching for the *Sumac*. There she was! Rounding the bend and heading for us as calmly as could be. It seemed like an eternity for her to reach us. Actually, with the fast current, we were probably moving faster toward her then she was toward us. The *Sumac* pulled alongside and lifted the small boat, with us in it, right out of the water and to the security of her dry deck. The Executive Officer (XO), Boatswain Mate Senior Chief (BMCS) Anthony, was not too happy to have his small boat swamped but was glad we were okay. As if nothing had happened we dried off and went back to work!

Working the navigational aids, known as day-boards, was another important deck hand duty that turned into an all hands evolution. Dayboards are huge, red and green, billboards positioned on land that help mark the channel. They also have a light beacon on top of them powered by a solar panel and battery system. We would pull the cutter into the river bank next to these day-boards and perform maintenance on the batteries, solar panels, lights, and overall condition of these river road markers. In the summer the brush would become really dense around them and almost block their view from the river. We would get out the chainsaws and machetes and have to hack our way to them, clearing a nice sight path so vessels could see them from the river.

Of course these overgrown riverbanks are perfect for cultivating Poison Ivy, Oak, and Sumac. All of which I am very allergic to! And man did I get it bad when we worked those day-boards. I would have it all over me by the end of the first day-board we would work. In a matter of days I was an itchy mess. In the evenings I would lay there in my rack covered in Calamine lotion and just itch. What even made it worse was that I still had to stand engine room watch in the 110 degree plus engine room.

Speaking of day-boards, on one occasion my good buddy MK3 Clay Tidwell and I had an unscheduled opportunity to explore a little bit of Herculaneum, Missouri. The cutter had sent me and the EM3 to go work the electrical system which was mounted on top of the day-board. We went over in the small boat and checked the batteries, replaced the bad bulbs in the light, and cleaned the solar panel. Somehow I left my prized Case knife up on the day-board somewhere. I had purchased that knife from a local gun shop back in Pennsylvania when I was home between the Army and Coast Guard and it meant a lot to me.

At some point after getting back on the tender I noticed I was missing the knife and was upset about leaving it on the day-board. When we pulled back into our moorings in St. Louis, Clay and I decided to see if we could find the light and retrieve my knife. We figured the day-board was someplace around the town of Herculaneum. My only reference from the river was this huge refinery, or grain elevator, which I could see from the day-board. Other than that it was all just river bank and trees. Now this may seem like an easy task, but these day-boards are meant for river traffic and may not even be accessible from any road.

It was about an hour drive south to the town of Herculaneum. It was a chance to get out of the city and the hour flew by. We kept thinking we were getting close to the day-board, but it seemed like we were driving in circles. Everything looks different when you're standing on land and looking out at the water verse our normal perspective of being on the water and looking back at land.

After several hours of back and forth along the dirt roads paralleling the river we determined that the day-board was only accessible by going through a huge guarded lead producing plant. When we pulled up to the guard shed the guard looked pretty intimidating. Clay and I flashed our military ID cards to the guard like we were FBI agents and were let right in! In about 30 minutes we had located the day-board and I had my prized Case knife in hand.

I had the chance to work on another day-board which could have been disastrous! We were in home port and the command needed to work a day-board that was only 30 minutes way. It must have been an important one for us to service it while in port and not just wait a few more days until we got underway. The command selected four of my friends to take the government truck to repair it.

My friends were going, which meant I really wanted to go, and I was pretty upset when I was told I was staying behind. Turns out the guys that went had one of the truck front doors sheared off by a train! They had picked up some beer on the way to the day-board and somehow parked the truck parallel against the train tracks with the front doors open. They had to walk down to the day-board and climb up the 50 foot or so tower to work on the light. While they were up there, a freight train came down the tracks and took off the truck door!

There was an investigation and things didn't turn out too good for my friends. They could have gotten away with leaving the door open as a stupid mistake, but add the beer while on duty and you have trouble. They were brought up on charges under the Uniform Code of Military Justice (UCMJ), found guilty at captain's mast, and given punishment. I was getting close to going to machinery technician school and if I had gone on that trip I would have been removed from the school list for bad conduct. I dodged a bullet!

When we were underway port calls were every night. We never steamed after dark. I'm not sure if it was a regulation or that the CO's just didn't feel comfortable doing it. We would try and hit a town with a pier but they were few and far between so we usually just pulled over to the river bank at sunset. As we would slowly edge our way close to the bank there would be a guy on the front of the barge and one on the back of the tender with long poles. They would stick them into the water feeling for the river bottom. You would hear them yell up to the captain, "No bottom!" every couple of seconds and then eventually, "Ten feet aft! now nine feet aft!" as they started to hit the rivers bottom. Once the captain felt he was close enough to the bank, and still had enough water under the cutter, we would tie up to a tree and set the spuds.

Spuds are a river tender's version of an anchor. They are two huge vertical metal beams toward the bow of the tender that are lowered by motors into the riverbed and they hold the cutter in place. These spuds pass right through "spud wells" which are openings in the tender's deck. It was a ritual for the new guy to fill the spud-wells with bucket upon bucket of water. It's a pointless task because the spud-wells are open to the river.

The first night we were underway after I arrived I was told to get a bucket and fill the spud-wells. So I got a bucket and started to pour countless buckets of water down the opening of the tender where one of the spuds was sticking out. Eventually, when the crew had their laughs, they told me to stop. I asked them, "How do you know when they are full?" The reply was that the only way the spud well would fill up with water is if the tender was sinking! This would surely not be my last initiation in the Coast Guard.

We ran a one-in-four duty section which meant every 4th day you had duty and had to stand a 24 hour watch aboard the tender. If you did not have duty, and had liberty, you could leave the tender after mooring up and walk into town and get a drink, or just sightsee. That is if there was even a town nearby. Usually these towns were very small and had only a

130

few houses. Sometimes we would just pull along the river bank in the middle of nowhere. In that case we would just sit around listening to music and telling sea stories.

These small backwoods towns were friendly but cautious of strangers. Some were predominantly white and didn't take to people of color. We had one or two black crew members and some of these small river stops were not friendly places to them. The CO, sympathetic of their desire to go on liberty, also knew the danger these places posed and would ask them to stay aboard. They understood the situation and never made a fuss or complained.

The white crewmembers were bothered by it. We all worked hard together and wanted to go into town together and blow off some steam. There was no discrimination on our cutter or in the Coast Guard that I knew of. During my time in the Army I never encountered any type of discrimination or racism, and I was stationed down in Louisiana! I never really discussed race while I talking about my Army experience because it was never an issue. The Army was totally integrated as far as I could see. My recruiter was black as were both my roommates at Fort Polk and the majority of my sergeants at all my units. In Korea and basic training it was always a melting pot of ethnicity.

So I was surprised when four years into my military career I encountered a strange incident aboard *Sumac* that I would consider more stupidity and ignorance than discrimination or racism. Although, I'm sure he may have had some questionable upbringing. We had received a new recruit from Cape May. He was a young white kid and as usual for young kids he went out and got drunk with the rest of us on liberty. We had a black seaman by the name of Cliff Fuller who had been on board for a while. He was older than most of us and we looked up to and respected him. He was old for being a seaman and I'm not sure if he was prior service or just happy being a seaman. It was common at that time to not promote if you liked where you were stationed. By not promoting you would not be transferred early and you could just homestead; meaning you could just stay at your current assignment.

So we came back from town all liquored up and passed out in our racks. In the middle of the night I woke up to this commotion and find a group of guys around Cliff's rack holding the drunken new seaman on the deck. Turns out he had tried to see if Cliff grew a tail at night! I had never

131

heard of such a thing. I guess it's some sort of folk lore or something. The seaman got roughed up a bit and it was only a matter of a few weeks before he was transferred over to the base. Maybe I hadn't been exposed to any type of discrimination or racism over my short career, but Cliff seemed use to it and just shrugged the incident off.

I had a nickname, like most of us, and Cliff gave it to me. Cliff had glassy eyes and smoked menthol cigarettes which always seemed to make his eyes water. He looked at me with those watery eyes one day, cigarette dangling out of his mouth, and said, "You look like a JABO to me. Yep that's what I'm going to call you, JABO." So my nickname while I was aboard *Sumac* was JABO. I later asked Cliff what JABO meant and he coolly replied, "Just Another Buoy Observe!"

Living conditions were pretty tight for an all-male crew of 21. The CO and XO had their individual staterooms forward on the upper deck and shared a head. The MKC and boatswain mate first class (BM1) had their own staterooms along with the senior petty officers, who shared a berthing area, on the main deck forward. They all shared a head up forward. The remaining 15 junior enlisted lived all the way aft. Our racks were stacked three high. I was in the top rack in a set of six that were side by side with no dividers. Since they were stacked side by side with no dividers, the guy in the rack next to you would always be rolling over into your rack. It was like sleeping in the same bed with the guy!

Our head was aft of our berthing area and it had two sinks side by side, two toilets side by side with no divider, and two showers. There is nothing like sitting there on the toilet with a guy next to you. I'll have to say that you lose whatever hang-ups you have real quick! With tight living conditions we kept things clean. Every day we swept and mopped the berthing area. The head was totally wiped down, swept and mopped. All garbage and butt cans were emptied. Once a month or so we aired our mattresses out on the deck which was above the berthing area. The CO ran a clean cutter!

Meal time was piped using a boatswain's whistle. It was done in the old tradition and manually piped by one of the boatswain mates. We had a cook on board who cooked us three meals a day while underway. In port he would cook breakfast and lunch during the work week. After hours and on the weekends we had an open galley, which was basically fending for yourself. The cook would leave the refrigerator and freezer in the galley unlocked and we would just help ourselves to what we wanted. Our main food staple was making hamburgers on the grill top and fries in the deep fat fryer.

It was my first interaction with the substance specialist (SS), which is the rating for cooks. The two that were on board during my limited time were eccentric to say the least. The first cook had the longest hair I have ever seen on an active duty person. He would sort of gel or grease it so it was compact and looked short. But when he took all that grease and gel out of his hair he looked like a hippie! He was actually pretty famous because of the antics of his wife. At some function on the cutter before I had arrived, she either lifted up her shirt to show off her breasts or dropped her pants and mooned the captain! Heck I liked both stories.

The second cook was a big jolly fella with bad smelling feet. They wouldn't let him keep his boots in the berthing area they were so bad. He had a car that was hand painted with deck grey paint. Deck grey paint is what's used all over the cutter on the decks. The car looked awful, it leaked oil really bad, and he was always asking for oil from the engine room. So his car was painted with Coast Guard paint and lubricated with Coast Guard oil! I will have to say that he did make the best creamed beef, just like my mom's.

We had a pretty good sized recreation room (rec-deck) up on the barge. It was a huge room with sofas, chairs, and a pool table that we used to hang out and watch TV. This was the general hang out for everyone. It had a window air conditioning unit that kept it cool on those hot summer days working the river. It was a nice place to wind down at the end of the day. Especially if we were spudded down next to a river bank!

I remember on the 28th of January 1986 hearing that the space shuttle Challenger had blown up during its launch and running up to the rec-deck to see what was going on. We all sat there amazed that such a thing could happen. Back then the space shuttle was a big deal.

Up to this time the Coast Guard mandated retirement age was 62 and you could stay in at pretty much any pay grade. In 1995 they enacted a retirement program that limited members to 30 years of service and instituted mandatory pay grade retirement milestones. For instance, you had to make E-6 by 20 years or you were out. So we had quite a few older guys aboard and some who had been in the service for as long as 10 years but were still low level enlisted. This was largely due to the fact that they liked where they were and didn't want to transfer to take a promotion and/or they were just happy being in a position of no authority or responsibility. They had job security, a steady paycheck, and that's all they wanted.

In July of 1986 the CO's tour was up and he was being replaced. Our new CO, BMCM Nadeau, made a trip south with us down to Cairo, IL and back. During this trip the outgoing CO was transferring responsibilities of the cutter over to BMCM Nadeau who didn't say much of anything to the crew, just observed. The BMCM must not have been happy with what he had seen on the trip with us.

Every morning we would have muster on the aft deck of the tender which covered the engine room, mess deck, and berthing area. They called it the "Texas Deck" because it was the biggest deck on the tender. The first morning that BMCM Nadeau took over we mustered on the Texas Deck as usual. The BMCM walked up to all of us standing in formation and said that he had reviewed all of our personnel records and he was cutting out the dead wood. He took a handful of personnel records and dropped them on the deck and said, "If you belong to one of these personnel records get your sea bag and get off of my boat." And so a few of the long time seaman packed up their sea bag and headed up to the base barracks to await another assignment or possibly even discharged from the Coast Guard.

My record could have easily been in that pile if not for an incident a few months earlier. We were working up north covering an area for another cutter. I was floundering; drinking and partying was my priority. My supervisor, MK1 Dave Smith, caught me alone in the galley one evening. We were getting something to eat and he saw his opportunity to engage me. He said, "Ed, you have such potential, why are you wasting it? I can help you get to MK school if you make it your priority."

He had caught me at just the right time –I was ready. All the other nonrates were going no place and I could see it. I realized I needed to get it together and now. So I took him up on his offer. From that day forward I totally immersed myself in getting to school. In the evenings, after work, instead of going out on liberty I stayed on the cutter and MK1 Smith taught me the fundamentals of engineering. If I hadn't listened to him that night, I have no doubt my record would have been laying there on the Texas Deck.

My generation of Coast Guardsmen considers a major milestone in the Coast Guard to be when the Commandant of the Coast Guard, Admiral Gracey, was replaced by Admiral Yost, in May of 1986. Admiral Yost wasted no time banning the age old seafaring tradition of wearing beards. He also introduced a slew of unpopular, at least with the junior enlisted, budget cutting measures. Scuttlebutt at the time with us junior enlisted was that he wanted to ban alcohol sales on base and close all the base clubs down! We jokingly referred to the new Coast Guard under Admiral Yost as the "Yost Guard." The transition would be very evident to me while on the *Sumac* as I saw these new changes take effect. No one likes change, especially those that affect tradition.

After headquarters came out with the initial message that they would be banning beards on a set date, it was like watching condemned men waiting for their final day. The person that took it the hardest was BMCS Anthony, the XO. He had a really nice long beard that just looked nautical. He reminded me of one of those German U-boat captains you see in the movies. When he came into work the day the ban took effect I didn't even recognize him. Needless to say he was not happy and we all gave him a wide berth!

I wasn't worried about the beard issue as much as I was worried about the banning of alcohol on base. While in port one of my favorite daily routines was walking up to the base with friends at lunch and getting a beer out of the beer machine. It was just like a soda machine but was filled with beer. At lunch we were allowed two and we always at least had one. Drinking was a big part of my life. I was young, single, and living for the moment.

One of the Coast Guard's primary missions was search and rescue. Even at my age I knew not everyone would make it. I sort of expected to come across a corpse at some point in the Coast Guard. It seemed like that would be a part of the job. My first Coast Guard experience with a dead body happened on an in-port duty day. I was sitting up on the bridge watching the river traffic go by when a police small boat came alongside the pier. The local police had pulled a "jumper" from the water and were laying the body out on the pier. It was common for people to jump off the Bernard F. Dickmann Bridge, also known as the Poplar St. Bridge, which was just up river from our moorings. It is a major interstate bridge which crosses I-55 and I-64 from Illinois to Missouri. This body had been in the water for a while and was bloated. They had draped a sheet over it and I will never forget the smell that filled the air. I dealt with it much the same way I did the kid that killed himself at the holding camp in Germany; I put it in its place and didn't assign it an emotional attachment. It was another day and when the body moved on, so did I.

I once heard that a study of people over 100 years old showed that if you can compartmentalize grief or stress in your life you live longer. It's not that you're uncaring or shallow; it's more that you can deal with it, put it in its place, and move on with your life.

During an extended in-port we overhauled one of the three Caterpillar Diesel engines that powered the *Sumac*. It was the middle of the three engines known as the "keel main." To assist us we had an MK1 come down from the area material assist team (MAT) which was located across the river in Granite City, Illinois. He specialized in overhauling engines and maintained all the special tools needed for the job at the MAT team. He was a very relaxed guy who just blended in with us and seemed like part of the crew. Seeing his extensive mechanical knowledge and independent duty; traveling on his own, started to reinforce my interest in the MK rating.

The engine overhaul had us working from sunup to sundown. Each day always ended with us grilling burgers and making fries in the galley. Although we were all relaxed and having a good time, the MKC was a nervous wreck during this whole evolution. He was a heavy smoker and drinker who always had a cigarette in his hand. We were more than likely under a time crunch to get the engine back up and running so the cutter could get underway and the chief was showing the pressure. I will never forget overhauling that engine, with him yelling at us with a cigarette in his mouth, one in the ashtray, one in his hand, and two lying on the engine someplace! I would be wiping down that engine weeks later and still find cigarettes lying on the engine with an ash trail where it had burnt down to the filter.

When we went to start the engine up for the first time it kept overheating. After a lengthy investigation we found out that "someone" forgot to cut a hole in one of the homemade jacket water gaskets and the engine could not get any cooling water. Of course the chief was super pissed! I knew my boss MK3 Tidwell had made the mistake, but I wasn't about to rat on him and have him face the wrath of the chief!

Everyone gave the chief a wide berth. He had taken a good part of my ass on several occasions and I avoided him like the plague. He was the type of chief that looked like he was going into cardiac arrest when he got mad. He had really thin, long for regulations, Brill Creamed hair and wore glasses. When he got on a rant that hair would be flying along with his hands and spit! And to add to his charming persona he had a boat propeller screw tattooed on each of his ass cheeks! And I know this because when he got liquored up he would drop his drawers and show them to you!

Once he caught me goofing off when we had a casualty with the barge crane cooler. The cooler had gotten plugged with river sand and we had taken it apart to clean it. The chief always wanted everyone present at a casualty. This always turned into him and the MK1 fixing it while the rest of us sat there and watched or occasionally fetched something. I usually didn't look at these events as a learning experience, more as total boredom!

On this particular casualty I could see that there were way too many people standing around so I slipped back to the tender to work on something a little more interesting - my hard hat artwork. It was trendy to have nice graffiti on your hard hat! The chief must have noticed I had slipped away and came up looking for me. He found me sitting in the engine room cutting out reflective tape into graffiti and placing it on my hard hat. He hit the roof! I would have to say after all these years it's still a very memorable ass chewing. He went up one side of me and started down the other. By the time he was done I was covered in spit. He was so close to my face yelling I don't think you could have slid a piece of paper between us!

And then there was the time Clay and I were tuning up the GM engine on the barge air compressor. We had been out there for a while and could not figure out how to set the valve lash on the intake valves. I reluctantly went to ask the chief as Clay had directed me. I should have suspected there was a reason Clay wasn't going to ask him. As soon as I had asked my question the chief's hair, hands and spit started flying. He yelled, "You fucking idiots, GM's don't have fucking intake valves, they have a fucking blower!" I'm sure there was a lot more said but I really can't remember anything past that initial bombardment! I should have told him Clay forgot to cut the whole out of the jacket water gasket back on the engine overhaul job!

Probably my last memory of the chief was a final port call when he lost his glasses. I had gone to see him in his stateroom for something and saw that he was pretty hung over and missing his glasses; all the ingredients for a nuclear meltdown. I didn't waste any time in exiting and leaving him alone.

While moored up in St. Louis, and working on that famous barge air compressor one day, I noticed animal tracks all over the deck. When the air compressor ran it left a small sheen of oil on the deck and some animal had walked through the oil and was tracking it around. Clay and I followed the tracks around and you could see that whatever it was - was pretty big. We wiped up the oil tracks and didn't really think much of it. A few days later we were doing maintenance on the air compressor and there were those animal tracks again. They were everywhere. We examined them pretty closely but neither one of us could tell what they were. We couldn't imagine what was getting on board and walking around unnoticed.

Later that week I had duty. I was sitting up in the pilot house listening to the barge traffic on the radio and waiting to go on my next hourly round of the cutter. It was late at night and I happened to notice something really big walking around up on the barge. Nothing should be up there at this time of night, so I headed down to the main deck to make my way up there. I had come out of the port side door on the tender and stepped onto the weather deck area which would take me up to the barge. This area is about three feet wide with the cutter's structure on one side and a three foot high solid steel wall on the other side.

As I started to walk toward the barge here came this huge, dog sized, raccoon down the weather deck toward me! I don't know who was more scared, me or the coon. I turned around, ran inside, and headed back up to the bridge. I don't know what the coon did after seeing me, but he was nowhere to be seen once I got back up to the bridge. Needless to say I was jumpy as could be the rest of the night. Every time I would have to go make a round I was waiting for that coon to come popping out from around a corner!

Base St. Louis was home port for two other newer river tenders, the *USCGC Cheyenne (WLR-75405)* and *USCGC Obion (WLR-65503)*. They covered other areas of the Mississippi River and surrounding rivers. Every now and then we would cover each other's operating area if one of us couldn't get underway. On one of those occasions we took the northern run of the Mississippi River and transited from St. Louis up river to Davenport, Iowa. This was a great break from our usual southern run. It would also be an unusual trip because we had to transit through all the locks on the Mississippi River. They end in St. Louis, just before our moorings, so they are not on our normal run. Our normal operating area on the Mississippi River was after the last set of locks at the Chain of Rocks Locks in Granite City, Illinois.

Going through the locks took time. The Mississippi River is a heavy commerce route for river tugs pushing barges loaded with cargo. Their loads consist of so many barges that they have to take them through the locks several at a time. It takes hours for these tugs to get all their barges through one single lock. Usually there is a line of tugs with their barges waiting their turn to go through the locks. As a government vessel we took priority and would go straight to the head of the line.

There was never any idle time when transiting the locks for us. While we were waiting for the lock to close, fill, and empty, we would fill our potable drinking water tanks from a hose provided by the Corps of Engineers who ran the locks. Because we didn't have a water maker on board and usually tied up to the river bank, this was our only means of getting fresh water. Sewage was never a problem. We would just pump our sewage overboard while transiting the river. Yes, right into the river. The chief said it was good for the catfish!

Working the upper part of the Mississippi also meant we had to change the way we set buoys. We used steel cable on the southern part of the river we operated on, but up north they used chain. It wasn't that much different to set them, except the chain was heavier and made a huge racket as it fed out unlike the wiz of the steel wire we used down south.

One evening while heading back home we ran hard aground. Scuttlebutt was the CO fell asleep at the helm. We were headed south and it was getting late. The captain got a report that some buoys we had just set behind us had been taken out by a commercial tug and barge. The CO decided to turn the *Sumac* around and replace the buoys since we were so close. I guess the plan was to head back north until it got dark, moor up, and replace the buoys in the morning. About an hour after we turned around I was back aft and felt us hitting hard. I walked out to the weather deck and saw we were right next to shore! I knew something was wrong right away because no one had said we were getting ready to moor and we should never, ever hit ground. We immediately made the rounds of the cutter making sure we had no damage or leakage, and there was none. The area had a sand and mud river bottom so we were lucky. After a lot of back and forth with the engines we made it off the river's bottom and continued on our way. I never knew for sure what happened to cause the grounding but given the rumor, no one ever brought up the incident.

On another occasion during this trip we were moored up to the river bank outside of Burlington, Iowa. We had just spudded down in the middle of nowhere. All you could see besides woods was this huge factory that loomed in the distance. Everyone stayed on the cutter because there was no place to go, so we didn't put over any type of ladder or gangway. It was dark and I was on the weather deck having a smoke with some shipmates. From the cutter's lights casting a glow on the water we noticed things swimming in the water. We turned on the spot lights and there were hundreds of rats trying to swim out to the cutter and get aboard! It was like watching a horror movie. Luckily they couldn't get aboard! They just swam out, couldn't figure out a way to get on, and swam back to shore.

On my last trip aboard the *Sumac*, as we headed home under the Jefferson Barracks Bridge which crosses I-255, the last bridge we went under before we got to our moorings, I had my last chance to screw up and stay aboard *Sumac*. It was a custom to get a glass jar of paint and throw it at the bridge pillar on your last trip and "paint the bridge." BMCS Anthony was very familiar with this unauthorized practice and he knew I was on my last trip. He had made the statement that the tradition was no longer approved of and he would punish anyone who did it. Well there I stood with a jar of paint in my hand as we came up on the bridge. And you know what, I didn't throw it. The old Ed would have thrown it, but I was no longer the old Ed. I was maturing from a live-for-the-day type of person, to one looking toward the future.

As we pulled into our moorings the river was at a historic flood level. It had crested at Graton, Missouri, which is just north of St. Louis, at 29.70 feet. It was the sixth highest crest ever recorded. Our pier was even with the parking lot of the base, unlike the 20-30 foot drop when I had arrived. I swept up my sea bag and headed off the gangway never looking back. I was on my way to USCG Machinery Technician "A" School in Yorktown, Virginia.

US COAST GUARD TRAINING CENTER YORKTOWN

MACHINERY TECHNICIAN "A" SCHOOL

YORKTOWN, VIRGINIA

13 October 1986 – 30 January 1987

Machinery technician school was somewhat of a return to boot camp. We had academic class, marched everywhere we went, pulled guard duty, had special details, and were monitored 24/7 by a cadre of instructors and class leaders.

The rating was formed in 1974 when the boiler technician (BT), machinist mate (MM), and engineman (EN) ratings were combined to form the machinery technician (MK) rating. I know you're probably wondering why the abbreviation is not MT instead of MK. Well the Coast Guard ratings follow the Navy standard due to the fact that the Coast Guard falls under the direction of the Navy in times of war. There was already a Navy missile technician (MT) rating so the Coast Guard had to change the abbreviation to something else, and they chose MK. Why "K" I do not know.

The 14 week curriculum was pretty intense for someone like me with a very basic understanding of mechanics, hydraulics, and electricity. I was still unsure about my ability to learn everything I needed to become a machinery technician. On the *Sumac* I just followed the directions I was given. I never really tried to comprehend the theory behind what MK1 Smith was teaching me about how an air conditioner or boiler worked.

But as with everything else I was exposed to in the military, there was a detailed process. No matter what your background was we started out with the very basics, such as recognizing what a screwdriver was and so on. So no matter what your skill level was before getting here, we all started out from scratch. In the following weeks it was basic machinery, electricity, then rebuilding an engine and so on. As my knowledge grew, so did my confidence for working on things.

Classes started at 0800 and ended at 1600 and ran from Monday through Friday. We were kept fairly busy on the weekends with duty and homework. We always had homework that would take us several hours to complete. You were there to learn and you were expected to keep up and maintain a passing grade. If you fell behind you had to stay behind for study hall. Simple academics that have been proven to work through the ages!

Our weekly studies involved mechanical engineering theory and our progression hinged on the Friday end of week test. In order to advance with the class you had to demonstrate proficiency. And it was always held over us that you didn't want to fail or you would be sorry! When there was a failure, the instructors converged on you in a tidal wave of information and you retested until you passed. Instructors didn't want you to fail. If you failed it reflected badly on their teaching ability, and then they had to stay after hours teaching you the information until you passed. And you didn't want to be cutting in on the instructor's liberty!

As a collateral duty I volunteered to be a member of the base honor guard. We all needed a collateral duty and I sort of picked this one without much thought. It turned out to be really challenging and took a lot of afterhours training. After class and on the weekends we would practice drilling and doing tricks with rifles for hours. You've seen it before when military members are twirling a rifle around and flipping them back and forth to each other. That's pretty much what we trained to do. Although it didn't really interest me at first, I am glad I did get involved with the honor guard because it was a nice distraction from the daily academic routine. We never performed at any ceremonies or were involved in any parades while I was assigned to the detail. But we did raise and lower the flag on board the training center, which was in my eyes an important responsibility.

Guard duty on the other hand was boring. It consisted of standing watch down at the small boat station known as Wormley Creek and front desk duty at the other buildings on the training center. The front desk duty wasn't as bad because it was sitting inside, but the Wormley Creek duty was tough because it meant standing out in the cold weather.

Our barracks were the typical three story brick buildings similar to those in Cape May. We were berthed on the second deck of Steuben Hall and I shared a room with three other classmates. The room consisted of two older style wooden bunk beds, four wooden desks, and four simple metal wall lockers. We all smoked so there was a constant haze in the room. Smoking inside was normal and we didn't think anything of it. The head was on the other side of the building and shared by everyone on the floor, referred to as a deck. It had a gang shower, which was an open area with shower heads and valves lining the wall. Finishing off the head was a row of sinks, and stalled toilets. The only other noticeable feature of the barracks was a recreation room on the main deck that had a TV and pool table.

MK "A" school roommates FN Duran, FN Hithcox, FN Shrieffer, FN Semler

We usually had a majority of the weekend off and caroused around off base or hung out at the enlisted man's club. I caroused around a little too much and got my first professional tattoo in the small town of Yorktown. Up until this point I had a few homemade ones created by two school-mates in Australia. They were applied using India ink, cotton, needle, and consuming a lot of beer! This was a very crude and unsanitary way of applying a tattoo. So I was ready for a professional one.

My buddy Bob Schrieffer and I had gone down to the local watering hole in the sleepy little town of Yorktown. After a few beers we got on the subject of tattoos. Bob didn't have any and I had been thinking about getting one for a while. So after a few more beers we headed over to the local tattoo parlor. We both went in but only one of us walked out with a tattoo! I picked something out on the wall of endless tattoo art and sat in the artist's chair. He copied the art onto my arm and reached for his needle gun. This was before the more stringent sterilization protocols of today. He pulled the needle out of a small jar of alcohol sitting on the counter, loaded it in the tattoo gun, and went to work. I wound up with a lovely likeness of the "Zig Zag Man." He was the cigarette rolling paper icon for dope smokers, which was probably totally inappropriate for the drug busting Coast Guard! I was still obviously hitting a few bumps on the road to making my transition to the new Ed!

Over the Christmas holiday we were given the opportunity to take a week of leave and vacate the training center. The alternative was to stay and field day the classrooms and heads for a week. I chose to head up to Pennsylvania and see my family since it was only about eight hours away. My buddy Bob Schrieffer joined me since it was too far for him to go back home to New Hampshire.

Before the command let us hit the road on leave they mustered us all in the training center's movie theatre for a safety briefing. In the briefing a man in a wheelchair rolled himself out onto the stage of the theatre and told us the story of how he was paralyzed in a car crash, all because he wasn't wearing his seat belt. Up until this point in my life I had never worn my seat belt. The man's story, and the way he delivered it, had such a profound impact on me that day that I have worn my seat belt ever since.

We arrived in Pennsylvania where Bob promptly got drunk with my Dad and I got my truck stuck in a back field at the Semler farm; and those were pretty much the highlights! Truly, I always enjoyed time with my family, both immediate and extended. I took the time to get back to see them any chance I could get.

The whole base at Yorktown exposed me to American and Coast Guard history. The original base was operated by the Navy from 1917 until it was transferred to the Coast Guard in 1959. It is located right in the middle of the American Revolutionary War battlefield of Yorktown. This

146

was a pivotal battle in the Revolutionary War. Victory by American forces led to the surrender of the British Army under Lord Cornwallis, the inevitable end to the war, and American independence. The area was also heavily fortified during the Civil War by Union forces.

Although the base itself was not a Coast Guard historical landmark, it was filled with Coast Guard historical artifacts. The galley in particular impressed me every time I entered it. As I sat and ate my meals I would gaze up at the walls that were covered in huge painted murals of past Coast Guard vessels and events. And in every available space on the deck were artifacts from cutters that had been long gone. The atmosphere was inspiring.

Talking about the galley reminds me of a funny story. A time when one of the students came walking in with bright yellow hair! This was a major infraction to the strict haircut regulations. It was Monday morning and the galley was full of students eating breakfast. The Coast Guard had strict regulations on hair length and color. Hair was to be no more than 1-1/2 inches in bulk, not touching the ears, tapered in the back, and your natural color. Well, in walks a guy who obviously had a bad weekend! His hair was colored bright yellow. It was so bright and unnatural that he stood out like a beacon. And when he walked in the galley you could have heard a pin drop. I'm not sure what punishment he ended up getting, but I can tell you that he was definitely punished!

This leads me to a more serious story; when a bunch of my classmates decided to have a pre-graduation celebration. They got a hotel room off base, got drunk, and had some prostitute over. The cadre at the school got wind of it and for some reason they made a big deal out of it. To the point that they wanted to hold everyone from graduating until they figured out if any rules were broken. Come on! Drunken sailors in a room with a prostitute seemed pretty normal to me.

Our class cadre got us all dressed up in our dress uniforms and marched us around the training center for hours. Up and down every road and into every parking lot where we conducted facing movements. Eventually we ended up in front of the chief's club where they left us standing in the parking lot at attention. They went in and had a few drinks and talked over what they were going to do with us. After a while they came out and marched us around a bit more and returned us to our barracks. You could tell that they wanted us to pay for our actions, but really did not want to get the command involved. They must have been satisfied with their punishment because that was the last we heard of it and we were all allowed to graduate. It seems they reached the same conclusion I had; typical sailors on liberty!

Several weeks before we graduated I had received orders to the *USCGC Seneca (WMEC-906)*, a new 270' cutter out of Boston, Massachusetts. I was starting to wonder what ever happened to all those nice small boat stations, with beautiful sandy beaches, the recruiter had shown me! I never recall him showing me any of these huge navy-like ships!

Graduation was a proud moment for me. It marked the day that I became rated and would get my "crow" designating me as a petty officer. Sure I had made E-4 in the Army, but it took so much more of an effort to get it in the Coast Guard. Unlike in the Army where I made E-4 solely on keeping my nose clean and longevity, I had to learn a skill to make E-4 in the Coast Guard. I was now Machinery Technician Third Class Petty Officer Semler, and heading to Boston to catch my ship.

USCGC SENECA (WMEC-906)

BOSTON, MASSACHUSSETTS

12 February 1987 – 18 January 1990

USCGC SENECA (WMEC-906)
In Baltimore, Maryland for a port call

I arrived at Coast Guard Base Boston, Massachusetts in the middle of a huge snow storm as a brand new MK3. The *Seneca* was out at sea and I waited at the base barracks until her arrival a few days later. The base had been there for years and was located right in downtown Boston in the North End section. Right across the inlet were the historic Navy piers where the *USS Constitution* was moored.

The accommodations at the barracks were dated but pretty nice; I had my own room and a shared head. My room was several stories up and my window looked right out onto Commercial Street and the busy North End. I was just getting comfortable when the *Seneca* pulled in.

The *Seneca* was a newly built 270 foot medium endurance cutter, the sixth in the "Famous Cutter" class. She was named in honor of the cutter

Seneca which served from 1908–1936. The older *Seneca* distinguished herself over her service life conducting ice patrols, sea rescues, and convoy duty during WWI. During the war she lost 11 crewmembers who had volunteered to man the torpedoed *SS Wellington*. The *SS Wellington* was in a convoy being escorted by *Seneca* when she was torpedoed in her bow by a German U-boat and started to sink. Nineteen *Seneca* and eleven *SS Wellington* crewmembers volunteered to try and keep her afloat and sail her back to France while *Seneca* and the rest of the convoy continued on. After getting her stable and commencing the transit *SS Wellington* ran into rough weather and sank. The water was extremely cold and 11 *Seneca* and 5 *SS Wellington* crewmembers perished before the remainder were rescued.

The new *Seneca* was just coming out of refitting at the Coast Guard shipyard in Baltimore, Maryland and was heading back to home port. She had a new crew of plank owners on her. A plank owner refers to a crewman assigned to a newly commissioned ship. At this point she had only gotten under way for sea trials in Newport, Rhode Island where she was built and for refitting in Baltimore. She had yet to make her first official patrol.

I would end up completing eleven patrols on her; two District 1 North Atlantic fisheries patrols, six District 7 Caribbean drug and migrant patrols, and three refresher training patrols at Guantanamo Bay, Cuba and Little Creek, Virginia.

Patrols ranged from six to eight weeks underway with four to six weeks in port for maintenance. It was mandatory to be underway at least 180 days a year. When we came back from a patrol we were usually given 72 hours of liberty, unless you had duty, and then it was a straight Monday through Friday 0800-1600 work schedule. I stood a straight one-in-four duty rotation, which meant every fourth day I had a 24 hour duty aboard the cutter. This was the standard duty rotation and a majority of the crew stood it. With that type of duty schedule in-port free time and liberty were scarce.

While underway we would stop for two day refueling, supply, and liberty port calls about every two weeks, or twice a patrol. These port calls included Puerto Plata, Dominican Republic; Roosevelt Roads, Puerto Rico; Guadeloupe; Guantanamo Bay, Cuba; Mobile, Alabama, Miami and Fort Lauderdale, Florida; Governors Island, New York; Halifax, Nova Scotia;

St. Thomas, U.S. Virgin Islands; Little Creek, Virginia; Annapolis and Baltimore, Maryland; Rockland, Maine; Wilmington, North Carolina; New London, Connecticut; and Newport, Rhode Island.

The cutter had a crew of 100, consisting of 14 officers and 86 enlisted. When I initially reported aboard there were two female junior officers. They left about halfway through my tour on normal rotation for their next duty stations. They were replaced with two male officers. In order to have a female officer aboard they needed to be assigned in pairs because of the limited berthing.

The officers had their own berthing area in the upper forward area of the cutter. It was made up of single and two man staterooms with their own head in each stateroom. Their dining and recreation area, called the wardroom, was on the main deck amid ship.

Our captain was Commander (CDR) Jay Creech. Captain Creech had been in a while and had plenty of sea time, which we called "salt." He entered the Coast Guard Academy in 1964, the year I was born. He was a Vietnam veteran having served in the *USCGC Mendota (WMEC-69)* and returning for a second tour ashore in Vietnam with an explosive loading detachment.

At my level there was no interaction with the CO. I would only hear him over the intercom system or pass him on the decks or in the passageways. Back then, when the CO came walking down the passageway you got out of his way, squared it, and gave him a greeting. If he walked into a compartment you were in you snapped to attention and yelled, "Attention on deck!" If you passed him out on the weather deck you gave him a smart salute, a greeting, and kept moving. He ran a tight ship. When we got underway, everyone got underway. It didn't make a difference if your wife was giving birth or you had a broken arm. When we sailed everyone sailed until the patrol was over.

Our day to day interaction at quarters, musters, and having important paperwork signed was with the Executive Officer, Lieutenant Commander (LCDR) James Morton. He was another good man and would later assume command of another 270, the *USCGC Forward (WMEC-911)*.

The chiefs had their own two man staterooms, heads, and dining and recreation room known as the chief's mess at the rear of the cutter. The rest of us junior enlisted had our berthing areas spread throughout the cutter in mostly 21 man berthing areas, depending on which department you worked in.

Engineering berthing was a little forward of amid ship and was comprised of both a twenty-one man and a nine man berthing area. The twenty-one man was on the main deck and had three high racks with an attached head. The head contained three sinks, one urinal, three toilets, and two showers. The lockers for twenty-one man were across the main passageway, which pretty much ran the length of the cutter. Nine-man was one deck below and had three high racks with an attached head. The head contained two sinks, a shower, and a toilet. The stand-up locker space was also attached to the berthing area.

I lived in nine-man and had a top rack, just like on *Sumac*, which I liked. We had curtains on the rack for privacy and a metal panel in between the stacks of racks. The metal panel was perforated to aid in air circulation so it wasn't total privacy from your neighbor. My primary storage was under my rack which was accessible by lifting up my mattress. It was sort of a hinged box with a mattress on top. They called these "coffin racks" because it was like a coffin, only you slept on top and your gear was inside. The mattress was the standard three inch thick foam type. All my important personal items and daily clothes were kept in my coffin rack. This meant that every evening before I went to bed, and every morning, it had to be lifted and propped up. It was not a big deal in the middle of the night, but in the morning when all six of us were getting out of our racks and trying to get dressed in the three foot isle between the sets of racks, it was tough.

The standup lockers were used for dress uniforms, things that needed to be on a hanger, and boots. They were the size of high school lockers and didn't afford a lot of room. Our laundry bags and towels were affixed to the outside of the lockers. We didn't want these in the berthing area because they would start to smell funky!

The engineering junior enlisted recreation room was outside nine-man and held a TV, sofa, table and chairs. You were allowed to smoke on the cutter, with the exception of the berthing areas and mess deck during meals, and that small rec-deck would always be so filled with cigarette smoke you could cut it with a knife! The TV wasn't used much, except in port when the antenna was attached. Underway it wasn't used. There was a stereo system but it was never used either because it was an eight track player! When the cutter was designed eight track players were cutting edge technology, and that was what was ordered and bought for all the cutters being built. By the time *Seneca*, which was sixth in her class, was built eight 8 track players were long out of date.

Seneca was commissioned on May 9th 1987 by Admiral Gracey's wife, Dorcas "Randy" Gracey. Admiral Gracey is the commandant I described earlier when I was on the *Sumac*. Until *Seneca's* commissioning we only made small trips down to Little Creek, Virginia for shipboard training in firefighting, engineering, casualties, seamanship, and navigation. The cutter also became certified to land helicopters and take on fuel and supplies from other ships while at sea. Now that *Seneca* was officially commissioned, and her crew certified to operate her, we were ready to go on patrol.

I was assigned to the engineering auxiliary division. We were in charge of the operation, maintenance and repair of equipment such as the water making distilling plant, water tanks, steam heating system, air conditioning system, fuel system and tanks, food refrigeration, galley equipment, and helicopter fuel storage and refueling operations. We were responsible for just about every mechanical system outside of the ship's engine room, which was controlled by the other engineering division, main propulsion. Auxiliary was known as "A-gang" and consisted of an MKC, MK1, MK2, two MK3s, and four FN/FAs.

Our first MKC was a portly and friendly fellow named Wayne Patton. He was addressed strictly as "Chief" to his face, but known as "Pappy" behind his back. He was from Maine and what we called a "chummy." A chummy was a common nickname for someone from Maine. A lot of guys on the cutter were chummys, because Boston was as close as they could get to being station back home in Maine. I got the impression that chummys didn't like to stray too far from home.

There was no PT like back in the Army and weight standards were pretty much non-existent. There was a maximum weight limit but this was loosely enforced throughout the Coast Guard.

When we were underway Pappy's belly was so big he couldn't get down the 24 inch diameter scuttle into the machinery spaces where most of our important equipment was located. It was always a big pain in the ass when he needed to get into one of these spaces because we had to lift up the entire monstrous four by six foot square hatch, instead of just the two foot circular scuttle in the center of the hatch. Lifting the hatch required several guys because the hatch had to be unbolted from the deck and then lifted up and secured open. They were so heavy they had huge springs so that when you lowered it, the weight of the thing wouldn't slam down and take off your fingers. We always dreaded hearing, "Chief wants to go down into a machinery space!"

One time when we were down in Little Creek we had to run over to the Coast Guard base in Portsmouth, Virginia for parts. Chief was with us and he had this huge golf ball sized cyst on the back of his neck. He was sitting up front in the van and we were in the back seat trying not to get directly behind his cyst for fear of it exploding! We were sitting there in the back starring at this thing the whole trip. He kept asking us if it looked bad, and we kept saying it looked fine so he wouldn't worry about it. When in reality we had never seen anything so huge and swollen! It finally got so bad that he did have to have it lanced, but he waited until the very last minute.

Pappy, along with most of the other chiefs on the cutter were pushing, or were over, their 20 year mark and spent most of their time in the chief's mess. Twenty years is the milestone in which you can retire. As I mentioned previously you could stay in until you were in your 60s, so some of those chiefs were getting pretty old and mean. We always steered clear of the chief's mess, also known as the "goat locker," and stayed out of their way.

Word was our chief was famous for drinking endless amounts of chocolate syrup in the mess. Since we were not allowed in the mess, we heard this through the mess cook. Mess cooks were used in the officer's wardroom, chief's mess, and enlisted mess. All the non-rates rotated through this duty on a monthly basis while awaiting their "A" school. Mess cook duties for the officers and chiefs entailed setting up and cleaning the eating area, getting them their meals, cleaning their rooms and heads, and doing their laundry. The enlisted mess cook took care of cleaning all the pots, pans, dishes and kept the enlisted mess deck clean.

Guys actually enjoyed mess cooking for the chiefs and officers because they would pitch in and give their mess cooks money at the end of the month. The mess cooks for the crew didn't get anything but a hard time! Mess cooks were always the fly on the wall in the wardroom and chief's mess and the scuttlebutt usually started with them!

The chief of A-gang and the chief of main propulsion typically have a little rivalry going on. They are both MKs, so they both want to outshine each other and have the better division. The main propulsion chief was a gunslinger by the name of Bill Pitkin. He was a young chief, probably the youngest in the chief's mess. He was starting to break the stereotype of the "old chief" by spending more time in the work place, his engine room, than in the goat locker.

One day he was up working in our A-gang shop using the huge industrial metal lathe we maintained. There is a shop rule that when you use the lathe you clean the machine so it's ready for the next guy. When Chief Pitkin was finished he left without cleaning up the lathe. I'm sure he was busy with his project and just forgot- hey, he was a chief, no problem. Well Pappy comes in and sees that the lathe is a mess and asks if Chief Pitkin left the lathe like that. I said, "Yes chief." Pappy was not happy and instructed me to go tell him to clean it up. Now I was only an MK3 and even I could smell danger all over this. I questioned Pappy about me going to tell him, and Pappy said "Yes you. Now get going!"

Against my better judgment, but not wanting to disappoint Pappy, I caught up with Chief Pitkin. He was up forward by 21-man engineering berthing in the main passageway where the ladder heads up to officer country or down to engineering nine-man berthing. The location will forever be burned into my memory. I casually said, "Excuse me chief, Chief Patton said you need to go clean up your mess on the lathe." Well that's about the time I felt the heat of Chief Pitkin's breath and the wetness of his spit as he was about a millimeter from my face yelling and screaming about how I will never, ever tell him anything! It seemed like a simple statement, but it drug on for quite a while with a lot of profanity and a lot of "Yes, chief" coming out of my mouth. Chief Pitkin gave ole Chief Trofhos a good run for his money, but I always had that feeling that Chief Trofhos would actually hit me at some point; I didn't get that feeling with Chief Pitkin! Needless to say Chief Pitkin didn't go back to clean up the lathe, I did!

Speaking of ass chewing machines, BMC Pawloski, the chief of deck department was a legend. His favorite ass to chew seemed to be those of engineers, but all the ratings gave him a wide berth. The boatswain mates, which comprised deck department, were known as "deck force" and on every cutter they always seem to butt heads with the engineers. BMC Pawloski was an older tall guy who sort snuck up on you. He was a heavy smoker and had these noticeably big white teeth, which I assumed were false. My vision of him is standing there with a cigarette in his hand, mouth sort of open in a grin, his teeth clicking together, twitching a bit, and him yelling some profanity! You could tell he was about to unload when his teeth started clicking together and he began to twitch. That was a warning sign to get the heck away from him!

One day our new auxiliary division officer, Ensign John Metcalf, asked me to get the rigid hull inflatable (RHI) small boat ready. He wanted to take it for a spin to make sure recent repairs made to the engine were correct. Ensign Metcalf was fresh out of the Coast Guard Academy and full of energy. The RHI belonged to deck force, we just maintained the engine. I didn't think anything of it, and we loaded up, and started to spin around the pier area there in our homeport of Boston. After about 30 minutes I looked over toward the pier and there was Chief Pawloski, smoking a cigarette and motioning with his finger for us to come over to him. I'm no dummy and I knew that this was not good! As we maneuvered the RHI over to him I could tell that the young ensign, who out ranked the chief, didn't know about the ass chewing machine known as the BMC.

Now in the military there is a definite difference between positional authority and coercive authority; and the young ensign was about to get a lesson in the difference. When we got close to the pier I could see the chief's teeth clicking and his face twitching. I wished I was anyplace else. BMC asked the ensign "Why in the fuck are you driving around in my boat without me fucking knowing about it?" There was no place to hide in the tiny RHI and I just kept my mouth shut. After a good ass chewing we took the boat back to the cutter in silence.

A few months later while in a port call, a few other engineers and I came back with a good buzz on. It was late and the cutter was quiet. We were scavenging for food on the mess deck with no luck. We knew the chief's mess always had food, but it was off limits. We were drunk and decided to throw caution to the wind. A couple of guys kept lookout in the passageway and I cracked the door to the chief's mess to see if anyone was in there. It was empty and I slid in. I spotted some peanut butter and jelly and started to head out with it when I saw the BMCs hard hat sitting there on the corner table. I couldn't resist and put a big glob of peanut butter in it before heading out the door! It wasn't worth it. For the next year I sweated it out thinking that at any moment I would be found out and the wrath of the BMC and the rest of the chief's mess would come down on me like a ton of bricks!

About six or seven months after I arrived "Pappy" retired. His retirement ceremony on the *Seneca's* flight deck was the first time I had ever seen someone retire. The CO's address still sticks with me to this day. He said something to the effect that the term, "Being in the service" refers to the fact that you're committing yourself to the service of your country. I had never really thought of what I was doing as service to my country. Odd as it may seem, I had always thought of it as just a job. That speech started me to think of service before self a bit more.

Our second MKC was Bob Hodgden. He was a very good mechanic but seemed nervous and unsure of himself most of the time. He popped antacid pills like they were candy. I don't know if it was pressure from the EO, the chief's mess, or his family, but he always seemed to be stressing over something. The technology of the newer 270 cutter may have been a bit too much for him. It also seemed to intimidate Pappy, who never seemed too settle into the modern equipment either. This was the newest class of cutter in the Coast Guard. Its state of the art computerized engine room and auxiliary equipment were a night and day difference from the manual engine rooms and equipment on the older 210, 327, and 378 cutters which were built in the 1930s and 1960s. These older cutters are what MKC Hodgden and Pappy had cut their teeth on.

Our MK1, Dan Bartlett, was the only thing that held us together most days. Chief Hodgden wasn't a bad guy; he just seemed overwhelmed and didn't seem to have confidence in himself. As time went on, we started to lose confidence in him as well and as a result showed him little respect. I wouldn't appreciate what he was up against for a few more years, when I would make chief and be assigned to another 270. It's a tough job managing people, keeping machinery operational, dealing with the chief's mess, and maintaining a personal life. But at that moment we needed a chief with a backbone who would stick up for us, keep us focused, and lead us. It wasn't happening with MKC Hodgden.

One morning he and I had lite-off duties in the engine room. Lite-off duty meant you were in charge of getting the engineering plant ready to get the cutter underway. The bulk of it involved starting all the engines and equipment, shifting from shore power to ship's power without losing power, making sure all water tanks were full and the sewage tank was emptied, and all shore connections were disconnected.

We had started the generators and had shifted from shore power to ship's power without incident. Chief had to visit the head, which was next to the control booth in the engine room. I was sitting in the control booth monitoring the engines and going through our checklist. Next thing you know I heard the generators start to wind down, the breakers on the power panel trip, and we went dark. The chief comes running into the control booth with his pants half down, holding a roll of toilet paper, yelling and screaming, and wanting to know what's going on! It was just a mechanical glitch and we had everything back up and running smoothly right away; everything except for chief's nerves.

On another occasion he started to get paranoid about accountability for the tools in the shop. We never kept anything locked up because someone was always working 24 hours a day. Nothing was ever missing, so I don't know what his concern was. Anyway, chief decided he was going to put pad locks on everything and we had to see him for the keys. It's hard to express the mounting frustration that I and the other A-gang members were feeling as we attempted to work on casualties. Our progress was continually delayed because we couldn't access our tools. After several days of trying to work on equipment and having to stop to track him down for keys, I lost my temper. He was in the shop and I asked him to reconsider locking everything up. He dismissed my request and my frustration with a curt "no" and walked out of the shop. I have always been a patient man with a slow burning fuse, but when he walked out that door I slammed it behind him and threw the wrench I had in my hand at the door. All my respect for his positional authority evaporated.

I transferred off before he did but I heard through the grapevine that they ended up taking him off on a stretcher while in a port call. I was told he ended up with a bad case of kidney stones. Years later I would come to understand the stress Chief Hodgden was dealing with when I was placed in his same position. It's easy to second guess your boss. At the time I had no concept of the responsibility and pressure he was dealing with, not to mention the politics he faced in the chief's mess. Add in whatever personal issues he might have been dealing with and it's easy to understand how anyone could become overwhelmed.

In March of 1987 I was sent to the Navy's JP-5 fuels school in Little Creek, Virginia. JP-5 fuel is highly refined and is used in helicopters. I was sent with another MK3 in Auxiliary by the name of Brian Schuette. Schuette was a great spiritual guy who was always upbeat and happy. The only thing that worried him was being away from his family. He was prior Navy and had done a tour on an aircraft carrier working up on the flight deck. He left the Navy because of the long deployments they made. When he joined the Coast Guard, like me he thought all they had were small boat stations. We were both shocked to find out otherwise!

When we arrived at Little Creek we were shown our sparse living quarters, which was a room in a three story barrack that we shared with two other guys. The room had four beds and that was about it. I got the impression everything else had been stolen and what was left wasn't worth taking. The Navy did not impress me. I gained a little knowledge attending the class, and took away the fact that I was glad that I hadn't joined the Navy. The projects in inner city Chicago seemed in better condition than the barracks; and the Navy folks seemed like they could care less about anything except for their own survival.

When I returned to *Seneca* I was assigned as the JP-5 aviation fuel supervisor. I was responsible for maintaining, testing, and refueling helicopters that were either assigned to us during a patrol or just needed to land and refuel. Schuette would be my back up if I wasn't able to perform my duties. I was also responsible for helping with all the other A-Gang equipment, but personally held accountable for the JP-5 system.

When we left homeport on patrol we almost always had a helicopter assigned to us. The flight crew usually consisted of two pilots, who were officers, and three crewmembers who were enlisted. These flight crews rotated within the aviation community so we always had different helicopter crews. The flight crew would have their gear sent to the cutter before we set sail and then fly the helicopter out to us once we were out in open water.

It seemed to me that aviators didn't like being out at sea because they would wait until the last possible moment to fly out to start the patrol. And as soon as we were released from patrol to head home, called "out chopping," they would fly the helicopter off the cutter and head for their air station. We would usually still have about a week of transit time left to get back home when they would fly off. Once the cutter arrived back in homeport we would have their gear shipped back to their airfield.

Once aboard, the helicopter was flown at least twice a day looking for go-fast drug boats, suspicious vessels, migrants, or for search and rescue (SAR). I refueled the helicopters several ways. The easiest way was an on deck, cold engine refuel. The helicopter would land, be secured to the deck, turn off its engines, and then be refueled like a car. Another way was the "hot refuel." This involved the helicopter landing and being secured to the deck. Then while it was still running with the blades spinning, I would go out and refuel it. This was done usually once or twice a day and the preferred method so there was no wasted time getting the helicopter back into the air. The third method was in-flight refueling. The helicopter would hover over the flight deck, lower its hoist cable, and the refueling rig would be raised up to it. The helicopter would then drift off to the side of the cutter and refuel. Once done it would hover back over the flight deck and lower the refueling rig. This was not a common method, but I did do it several times over my tour on *Seneca*. Once when we had a broken helicopter on deck and needed to refuel another helicopter, and several other times when a SAR helicopter from another location needed to refuel and the weather was too bad for it to land. This type of refueling really gave the helicopters a greater range during SAR cases. For example, if a vessel went down 200 miles off the coast, and we were 100 miles off the coast. A helicopter could fly out to us and refuel, rescue the sinking vessel's crew, fly back to us for more fuel, then return to shore without ever landing.

Every day I would have to make sure that the JP-5 aviation fuel on board was filtered and tested before flight operations at dawn. This would take about two hours and the test results were logged and provided to the air crew. As I refueled the helicopter, I would also take a sample in a glass bottle right at the point of entry into the helicopter. This was in case there was a crash; they would want to see what the fuel quality was that actually went into the helicopter.

My only major mishap with JP-5 happened while operating around the Fort Lauderdale, Florida area. It was the first time we had used the system and we were conducting helicopter operations to get the cutter flight certified. MK2 Mike Stanford, who we called "Stitch," was trying to show me how to line up the piping system so we could purify the JP-5 by recirculating it through a filtering system. There was a maze of pipes and valves and we configured the system the way Stich was shown in the shipyard. After running the system for about 30 minutes we received a call down in the JP-5 space to secure what we were doing immediately! Apparently the system's lockable overboard valve was installed without a lock at the shipyard during construction. The valve is for emergency jettison of fuel and is supposed to be locked closed to prevent fuel from going overboard during normal operation. The valve was mistakenly opened, since it wasn't locked. By the time the fuel slick was spotted in the water we had pumped several thousand gallons of JP-5 over the side! I thought we would be in big trouble, but the command recognized it was an accident out of our control and we moved on.

When I first started refueling helicopters I started out on these old Navy HH-3 reserve helicopters out of South Weymouth, Massachusetts. They were like Korean War vintage, with the pilot and copilot sitting up high and a crew and cargo section below them. They would come out to land and we would always hot refuel them because they were afraid that if they shut the helicopter off they wouldn't be able to restart it! These Navy Reserve pilots were what I would call mavericks compared to our Coast Guard pilots who followed a very strict protocol. These mavericks would hop out with their helicopter running, looking like they just came out of a war movie, and would go into the cutter and have coffee and bullshit while I refueled their aircraft.

It was always very peaceful out there refueling and my only mental sanctuary from the cramped confines of the ship. I felt like I was in my own little world. With the helicopter making so much noise I couldn't have heard anyone if they were screaming in my ear. I would stand there gazing out at the ocean and sometimes I would be able to see the shore line on the horizon. Meanwhile the rotor blades and racing engines of the helicopter drowned out the rest of the world with that overwhelming thump-thump sound.

The cutter would be at flight quarters during refueling, which was an all hands evolution. I would be dressed in the refueling team color purple, the tie down crew dressed in blue, firefighting teams dressed in red, and landing safety officer (LSO) dressed in yellow. The color coded vests also acted as life preservers in the event we were blown overboard. We also wore helmets, ear muffs, goggles, and fire proof hoods and gloves.

Once the helicopter was in position, either on the deck or in the air for refueling, the LSO would give me the okay to refuel. Everyone would be huddled in front of the cutter's helicopter bay watching and waiting for me to finish my job. Once the helicopter crew gave me the wave off that they had enough fuel, usually about 100 gallons, I would disconnect and head back to the helicopter bay with the others and wait for the helicopter to depart and the cutter to secure from flight operations.

My only gripe with being out under the spinning blades of the helicopter was that I wasn't getting the extra flight deck pay that my co-workers were drawing. I argued the point with my supervisors and the yeoman who handled the ins and outs of the pay manual to no avail. Eventually the Coast Guard would give the JP-5 person flight deck pay, but long after I was done working under the spinning blades.

The Coast Guard loved to get their money out of you and just about everyone had several collateral jobs on board beside that of their rating. In addition to my rating job and being the JP-5 king, I was also a damage control petty officer (DCPO), and in the firefighting team for repair party #2 (RP2).

As a DCPO I was assigned a zone of the cutter to maintain that had about five compartments. I maintained all the damage control markings, fittings, and listings for these spaces. Every space on a cutter has a sheet posted next to every entrance which listed every fitting in the space and its damage control classification. This listing was called the compartment check off list (CCOL). I was also responsible for securing and resetting these fittings during a casualty or drill.

The more common and mostly classifications of fittings were x-ray (X), yoke (Y), and zebra (Z). X-ray was the most relaxed condition and suitable during the daytime while in port. Yoke was an intermediate condition used in port after 1900 and at all times while underway. Last, and the most critical, was zebra. Zebra was the most secure the cutter could operate and was set when in extremely heavy weather, attack, or when damage was declared.

When material condition x-ray was set, all x-ray and circle x-ray fittings were closed. When yoke was set, all x-ray, circle x-ray, yoke and circle yoke fittings were set. When zebra was set, all x-ray, circle x-ray, yoke, circle yoke, zebra, circle zebra, and remaining fittings were closed. Remaining fittings are William and circle William for ventilation and dog zebra for port-hole coverings. It sounds confusing, but is actually pretty easy to set as long as you know your alphabet!

When general quarters (GQ) was sounded, which was a loud repeated gong sound, it was my responsibility to rush to my DCPO zone and set all the fittings to material condition zebra. Once done I would rush to RP2, report my zone was set, and then don my battle dress. Setting zebra was critical and the whole cutter had to be set and reported to damage control central (DCC) within a matter of minutes.

I would then await my orders from the RP2 locker leader to either dress out in my firefighting gear or battle dress depending on the casualty. Battle dress was long sleeved shirts, collars up, top button buttoned, pants tucked into your socks, and flash gear. Flash gear was a thin fire retardant hood and long elbow length gloves.

If it was a fire I would don my firefighting suit and oxygen breathing apparatus (OBA) and await orders as the #1 nozzleman to head to the fire. I was a part of the firefighting team which consisted of an on scene leader (OSL), a #1 nozzleman, #2 nozzleman, #1 hoseman, #2 hoseman, Plugman, and an accessman.

We rotated around a bit at the positions to cross train but my assigned billet was the #1 nozzleman. When we had a fire the OSL would be in charge of the firefighting team. He would direct us to the fire and communicate back via messenger with the locker leader in RP2. We didn't use radios to communicate back to RP2, a messenger and hand written damage control shorthand was used.

When we reached the compartment on fire we would position ourselves with the accessman next to the door, the nozzleman, hoseman and OSL piled up ready to enter, and the plugman manning the nearest water valve. You have to imagine that the passageways on the *Seneca*, like most Coast Guard cutters, are about the same width as a hallway in your house. Now imagine that hallway filled with five guys in firefighting gear and oxygen tanks all trying to get through at once!

It usually was an orderly process, starting with the accessman feeling the door for heat. He would then tell me, the #1 nozzleman, to either apply water to cool the door or, if the door was cool, he would open it and we would enter. The accessman would swing the door open and get out of the way. The nozzlemen would apply water to beat down the heat and flames and the OSL would direct us to the fire. We would battle it until it was out.

We were the first line of defense. If we went down or the fire was too big for us to contain, repair party #3 (RP3) would be called in. RP2 maintained responsibility for the forward part of the cutter and RP3 for the aft part. If there was a casualty up forward, RP2 was the responding repair party and RP3 the back up. If the casualty was aft, RP3 was the lead and RP2 the backup.

Drilling was relentless underway and in port. Every week underway one or two days were set aside for drills in firefighting, flooding, collision, attack, and nuclear and biological warfare. In port the duty section ran a drill every evening. We had to know how to save ourselves, because no one else was coming to save us out in the middle of the ocean.

Constantly working around machinery and helicopters I always had a pair of orange plastic earplugs stuck in my ears. The orange earplugs had these one inch stems on them so you could put them in and remove them easily. All the guys would take theirs out when done standing watch in the engine room. After my watch in the engine room I had JP-5 to recirculate and a whole host of work to get done throughout the cutter around running machinery. So I was always seen walking around the decks with orange ear plugs hanging out my ears. Someone ended up giving me the nickname "spuds," I think MK1 Bartlett, because it looked like I had potatoes growing out of my ears. I thought the nickname would disappear when I left *Seneca*, but it would get resurrected wherever I went.

About this time the Coast Guard rolled out their new helicopter known as the Dolphin HH-65. It was a really nice small helicopter, but it had its initial problems. One blew an engine while on the flight deck and we had to go in to port and crane it off. That wasn't really too bad because they wanted it craned off in Savanna, Georgia which was always a great port call. While off of Puerto Rico another one was so new it didn't even have tie downs on the side of it to secure it to the deck. When the helicopter landed, and the tie down crew sprinted out to tie it down, the tie downs were missing and the helicopter had to fly back to Puerto Rico.

We sailed to Little Creek, Virginia and conducted our final shipboard shakedown training from 8-26 June 1987 with the Navy's Fleet Training Unit. Completing this training would demonstrate that we would be able to perform all required shipboard operations and casualty control evolutions satisfactorily. Luckily we passed with an excellent grade of 89.4 percent and headed home proud to be able to get out on patrol! Finally after all the preparations and certifications we could finally do our job.

On one of our early patrols we headed down to the D7 Caribbean Sea area to participate in Operation Checkmate 88. This was an ongoing counter narcotics operation to stop the flow of marijuana and cocaine via air and sea from entering the United States. In early September of 1988, while still in the Caribbean Sea, we landed in the middle of Hurricane Gilbert; a class 5 hurricane with 185 MPH winds. At the time it would be the most intense storm of its kind. We knew it was coming and it was decided that we would pull into Guantanamo Bay, Cuba (GITMO) and the safety of the inlet there. The *Seneca* could only make about 19 knots full speed, so it would have been impossible to out run the storm. When we arrived in GITMO there were several navy ships there and the place looked like they were preparing for WWIII. Everything on shore was covered and strapped down. They were in the midst of pulling everything they could out of the water. And the ships there were tripling up on their mooring lines.

As the storm grew closer on the 12th we learned it was bigger than anticipated and was bearing right down on us. Although we originally sought the protection of the small inlet, it was quickly determined it would do us more harm than good. Extremely heavy weather could cause the cutter to beat itself against the side of the pier and sink. It was decided that all the ships, Coast Guard and Navy, would have to head out to sea and ride it out in open waters. We prepared for heavy sea and tied down everything we could. The storm clouds were brewing as we slipped out of GITMO and it started to get dark. I was sitting up in the flight deck hanger, with the huge hanger door open about half way, watching Cuba fade into the distance. As she disappeared from view I could feel the winds whipping up and the sea state getting worse and worse.

We were headed right out into the middle of hurricane Gilbert which was now a class 3 hurricane with 140 mph winds. For the next several days we just sat out in the huge lashing seas being carried to the top of a wave and then dropped 30-40 feet or more into its trough. We were like a cork being tossed around out there in the middle of the ocean. Our only goal was to keep our bow into the waves and ride them to the crest. If we got sideways we could capsize. All you could hear day and night were the waves crashing against us and the sound of things breaking loose inside the ship and crashing to the deck. The waves would hit and the whole ship would give out a big shudder as it absorbed the impact.

Storm or no storm the routine still rolls on and we still had to stand our usual four hour watch once or twice a day. It was dangerous going in and out of scuttles and hatches accessing compartments to make our rounds. It was hard enough to stand let alone maneuver around the ship. We had set material condition Zebra, which meant every hatch, scuttle, and door, was secure and could not be opened unless approved by the officer of the deck on the bridge. Everyone just hunkered down and stayed in there racks if they were not on watch. The galley was pretty much secured, and no one really felt like eating anyway.

The storm finally passed and we began to clean up the ship, regain our wits, and continue on with the patrol. I would face many more storms throughout my almost 11 years at sea and each one seemed just as rough at the time. But in the end, Gilbert would be the biggest and scariest storm I ever had to ride out.

For the most part you got your sea legs a day or two out of port. I would say the rough seas on any given patrol affected everyone in one way or another. I was lucky in that I never got physically sick at sea. A lot of guys would get sick all the time. That didn't get them out of anything, it just made the day longer and far more miserable for them. Some members would carry a plastic bag around with them and when they couldn't hold it back any longer, they would just puke into their bag and continue on. I felt sorry for them because it was only a matter of time before they hit the dry heaves. Eventually the sea state would die down and they would get better.

It was like everything else with ship board life, it took some getting used to. Water conservation was huge since we made our own water. Auxiliary was responsible for the two stage steam evaporator which produced the potable water from sea water. Peak output was about 6,000 gallons a day. We had a crew of about 100 and the average person uses about 100 gallons of water a day. Do the math and even at peak output we would come up short every day. And the evaporator never ran at peak output!

So you had to take what were known as "sea showers." The shower head had a little button on it that turned the water on and off once you got the temperature set. You got in and wet, turned the water off, lathered up, then turned the water on, and rinsed off. Sinks had those annoying spring lever handles which you had to hold open to use.

The toilets were low flow vacuum toilets that used almost no water and were very prone to clogging. It seemed like the damage control rating, who were responsible for the sewage system, was always taking it down because of a clog. We pumped sewage overboard liberally at sea, but once within 12 miles of land we had to hold sewage in the 1500 gallon holding tank. This usually wasn't a problem unless we were heading into a port, up a river or long inlet, which took several hours. Sewage would usually have to be secured because the tank would fill before we reached our moorings. Unfortunately, that wouldn't stop folks from using the toilet!

Meals were three times a day with an extra meal known as "mid rats" for guys going on the midnight (mid) watch. In between meals the galley was secure and there usually wasn't anything placed on the mess deck to snack on. Occasionally there may be some fruit or leftover sheet cake after leaving port. Once underway food was conserved and fresh vegetables and fruit only lasted the first week at best, after that it was canned or frozen food.

There was a night baker that made bread and pastries and the whole ship would be filled with the smell of fresh baking. Occasionally on the mid-watch the engineering security watch stander would come back from his round of the cutter and state that the night baker was making cinnamon rolls. The watch stander was always under orders to keep an eye out for snacks left over from mid rats and what the night baker was up to. If cinnamon rolls were being made we would open up the engine room escape hatch, which luckily for us opened up right into the mess deck. And the night baker, after a little prompting, would hand us down some fresh baked cinnamon rolls.

The chief cook was a Filipino by the name of Virgilio Manalo and he took pride in his galley and the food that was prepared. We always ate well and so did his fellow Filipinos on board. SSC Manalo always had some rice or fish cooking especially for the Filipinos instead of the tradition western food, which I assumed they didn't really favor. Whenever

167

SSC Manalo came walking through the mess deck and saw us lounging around, smoking or bullshitting, he would always say to us, "No work no eat!" That was his way of saying, "Get the hell off my mess deck and back to work!"

Morale on the cutter was high and we were a tight knit crew. This was in the days before internet and computers. After working hours we kept busy playing cards and board games, reading, and of course sleeping. In the evening there would be a movie shown on the mess deck with a projector. If the weather was nice, and we were not in a secure operating area, they would show the movie on the fight deck and shine the projector against the flight deck hanger door.

Once we left the pier on patrol we were isolated from the outside world. Our only contact was through mail when we reached a port call or a phone call when, and if, we would pull into an American port or GITMO. Our homeport would forward our mail to our next port of call and hopefully we and the mail would make it there at the same time. Sometimes operational changes diverted us from a scheduled port call and the mail would wander around trying to catch up with us. Once or twice it never did reach us on patrol and was just sent back to Boston.

When we would pull into GITMO there was a phone exchange and you could make a call home. The phone exchange was located at the far end of the base and you had to walk or catch the cattle truck out to it. Yes, just like back in the Army they had these cattle cars that were sort of shuttle buses that transported folks around the base. Once at the phone exchange you walked up to the teller/operator, told her the number you wanted to call, how long you wanted to talk, and paid. Then you had a seat and waited, and waited, and waited for your turn in the one of about 20 phone booths. These phone booths looked like something out of a 1950s movie. They were metal, all in a row, and had a sliding door for privacy. When you got into the booth you were connected to your party and you got to enjoy a conversation hampered with an annoying delay. By the time you got the cadence of talking with the other person because of the delay, your time was usually up and your call over. If there was an emergency back home the only way to get in contact with us was through the American Red Cross. Your family member would contact the Red Cross who in turn would get a message out to the cutter via coded message traffic.

Let me make this clear right now, I hated to go on boardings. The cutter was a nice and safe place with a warm shower, clean rack, and hot food. The boats we boarded were stinky, smelly, rat infested vessels that we usually got stuck on for a day or two. The engineer on the boarding team was sent over to repair engineering casualties, which usually involved trying to get some ancient broken down piece of junk equipment started. And while we worked on the broken equipment we were also supposed to look for drugs, contraband, and illegal migrants. While on one of our Caribbean patrols we came across two 70 foot cargo boats from the Dominican Republic adrift at sea. One had a broken rudder and the other had a casualty with their only engine. Apparently the one boat was towing the boat with the broken rudder when their engine went out. I was sent over with a boarding team to see if we could get the boat with the engine problems fixed.

MK2 Phil Cultrera and I would be the engineers on this boarding. We loaded up with the other boarding team members into our small boat and were lowered into the water for transit to the broken down boats. Once at the Dominican boat with the engine problem we pulled alongside and hopped aboard. Other members of our boarding team rounded up the crew for interviews as Phil and I headed to the engine compartment to investigate. The boat was bobbing around pretty good as we made our way down into the engine compartment. The compartment was below the water line and in a space about 12 feet long by 12 feet wide. It was hard to tell how deep it was because it was filled with water halfway up the engine. I looked around and the whole compartment was filled with Carnation milk cans. I'm talking case upon case of canned milk; I guess that was their cargo.

After working on the engine for an hour in the slowly rising water that was now up over my knees, we determined that it was beyond repair. The boarding team had determined the Dominican crews on both boats were not a risk and the cutter radioed over that they would be taking our boarding team off, except for me and MK2 Cultrera. We would stay behind and monitor the boats as the cutter towed them into the nearest port. I knew it! I knew I would end up getting stuck overnight on this dump!

By the time our crew hooked up the tow rope between our vessel and the broken Dominican vessels, Phil got really sea sick and started throwing up all over the place. He and I had been working on the engine while the others were working on hooking up the tow. The small engine compartment wasn't well ventilated and there was the smell of fuel and rot. Not helping matters was the constant rolling and pitching of the small Dominican boat bobbing in the open ocean. When Phil started to feel sick there was no place to let it go except right there in the engine room water. So there we were in that little engine room with rising water and Phil's vomit sloshing all around us!

When our small boat came along side to pick up the boarding team and drop off a dewatering pump to help with the water in the engine room, Phil was so sick and dehydrated that he was also taken back. That left just me and the Dominican crew, who were deemed to be no threat! Since I didn't want to sink on the dump, I thought I had better get the pump operating before they started the towing process. I set the pump up on the deck and lowered the suction hose down into the engine room. A couple of pulls on the pull starter and I was happily starting to pump out the water, along with Phil's yak.

About this time it was getting dark and the cutter was commencing the tow. They radioed back to me to check how things were looking with the towing bit on the bow. As I moved toward the front of the vessel a nice sized wave came crashing over the bow and drenched me, filling my boots with water! Oh great, just what I needed to start my evening. I radioed to the cutter that we were going too fast and taking water over the bow. Their reply was this was as slow as they could go without going backwards, and I would just have to keep a close eye on things. Wonderful! I've got water coming over the bow and I've got water coming up through the engine room. I'm soaked to the skin and I'm stuck on a boat with a bunch of people who are "deemed to be no threat" but they can't speak English. The only thing going for me at the moment was a calm sea state.

I wandered back aft to make sure the pump was running properly and to try and dry off. There was a Dominican who actually had his little sleeping area on the landing about halfway down to the engine room and I sort of used him as a gage for how the water situation was. I would shine my flashlight down into the space where he was laying and he would give me a thumbs up or a thumbs down in which case the water needed pumping.

At one point while I was sitting back aft on the fantail watching the pump run a Dominican crew member walked by me and over to a bucket where he proceeded to squat down and do his business. When he was done he poured a little water in the bucket and emptied it over the side. I guess that's why the older term for the aft area of the ship is called the "poop deck!" I made a mental note that I would be holding my poop.

Sometime in the middle of the night I checked on the water situation in the engine room and I got the thumbs down, meaning it was filling up again. So I went to fill the pump up with gas before starting it. One of the crew members decided to light a match so I could see and I told him to put it out, I would be fine! Of course since I didn't speak Spanish, and they didn't speak English, this was all done in hand gestures. Because it was so dark and the small boat was rocking and rolling I ended up pouring a bunch of gas on my leg. So now wet and smelling like gasoline I sat and watched the pump run in the dark. Thankfully, the rest of the night was uneventful. I tried to stay aft, away from the occasional wave that would come crashing over the bow. When I felt like I was nodding off I would get up and check on the engine room water level.

The next morning the small boat came over, ironically with Phil to relieve me. There was no chit chat and I hurriedly jumped into the small boat before Phil got sick again and I was stuck for yet another day! It never felt better to get back to the cutter. Needless to say I didn't take a sea shower and spent a good long time washing the funk from that nasty boat off of me!

Boardings were a daily routine when we were in the operating area. We never knew when we were going to roll up on a suspect vessel or vessel of interest. And we boarded day or night and in pretty much any sea state. While conducting a boarding in the North Atlantic I was the small boat engineer and we were using the motor surf boat (MSB) small boat. This boat is stowed on the starboard main deck and it has to be dropped a good 30 feet or so to the water. The RHI boat was stowed on the fantail and was only about eight feet to the water line. Members of auxiliary rotated the boat engineer duty on a daily basis. As the small boat engineer I had to start the two small boats up in the morning and do the daily maintenance on them. If they were going to be used that day I went along as part of the boarding team in case there were any mechanical problems.

There is one day while patrolling in the North Atlantic as the small boat engineer that I will never forget. The sea state was choppy with swells of about four to five feet. We entered the MSB and I took up my position on the after falls. The falls are two cables with hooks that attach to the boat. When the boat is lowered the cable pays outs. There is one cable forward and one aft. When the small boat hits the water the coxswain starts the engine and then orders the aft falls released, then the forward falls released, and then the tow line connected to the cutter called the sea painter released. All this has to be done in that particular order. If anyone of those functions is done out of order, the small boat could be spun around and dragged by the cutter or capsize.

Also, as the boat hits the water great care must be taken to have enough slack in the falls until you release them so the small boat will ride a swell. If there isn't enough slack to keep the small boat in the water you will basically ride up the swell and as you start to drop off the swell you will get a serious jar. It is sort of like having the ground drop out from under you causing you to free fall several feet. That's what happened during this boarding. We rode up the swell, and about halfway down the swell the falls snapped tight and we all just got jolted off our feet. As I went up with the force of the swell I rose to an almost standing position and when the falls snapped tight on the way down I was slammed onto the steel clamp that holds the aft fall. Unfortunately, it was my crotch which took the majority of the hit! It knocked the wind right out of me and I crumpled to the deck in pain. Seeing there was a problem the crew operating the boat lowering equipment hauled the MSB back up to the cutter and the corpsman had a look at me. He had me drop my trousers right there on the flight deck to inspect the damaged area! He said everything looked okay, nothing was missing or detached, and I was just shaken up a bit. Embarrassed, I pulled up my trousers and got back in the MSB.

MSB being lowered into the water

I ended up getting very lucky on another boarding down in the Caribbean Sea. We had been boarding a suspected vessel and I was assigned as the small boat engineer. On this particular occasion the vessel we were boarding was considered to be a threat, so I would be armed with the 16 gauge shot gun. My job would be to cover the boarding team members as they boarded the vessel.

Everything was going fine but as usual the boarding was dragging on for three to four hours. It was decided to relieve the small boat crew so we could get on board the cutter and eat. I was relieved by FN Mike Bogue. After we ate, the small boat was heading back to the cutter so we could rotate the small boat crew again and Mike Bogue and the other reliefs could eat. As the boat was coming back it was slamming up and down on the choppy water. All that pounding had loosened the pin that held the metal mast and it came slamming down on Mike's hand like a meat clever, almost severing several of his fingers. He was in such pain, and incapacitated, that we had to lift him out of the small boat with a strap to get him on deck. He was then immediately taken to sick bay.

The boarding was still going on so I hopped down into the small boat to resume my duty as the small boat engineer. When I hopped in I realized I needed the shotgun and looked around for it. There on the deck, in about three inches of blood and water, was the shotgun! I scooped it up, poured the mixture out of the barrel, and off we went! Later, when I got back aboard the cutter, I went to check on Bogue to see how he was making out. He was lying in his rack in pain waiting for us to get him medevac'd ashore. Despite all that the corpsman was able to do for him it was unsettling to see him in such pain, knowing it would be awhile before we could get him to a hospital.

When we arrived back into homeport, at the end of our patrol, he returned to the cutter fit for full duty. Mike Bogue went on to damage controlman school and made chief. Our paths would cross many years later when we were berthed in the same barracks while attending separate schools at the Coast Guard Academy in New London, Connecticut.

Another memorable boarding we conducted down in the Caribbean was on a beautiful 70-80 foot sail boat. We boarded everything that wandered past us, looking for illegal activity. I was once again the small boat engineer. The sea state was really rough and suited for the MSB. But it was decided that we would use the RHI to do the boarding because of its rubber sides. The last thing you want to do when conducting a boarding is to scratch or dent up an expensive sail boat. In this rough sea state it would also be tough to get the boarding crew members transferred from the RHI to the sail boat. The sail boat was flagged from a European country and

174

there were young kids and a pregnant lady onboard. As we came alongside the vessel so the boarding crew could jump on I caught sight of them. I remember being concerned that a pregnant woman and young kids were sailing around out here. It didn't seem safe to me!

Well we got the boarding crew on but after numerous attempts we couldn't get alongside long enough to get them off. You have to imagine two vessels in rough seas trying to get close to each other. You're slamming into one another and bobbing up and down at different heights. At some point the sail boat could come down on top of us. The boarding crew eventually ended up jumping off the sail boat into the open water and we picked them out of the water once the sail boat had cleared. Getting back on our cutter was just as dangerous. But, there were a lot more controls that could be put in place which greatly helped. These included passing a line hooked to the bow of the small boat and cutter to help stabilize the small boat, and the cutter positioning itself to form a calmer leeward side. It was all still a dangerous evolution, just ask FN Bogue!

Looking for drugs kept us pretty busy, but stopping illegal migration into the United States kept us even busier. These patrols were named Alien Migrant Interdiction Operations (AMIO). Most of the illegal migration was from Haiti and the Dominican Republic. Haitians were being stopped at an increasingly higher rate than any other nationality and patrols were therefore deemed Haitian Migrant Interdiction Operations (HMIO). The average number of Haitians interdicted per year from 1987-90 was about 4000, compared to an average of 400 Dominicans over the same period. Running third were Cubans averaging 50 a year.

As a matter of fact our only drug bust while I was aboard came while conducting AMIO on the 29th of December 1987. It netted us a measly one pound of marijuana. It wasn't that we were not heavily involved in drug interdiction; it was because we typically acted as a command platform for other smaller assets. They actually conducted the drug seizure and therefore received the credit. The *Seneca* had state of the art radar and a control center which enabling her to act as a floating command center. This enabled her to coordinate air and sea assets to intercept illegal activity whether it was drugs or migrants.

One of the more memorable Haitian interdictions was a vessel that had about 20 of them hidden behind the bulkheads of the vessel. This space was tight and they could only stand side by side. Our boarding team had been inspecting the vessel and heard voices coming from behind the bulkheads. When they took down the bulkheads there were Haitians hiding behind them. I wondered how long they had been squeezed in there like sardines. It was sad.

On *Seneca* we had a huge telescoping hanger to house the helicopter in bad weather. When we had migrants on board, we would fly the helicopter off to the nearest airport and extend the hanger so the migrants had shelter out of the weather. I was detailed to stand guard duty over them one evening up in the hanger. It was the 0000-0400 mid-watch and they were all lying there fast asleep under their grey wool military issued blankets, whole families of men woman and children. It was my first time seeing them up close and I felt sorry for them; and thankful for all I had. They risked it all to try to reach America. Everything they had in Haiti or the Dominican was sold to pay for the transit. And now all they had was what they could carry, which wasn't much. When we would repatriate them back to their home country the Red Cross would meet us at the pier. The migrants would be fed and given a few dollars and sent back into the country, more than likely to try another transit to America.

Haiti and the Dominican Republic are two countries which share the island known as Hispaniola, which was founded by Christopher Columbus in 1492. The Haitian side is in much worse shape economically and politically then the Dominican Republic side, so the condition of the Haitian migrants was always much worse than the Dominicans. Haiti wasn't even an option as a port call for us because of the bad conditions there. As we would start to enter the Gulf of Gonave, heading towards the capital city of Port-au-Prince, you could smell Haiti before seeing it. The crystal clear waters would be transformed into a floating sheen of garbage and scum. We would waste no time disembarking the Haitian migrants and be on our way.

In the small amount of time we were in Port-au-Prince we would be surrounded by small, handmade, wooden canoes with venders hawking their goods. The bartering was done in broken English and hand signs. Once a price or barter was agreed upon the items were passed up to the cutter and down to the canoe via rope. Haiti was well known for their hand carved wood and that was the main item for sale.

When we would get into the operational area on an AMIO patrol, picking up Dominicans and Haitians, we would have an Immigration and Customs Enforcement (ICE) agent ride us and interview each migrant. If the migrant was deemed by the ICE agent to be seeking political asylum the migrant wouldn't be sent back to his or her home country for repatriation. Instead they would be sent to GITMO for further interviewing. Very few, if any, migrants were deemed to be seeking political asylum.

Once we had been doing migrant work with an ICE agent and pulled into the town of Puerto Plata in the Dominican Republic on a port call. As soon as my buddies and I walked across the cutters brow on liberty we were swarmed by these kids who wanted to guide us around town. When we walked through the gate that secured the pier I noticed there was a guard with a machine gun. I thought that was odd, and we kept on our way being led by the Dominican kids.

As the kids weaved us through town I noticed more guards with machine guns standing at the entrance to a bank. I started to wonder just how safe this place was! Finally the kids came to a stop in front of this building and gestured for us to go in, so we did. It was a whore house! None of us spoke Spanish but we gestured that we didn't want a whore house, we wanted a bar. The kids took us under tow again and off we went. A few minutes later we arrived at another building and were escorted in. Another whore house! Only this one had our ICE agent sitting there on a couch with a couple of lovely Dominican ladies hanging on him.

I went over and chatted with the ICE agent, frustrated that we were not making any progress. I told him we were trying to get the kids to take us to a bar and not a whore house. He explained that the kids get paid for customers they bring to these places. Well that explained it. I asked the ICE agent to tell the kids to take us to a bar and off we went.

In the summer of 1988 we were detailed to be the back drop for President Ronald Reagan's May 18th graduation address at the Coast Guard Academy in New London, Connecticut. The crew wasn't too happy about getting underway during the middle of an in-port and spending several days away from homeport. The trip down to New London and back would eat up a good four or five days. And once we were out transiting we were always susceptible to any SAR case that might come up.

In-port time was precious. We were under a mandate to do a required amount of days underway and it usually worked out to eight weeks underway and six to eight weeks in port. We ran a straight one-in-four duty section which meant that every fourth day you had 24 hour duty on the cutter. We also ran an eight hour work day Monday through Friday. Just because you had duty didn't get you any compensation time. So if you had duty on Monday, your duty hours were 0800 Monday morning until 0800 Tuesday morning. Then Tuesday you would work your normal work day from 0800 until 1600. So you would literally be on the cutter from 0800 Monday until 1600 Tuesday. This ate up a lot of valuable liberty time.

I had duty the day before we headed down to New London for the graduation address. The next morning at about 0700 we hauled in our mooring lines and got underway. All went well with the president's address. We were so far away we couldn't see anything going on. We were running an underway duty schedule and never switched over to the in-port rotation. I had engine room watch, which was just fine by me. I was told not to come above decks because I was in working blues. The rest of the crew was manning the rails in dress uniform.

As I made my rounds I encountered my first Coast Guard Intelligence (CGI) person. They are sort of the FBI of the Coast Guard. He was wearing a civilian suit and sitting in a chair up forward by the armory. He didn't say it, but it looked to me that he was guarding the armory and gun mount access. I said a greeting as I walked by and he acknowledged me. I was wondering why they need a CGI guy to guard our armory, didn't they trust us?

After the ceremony we set sail for Boston to resume our in-port. As we steamed back home, through the Cape Cod Canal, I looked forward to having three days of liberty ahead of me. Well that was about to get shanghaied.

One of the crewmembers, who was to have duty the day we pulled back in, complained to the command that the previous duty section- mine, had not complete a full 24 hours of duty before we left and therefore should have duty again when we got back. The command agreed and my section was to have duty again.

You mean to tell me because my section only did 23 hours and not 24 hours of duty we have duty again? I was super pissed! Yes, I stewed and stewed until I came up with what I thought was the perfect retaliation. I snuck into the complainer's berthing area while he was asleep and filled his boots with jelly! And it took time because all I had were those small jelly packs you get in a restaurant. So there I was, in the darkness of his berthing area, peeling open jelly packets, and dumping them into his boots. Yes it was immature, but it felt so good the next day when he was walking around complaining about his boots being filled with jelly!

About half way through my tour on *Seneca* the executive officer was replaced with a big man, both in heart and stature, by the name of Dave Ryan. He had graduated from the Coast Guard Academy in 1975 and had done tours in the *USCGC Comanche (WMEC-202)*, *USCGC Cape Hedge (WPB-95311)*, and *USCGC Bristol Bay (WTGB-102)*, so he was no stranger to being afloat. Little could I know at the time, but I would end up serving in two more cutters with then Lieutenant Commander Ryan.

Captain Ryan was highly admired by the crew. His interaction was stern when it needed to be yet we felt as if he woke up and put his pants on the same way we did, one leg at a time. One of my favorite stories involving the good XO is the one of him falling asleep in one of the enlisted engineer's racks one night. Seems he had been out drinking in a port call and was trying to make it back to his rack in officer country. Right next to the ladder leading up to his state room was stinky, messy, cramped 21-man engineering berthing. Well LCDR Ryan missed the ladder and somehow made it into 21-man berthing and into an empty rack. At some point later that night the owner of the rack stumbled in and found the XO fast asleep! The stunned enlisted man recognized it was the XO and decided to find another place to sleep. He made it down to the enlisted rec-room and fell asleep on the couch. When the XO awoke the next morning he found the enlisted man and apologized to him and told him the next time he should feel free to go and sleep in his rack in officer country! This actually went a long way with the crew, who perceived his action and statement as saying what's was good enough for them is good enough for him.

December and January of 1988-89 were spent in the Caribbean Sea operating area. We would conduct a patrol and go to GITMO to complete our refresher training (REFTRA) on shipboard firefighting and recertification. If we passed this certification with flying colors the ship and crew would be awarded the battle efficiency ribbon to wear on our uniforms, and the letter "E" would also be painted on the side of the cutter.

The certification takes several weeks and every department on the cutter is tested. It involves navigation, firefighting drills, engineering casualty training, gun firing exercises, helicopter operations, refueling and taking on supplies at sea, and so on. Some of the training is conducted at the pier but most requires getting underway daily. The normal routine was up at 0430 to get ready to get underway, get underway, drill, then moor back up before dark and conduct in-port drills. The cadre that came aboard was mostly Navy personnel, known as "riders," who ran a sort of boot camp type schedule with a lot of long days and plenty of yelling.

It just so happened that the U.S. Navy battleship *USS Iowa (BB-61)* was involved in operations in the area and had been firing her massive guns at the firing range on Vieques Island, located off of Puerto Rico. On this visit to the range she set a record, firing one of her 16 inch shells over 23.4 nautical miles. *Iowa* pulled into GITMO for several days of liberty while we were conducting our training. What an amazing ship. Commissioned in 1943 her 16 inch guns represented America's undefeatable sea power from that point on. She saw action in WWII, Korea, and the first Gulf War.

Getting underway every day we would pass the *Iowa* anchored in GITMO Bay. She was so big that she had to anchor out and use her small boats to ferry her crew back and forth to land. We, of course, were small enough to moor up to the pier. The *Iowa* was so massive that I was in awe of her when we would pass her, especially her stern which really let you see how wide she was. Her beam (width) was a massive 108 feet compared to our measly 38 feet and she was 887 feet in length, all massive battleship steel.

When we would go on liberty there on the base the *Iowa* sailors would be all over the place. They had a crew of almost three thousand so they just took over everything. It was like kicking an ant mound and watching them scatter everywhere. The shore patrol had their hands full. On special occasions, like the *Iowa* pulling in, the shore patrol broke out school buses that they used to transport the unruly personnel back to the small boat landing pier so they could be taken back to the ship. And they always had those buses full of unruly *Iowa* sailors.

Once we went up to the enlisted club and the shore patrol had five buses out front. As soon as they would load one up, off it would go to the pier. And I mean to tell you they were not loading those sailors up on a voluntary basis. The minute any *Iowa* sailor stood up and started yelling, or fell over, they were scooped up by the shore patrol and off they went to an awaiting bus. One night we were at the Marine Corps enlisted club at the end of the base. We had been drinking with some of the *Iowa* crew and offered them a ride in our cutter's shuttle van down to their pier. As we pulled into the small boat shuttle area, which was ferrying the *Iowa* crew back and forth, it was chaos! There were drunken sailors all over the place looking for trouble. We off loaded our *Iowa* passengers and got out of there fast. It wouldn't have surprised me if they tried to flipped our van just for fun!

The Navy REFTRA riders were also conducting training on the *Iowa* and seemed annoyed at the *Iowa* crew. They complained about them while they were drilling us. I guess the *Iowa* crew members were not the big push overs that we were and they just told the riders to pound sand. Tensions escalated and the riders were told to get off the ship! But the *Iowa* crew was great to us and even invited our crew over to take tours. I didn't take them up on the offer but several of my friends did and they said it was a great experience.

After REFTRA we continued on patrol in the Caribbean Sea. As we finished up our patrol we made one last port call at the Navy base in Roosevelt Roads, Puerto Rico. It was perfect timing because we got to watch Super Bowl XXIII between the San Francisco 49ers and the Cincinnati Bengals. We caught the game at the base club and wined and dined on beans and weenies provided as free hors d'oeuvres! They were a delicacy to us after being on patrol for over a month.

A few months later in April 1989 we were back on patrol in the Caribbean Sea and the *Iowa* was involved in the Navy's fleet exercise (FLEET-EX) 3-89 being conducted in the same area. On April 19th we were operating off of Puerto Rico in the same general area as the *Iowa*. She was conducting gun firing exercises at the gunnery range near Vieques Island when her #2 turret exploded during the firing exercise, killing 47 sailors. The bodies were offloaded at the Roosevelt Roads naval base in Puerto Rico. There was so much speculation about what might have caused the accident aboard *Iowa* that I think it is still debatable today. Stories ranged from the gun crew not being trained well enough to a homosexual love spat. All I can add was that the event was tragic. Everyone on *Seneca* was shaken by it. Those sailers were fellow sea farers and we had just enjoyed liberty with them a few months earlier. For all I knew I could have been drinking with those that perished up at the Marine Corps club. I will never know.

We were underway again in August after spending June and July completing an extensive dry-dock at General Shipyard in South Boston. The patrol was highlighted by a stop in Annapolis, Maryland to pick up the famous author Tom Clancy. He transited the Chesapeake Bay with us to our port call at the Inner Harbor in Baltimore, Maryland. Mr. Clancy was very gracious and took the time to sign copies of his books and spend time socializing with the crew. We would spend several days in Baltimore during the first week of September. The American Legion was holding their annual convention at the Inner Harbor and the waterfront was packed, making for an exciting port call! From Baltimore it was back to work and on patrol.

Probably one of the more unusual things to happen while underway was losing one of our huge rudders while conducting a North Atlantic patrol in the winter of 1989. We had been conducting search and rescue operations on a sunken fishing vessel in rough seas and the helmsman reported difficulty steering the cutter. Our small boat was out retrieving a marker from the lost vessel and was heading up behind us. The crew of the small boat was asked if they could see anything wrong with the after part of the cutter. As *Seneca* took a huge swell part of the aft end of the cutter came out of the water and the small boat crew could see that one of the huge, 15 foot tall by 10 foot wide, rudders was missing! Just the long shaft it normally rode on was present. We had just completed that extensive dry-dock period at General Shipyard, so this was weird. Emergency dry-dock preparations were made at the Derecktor shipyards in Newport, Rhode Island where *Seneca* was built. Derecktor was at this time still under contract to build the remaining new 270 class cutters and had one about two thirds of the way finished. They did not have an extra rudder to give us so one was taken from the 270 that was still in production. The *Seneca* was dry-docked, the rudder replaced, and we sailed back off to complete our patrol. The entire evolution took less than a week.

In dry-dock at General Ship in South Boston

Our D1, or North Atlantic fisheries mission, involved patrolling off the coast of New England all the way up to Canada. The area is a huge fishing zone known as Georges Banks. This area contains a lot of fishing exclusionary zones and foreign fishing vessels loved to come into U.S. waters and fish, which is illegal. I'm not talking small illegal fishing, but huge harvesting ships that catch and can huge amounts of fish. They are literally floating canning factories.

On one occasion we were monitoring the scallop harvesting off the New England coast. The fishermen were out of New Bedford, Massachusetts and usually stayed pretty close together. Our captain suspected that they were using illegal catching methods and wanted to sneak up on them early in the morning and catch them off guard before they had time to alter their catching method, or discard any illegal catch. This is all fine and dandy, but I was a little nervous because the last thing you wanted to do to a fisherman was come sneaking up on his boat unannounced. Fishermen carry firearms onboard for protection against pirates, and yes other fisherman. There are numerous stories of fisherman shooting at each other in open water over fishing spots.

In the darkness of the wee hours of the morning I boarded the MSB small boat as the boat engineer and another boarding team entered the RHI small boat and we headed off in the direction of the scallop fishing fleet. The *Seneca* followed behind, but stayed out of sight just over the horizon until we were amongst the fishing fleet. The horizon is about seven miles off so we were out by ourselves in open water in these tiny small boats. As we sailed toward the fleet we eventually lost sight of the *Seneca* behind us, but could not yet see the fishing fleet ahead of us. We stopped and attempted to contact the *Seneca* on the radio with no luck. We were unsure if we were even headed in the right direction as everything looks the same in open water. We realized we had to trust our compass course and hoped it was right. Finally, the fishing fleet came into sight.

As we came up on the scallop fleet we could tell they had not gotten their day started and were just getting up. As we came up on the first fishing vessel the boarding team leader shouted out that we were the U.S. Coast Guard and wanted to come aboard and do an inspection. You could tell by the look on the face of the fishing vessel's master that he was surprised to see us and he kept looking around for our cutter. Our sneak attack worked! We boarded the first fishing vessel and not long after the *Seneca* arrived on scene with her blue law enforcement light flashing from the main mast. Yes, just like a police car, the cutter had a big blue light we turned on when we were pulling a vessel over for inspection! We did find a violation with one of the vessels which led us to escort her into New Bedford.

A more frustrating event happened just as we were getting ready to pull into Boston after a long patrol. We had just completed six weeks away from home and had reached Boston too late in the evening to pull in. The normal procedure was to only transit into Boston during daylight because our moorings were way at the end of Boston harbor, which is tight to navigate. The captain decided to anchor out at the mouth of Boston harbor until morning.

As was usual the night before pulling into home port the cutter was abuzz with anticipation! We were so close you could see the bright lights of Boston and hear the planes coming in overhead for a landing at Logan Airport. The crew was busy packing and talking about everything we were going to do once back home. As I lay there in my top rack, too excited to sleep, the CO came over the intercom system and announced that our relief cutter, the *USCGC Tamaroa (WMEC-166)*, was unable to get underway from her home port of Portsmouth, New Hampshire to relieve us due to mechanical problems.

What a kick in the gut! The crew was totally dejected. All we could think about now was driving up to New Hampshire and kicking their asses! The *Tamaroa* was an old cutter built in 1943 so she was lucky to still be around, let alone get underway. In the end, after a week of patrolling for her, she had made her repairs and was able to get underway to relieve us. In 1991 *Tamaroa* would be caught in the "Perfect Storm," a large storm system that hit the North Atlantic coast and she would become famous for rescuing fishermen and a helicopter crew.

In January of 1990 my tour aboard *Seneca* had come to an end. I had received orders to the USCG Supply Center located in Curtis Bay, Maryland. I had arrived on the *Seneca* as an MK3 straight out of machinery technician school and was leaving as an MK1. That was an unusual accomplishment in promotions because I had promoted the first time I was eligible for both MK2 and MK1. I was no longer the apprentice that had reported aboard and I now felt confident in my abilities as a machinery technician. But it was more than that the Coast Guard was now my career.

COAST GUARD SUPPLY CENTER

CURTIS BAY, MARYLAND

15 February 1990–16 January 1995

The Supply Center at Curtis Bay, Maryland (SCCB) was located on the United States Coast Guard Yard in Curtis Bay, Maryland. The Yard was a huge facility steeped in Coast Guard history dating back to 1899 when it became a repair depot and the location of the Coast Guard Academy. During World War II the facility was also used for basic training. My Uncle, Joe Semler, passed through here in 1943 when he went through Coast Guard boot camp.

The Yard was one large base, nestled on an inlet off the Chesapeake Bay, and was home to the only Coast Guard shipyard, the SCCB, a buoy tender, a small boat station, and several small commands. The facility was always humming with activity.

When I had initially contacted my assignment officer while on *Seneca* we had agreed that I would be transferred from the *Seneca* to a small boat station at St. Inigoes, Maryland, or so I thought. After I had talked to a few friends they asked me if I was sure I was not going to St. Ignace, Michigan, since the names sounded similar. The station at St. Ignace, Michigan was up on the frozen Upper Peninsula and I had no desire to go there. I was concerned so I called the assignment officer to confirm I was going to Maryland, and he said that he had me down for Michigan! I was able to convince him that there had been a mistake, but he said the station in Maryland was already filled.

The assignment officer told me that he may have an opening at the SCCB in nearby Baltimore, Maryland. He had someone else penciled in but, since I had more sea time than him, he would bump him and give me the position. I was relieved I wasn't going to the frozen tundra of upstate Michigan!

A few months after arriving I ran into another MK1, John Whittemore, and we were telling sea stories about our last units. At one point in our conversation he said he had been planning to transfer there to SCCB, but the assignment officer had just called him and told him he was being bumped for someone with more sea time! I didn't say a thing. He was a good shipmate, and eventually went on to become an officer. Our paths crossed later on down the road when he was the EO on a sister 270 class cutter out of Portsmouth, Virginia.

The SCCB was a big organization and had more civilians then military. It was the Coast Guard's only logistics depot for the repair, overhaul, purchase, and storage of engineering equipment. Being a machinery technician I was assigned to the central engine overhaul (CEO) program. We didn't actually do any wrench turning overhaul work as would be expected. Instead, we wrote the specifications to have civilian contractors do the work and we would also go out and inspect these contractors.

CEO was a small team consisting of a warrant officer, MKC, and two MK1s. My major assignment was the overhaul of the Cummins VT903M diesel engine and attached reduction gear that powered the Coast Guard's workhorse, the 41 foot small boat. This was the small boat used at almost all of our small boat stations, and there were over 170 of them in service. My coworker was another MK1, Regis McClosky, and my immediate supervisor was MKC Dave Bannon. The head of CEO for the majority of my time there was CWO Rufus Beard.

CWO Rufus Beard was one smart guy and he always seemed to be up to something. He impressed me because his background was as an electricians mate, but he knew engines, management, and logistics like he had been working at them all his life. He came up through the ranks like the rest of us, starting out as a fireman, completing electricians mate school, serving in the fleet, and finally taking a commission as a warrant officer. He was also the master at schemes, angles, and back door deals that were always on the verge of getting him into trouble. It seemed like he always had something shady going on while seamlessly managing the office in a professional manner. When you ran into people that knew him they either liked him or hated him, no in-between.

That was the mysterious side of CWO Beard. He had all these friends, acquaintances, relatives, and enemies. And I never knew who was who!

And if you wanted to see a man work the system to get things done, CWO Beard was the guru. His knowledge of the Coast Guard and calm cool demeanor always got him, and us, whatever was needed. He was a wizard at piloting the treacherous waters of his personal agenda while simultaneously navigating official Coast Guard business flawlessly. I'm sure that's how his evaluation report read!

Chief Dave Bannon was a young chief who loved a challenge. He wasn't much into the politics of the Coast Guard logistical system, but thrived on working with the civilian corporate world. He worked the best when he was told, "It can't be done!"

MK1 Regis "Mac" McClosky was a fellow Pennsylvanian and was also from the greater Pittsburgh area. He had been around the Yard community for a long time and his wife, Anna, worked as a civilian item manager in our office. Mac was a networker who knew everyone from the guy that took out the trash to the captain of the base.

Although we had a structured chain of command we predominantly worked independently. All four of us managed different Coast Guard engine assets and we were constantly juggling between being in the office and out on the road at a contractor's facility.

Work days were Monday through Friday 0800-1600 with weekends off. We did have to pull duty, but it was only about once every 30 days. It was a standard 24 hour duty day running from 0800 to 0800 and consisted mainly of locking the buildings up after everyone had left at around 2000 and opening them back up at 0600 in the morning. After locking up the buildings in the evening I would go home with a beeper and be on call until I returned in the morning to unlock the buildings. Probably the most interesting thing I did on duty days was go rustle up some of the older enlisted and warrant officers who were drunks, and wouldn't show up for work. The command would send whoever had duty over to the missing member's quarters to get them up and into work. This didn't happen a lot, but enough for me to remember it!

The command wanted us to stand the 24 hour watch entirely there on base, and stay overnight in the barracks. This was in case we had to handle an emergent parts shipment. But the hang up was with the civilians. None of the civilians were going to stand watch over night, which was a fact! And they held all the critical positions which were needed to ship an item out. So with no civilians, there was no need to hang around all night. With work hours and duty like this no wonder so many active duty guys wanted to homestead here and not go to sea!

One of the civilians in the office was retired Coast Guard Senior Chief Machinist Mate (MMSC) Gil Parks. He was an old salt, as salty as salt gets. He rode the old Coast Guard 327 Secretary and 310 Casco class cutters. These were the old school cutters, with crude living conditions and ancient engine rooms, which ran on steam turbines powered by dangerous boilers.

Gil had been a serious sea going man who told me sea yarns about how he would come off of one patrol and walk across the pier and get on another cutter getting underway to fill a vacant position they had. He would do it just so he didn't have to sit in port. Gil was at the SCCB when they started CEO and he had worked in the position I currently held. He told me when they first started the program they were instructed to get all the spare VT903Ms from out in the field back into the supply center so they could have a pool of engines to start to overhaul. Everyone in the field was skeptical of the program and wanted to keep their spare engines. The situation got so bad that Gil was tasked with traveling all over the country rounding up these engines and having them shipped back to SCCB. He said he would just drive on board the Coast Guard stations and maintenance facilities unannounced and confiscate everything he could get his hands on, to the dismay of the facility's engineers.

He said his most memorable confiscation was up in Boston. They had a huge station and maintenance facility and managed numerous other stations in the area. So he knew they had lots of spare engines. After rolling onto the base and spending the day looking all over the place, he could not find one engine. These things are the size of a small car so it's not like you could just hide them anywhere. Frustrated, Gil headed for the club there on base. He was having a beer at the bar and struck up a conversation with another guy sitting there. They had a few beers and the guy began telling Gil what an easy job he had that day. Gil asked him what he was doing that was so easy. The guy replied that his boss told him to take a truck off base first thing this morning and not to come back until after working hours. His boss said he didn't care what he did all day just as long as he didn't come back with that truck until after hours. Gil asked the guy, "Where is this truck?" The guy had no problem going out and showing his new drinking buddy the truck. Gil swung open the back doors and found the truck was loaded with engines! Needless to say Gil confiscated them all!

One day Chief Bannon called me over to the window of our office space and pointed out the window at Gil. He was standing outside against the building in the cool winter air. He had his old P-coat on with the collar lifted up to protect his neck, taking a long drag off a cigarette. He looked like the lone Navy sailor at the U.S. Navy Memorial in Washington, DC. We looked at each other and said, "Now that's a sailor."

It was a sad day years later in 2007 that I read that Gil had crossed the bar, our term for passing away. Whenever I hear the term, "old salt" I think of Gilbert Parks.

This was my first interaction with civilians and retired military, and it was really interesting. The whole mixture of military and civilian members at SCCB felt like a family. I interacted daily with the item managers who managed our engines. They were mostly civilian ladies and seemed like sisters. One in particular, Rose, was like a mother to us. Their boss was a retired Air Force character simply known as "Hose." He was the guru of supply and logistics and the nicest guy you would ever meet. I would say 25% of the civilians were retired military of one branch or another, usually Coast Guard or Navy. Most of them had served in WWII, Korea, or Vietnam and were full of what we call sea stories.

Mr. Neil Briscoe was a Navy veteran who worked with us. He told me an interesting story about when he was in the South Pacific with the Navy during WWII. He worked in supply and thought he was relatively safe back toward the rear of the fighting. After taking an island from enemy forces, Neil and his unit set up their supply operation there on the beach. He was staying in a canvas tent they had pitched for their berthing. One day they heard the air raid siren go off and he and his comrades ran to the woods for shelter. When he came back his tent and cot were riddled with bullet holes! He said it was his closest call during the war.

The work place technology was pretty simple. We had computers to type up our specifications, but they were the first run of computer technology and had a simple light and dark green screen type and background. Everything on the computer also had to be saved to these dinner plate sized floppy discs. There was no internet. The phone system was on a party network and had about four lines. Everyone in that section of the building, which contained several offices, had the same phone number. When the phone rang whoever was free answered it and yelled out the name of the person the call was for.

The government contracting section was also made up almost entirely of civilians. I had a close relationship with them as they awarded and managed our contracts. Like the item managers, they were mostly civilian ladies and passionate about their work. We were like family and always concerned and interested with what was going on with each other personally. We worked very closely together and occasionally traveled together.

I did a lot of traveling, about once a week, visiting my various contractors in Louisiana, Illinois, New York, Virginia, South Carolina, and Ohio for the bulk of my contracts. Traveling was enjoyable believe it or not. Airport security was simple and the planes had plenty of room and were rarely ever full. During this time the first Gulf War was going on and the airports and airplanes were virtually empty. All my flight, hotel, and rental car reservations were processed through the government contracted travel agency. The government had just started to issue individual credit cards, Diners Club, which made traveling pretty easy. If I needed cash I took my orders and credit card to the pay clerk and was given an advance on those orders. When I finished the trip I turned in my travel claim with my orders. Usually I made a few bucks a trip because I never ate as much as they gave me in per diem. Life was good.

The contracts for overhauls on the VT903M and reduction gear would usually be for four years and we had several contracts let at any given time. When a contract was near expiration another contract was let out for bids. When this happened I would write the technical specification for how the engine package should be overhauled and then act as the technical representative for the Coast Guard when the contract was awarded. So at any given time I was managing a couple of different contractors performing overhauls and writing specifications for ones in the bidding process.

I had to make regular visits to the contractors' facilities to inspect their work and make sure they were following the specifications outlined in the contract. I would mostly travel alone for the day to day inspections, but for the final acceptance I would go out with a warrant officer from our quality assurance (QA) division. They had the authority to actually sign for and take acceptance of the completed engines once they had been dynamometer-tested. Dynamometer-testing was an operating test to make sure the engine ran at the required parameters.

Several of my contractors were down in Louisiana. I loved going down to Louisiana, and usually made the trip with Chief Bannon. Chief and I usually traveled to Louisiana together because we both had contractors down there and several of them were in the same facility. I never would have thought I would love going to Louisiana after my Fort Polk days, but this was different because I could come and go as I pleased!

Our first stop after picking up the rental car was the drive-through daiquiri stand, and then the all you can eat catfish restaurant. Louisiana was poor and run down but it had that deep south warmth to it. The first time I went down to see this particular contractor I went with Chief Bannon. The facility was also overhauling engines for the 82 foot Patrol Boat, which he managed. When we pulled up to the facility the chief said, "We are going to have our hands full with these guys." I asked why and he said, "They spelled diesel wrong on their sign!" I thought to myself; this is going to be a long contract. It actually turned out to be a very short one!

A few months later chief and I returned to inspect the contractor once again. After getting our daiquiri and filling our stomachs with catfish we drove over to the facility. This time when we arrived the place was pad locked and there was no one around. A note on the door said the sheriff had impounded the facility! Chief called the sheriff's office and told them there was government property in the facility and we needed to get it out. The sheriff was accommodating and said he would come and open the place up, but we would have to get our stuff out quick, like in a couple of hours quick.

The chief's engines were about the size of a Volkswagen bus and mine were the size of a small compact car so this was not going to be easy. The facility had these engines in various stages of being rebuilt so there were parts all over the place. I was thinking there is no way we are going to get all this crap out of here. The chief didn't seem too phased about it. Like I said, he loved a challenge. He simply got on the phone back to SCCB and arranged to get a moving company to assist us. Within an hour several semi-trucks from a moving company came rolling in and we had a majority of our stuff loaded up by the end of the day!

The remaining engines, which were mine, we loaded up onto a borrowed truck and trailer we had called in from the nearby Coast Guard base in New Orleans. After getting them loaded up I drove them back across the set of bridges known as the Crescent City Connection into New Orleans and onto the Coast Guard base. The guys at the base were more than happy to get them because the base had a repair facility that also over-hauled engines for us. Their shop was a mix of active duty and civilian government workers and they were always looking for us to throw them work. They didn't like the civilian companies that did overhauls for us because it cut into their workload. Without overhaul work they really didn't have a reason for being around and they didn't want the overhaul facility disbanded.

It was always fun to go down and visit these guys around Mardi Gras. Work would just about come to a standstill as the whole city went into party mode. The shop had a tradition of buying what is known as "king cake." King cake is a sort of highly decorated sheet cake with a small plastic baby baked into the cake. As the cake is cut up and passed out, whoever ends up with the baby in their piece of cake buys the cake for the next day. They were a group of close knit guys and it was fun to work with them.

I had another company down in Norfolk, Virginia. This company was basically a junk yard that had gotten into the engine business to make a little extra money. The facility was at the end of a dirt road and consisted of a steel garage with a concrete floor and a huge garage door at one end. The owners were a very nice elderly couple with a whole lot of southern charm. The wife was the company president so they could claim the business as woman owned. This would get them into the lucrative "small business set aside" arena of government contracts.

On my initial inspection of the facility I had recommended that they not be given the work because the facility didn't meet our basic requirements for quality control. I was over ruled and the contract was awarded. The contracting officer, I assumed, needed to meet a quota of small business contracts and needed this contractor whether they were good or bad.

Great, this meant that I would need to spend a lot of time on site with this contractor walking them through just about every step of the contract. Starting a new contract always lent itself to a learning curve, but most contractors knew the industry and just needed to modify their production line to incorporate government specific requirements. This contractor was starting out as new to this as I had seen.

When they were assembling their first engine I went down to see how they were doing. The garage door was wide open and the engine was up on an engine stand about a quarter of the way done. The mechanic was putting in the pistons and every time a vehicle would come up or down the dirt road the garage would fill with a mist of dust, which would settle on everything in the facility. As far as engine building goes, this was a big no-no! When building engines you need a very clean environment, hence a high standard of quality control to monitor these things. Any dirt that gets into an engine can cause catastrophic failure as it wears all the internal parts, especially bearings. I talked to the owner about the situation. He was of the opinion that he had been doing this type of work for a long time and everything was going to be okay. Needless to say the first engine they built didn't even make it 15 minutes on the dynamometer-tester before it failed. The contract dragged on for over a year, and everything they produced failed either on the dynamometer or out in the field.

With all that said the contracting officer still wanted us to keep going instead of terminating. I learned real quick that the government doesn't operate on good business common sense all the time. In this instance we seemed to be doing charity work and punching our card for having a small business set aside contract.

One of my bigger contractors was a company up in Woodstock, Illinois, north of Chicago. They had been doing engines for years before I arrived and had a good reputation. I had been paying them regular visits, inspecting them along with the QA warrant officer, CWO Mike Vest.

CWO Vest was a smart man. He was a southern boy who really enjoyed a cigarette. He was a slow moving, really skinny, guy and when he lit a cigarette you could tell he really enjoyed it. He would take long slow drags, exhale, and then make a statement, take a long slow drag, exhale, and make a statement. He sort of reminded me of Peter Falk's character Colombo. Not in the way he looked physically but in the way he acted and dressed. CWO Vest always looked disheveled like Colombo. What hair he had was messed up and his uniform looked like he had been wearing it for several days. And of course his shoes were never shined. Like Colombo people would look at him and write him off, but he was as smart as a fox. Or like my grandma Churilla would say, "Dumb as a fox!"

The contractor produced a good reliable product and they had a good facility with good technicians. Nevertheless, we still inspected them like everyone else. We were conducting our inspection and CWO Vest was out talking to one of the mechanics. The mechanic was grinding on an engine block and CWO Vest asked him what he was doing. Just like Colombo he was asking a lot of seemingly innocent questions. The mechanic said he was taking off the serial number and replacing it with another serial number. When CWO Vest was done watching he casually walked over to me and said in his southern drawl, "These boys are grinding off serial numbers on our engine blocks and putting new ones on and charging us for a new block, that's illegal." I was surprised! But if CWO Vest said it, it must be true. Sure enough, we inspected the inventory against their records and it appeared that they were defrauding the government by selling us our own used engine blocks back to us as new. They eventually lost the contract.

Because of a couple of failed contracts like the ones I just mentioned, our inventory of overhauled engines had drawn down to a very low level. It was decided by the contracting officer to go out on an emergency contract to overhaul about 20 engines. Deeming the contract critical, and in an emergent situation, allowed the contracting officer to bypass a lot of the required contracting rules. Instead of a six-eight month contracting process we could award a contract within weeks.

The contract was awarded to a very well-known Cummins engine dealer in the Bronx, New York. It was important to get these engines done quickly and I was tasked with going up to the facility for the next couple of weeks to watch the engines being overhauled. One of the QA CWOs was also assigned to be on site to verify the dynamometer-test for acceptance.

I had never been to this Cummins facility before. When I arrived it was in the middle of the Bronx and surrounded by barbed wire with razor wire on top. I figured it would be a good idea to pull into the facility and park up front. When I walked in and met the manager the first thing he asked me was, "Did you pull inside the gate?" I told him I did and I was parked right out front. He said "Good! Never leave your car outside the gate or it will be stolen in a matter of minutes!" Obviously this was a bad neighborhood and his statement reassured me that he was aware of that and our government property was safe and in good hands!

Watching these guys at work was impressive because they followed the contracting rules. The government's requirement of documentation and quality control was meticulous and always seemed to throw contractors off. The contracts called for detailed step by step reports and approval before proceeding with the next step. A majority of contractors always assumed that once they had the contract they would do it their way and the government would be happy because the end product was great. This always caused big problems. Well, this contractor had it together and with the exception of one or two glitches had a smooth system that met our requirements.

They had a really nice assembly line for tearing down the engines along with several rebuild stands. They were able to rebuild multiple engines at a time, instead of the one at a time operations I had been used to. Once they got moving it was only a matter of a few days and they had the engines through every phase of tear down, rebuild, dynamometer-test, and out the door and on their way back to SCCB.

Chief Bannon and I joined forces on another venture to resolve an issue of premature failures with the VT903M engine package. The engines were failing at an unusually high rate, even for our extreme working environment. At around $25k an engine package, and two per boat, this was a big deal. From what I had seen at the overhaul facilities it looked like there was a lubrication issue causing abnormal wear. While brainstorming in the office we felt that the operator, known as the coxswain, was not letting the engine get oil pressure before giving the engine full throttle. This was only a theory and we had to prove it.

Cummins Engine Company had their main diagnostic testing center down in Charleston, South Carolina and we contracted with them to do an analysis on our engines. Chief Bannon and I headed down with several failed engines to assist with the analysis. After tearing down the engines it was clear, by the main and connecting rod bearing wear, a lack of lubrication was at fault.

After the engines were rebuilt on site they were run through Cummins intense dynamometer-testing. The test simulates running the engine for weeks, even months, at loaded speeds to simulate a real operating environment. They would start one up on the dynamometer and I would come back down a few weeks later and it would still be going! After it was done running we disassembled the engines and found normal wear.

The problem had to lie in the way we were starting, stopping, or maintaining them, and not how we ran them.

There was a Coast Guard station there in Charleston and the Cummins tech guys recommended that they go over and install some data collecting devices on the engines to see if they could come up with anything to substantiate our theory of a problem with oil pressure at start up. Bingo! The data showed that the engines were being loaded and given full throttle before attaining the critically needed oil pressure.

We discussed the matter with the operating side of the Coast Guard at the headquarters level. Their position was that because they needed every second to get a rescue crew on scene, they didn't want to wait the four to five seconds needed to obtain oil pressure. The compromise was to install an oil pre-lube pump that would supply oil faster to the engine and cut down the oil pressure wait time to about one second. But if the coxswain couldn't wait the one second, he could bypass it. This saved the Coast Guard a huge amount of money on maintenance and future overhaul costs.

In March of 1991 I received orders to attend Coast Guard Senior Petty Officer Leadership and Management School (SPLOLAM) at the Coast Guard base in Petaluma, California. Attending the school was a requirement after making E-6, and I was more than happy to head out to California on the government's dime. After a cross country plane ride I had to catch a bus from San Francisco airport up north to the base at Petaluma.

The base at Petaluma was over an hour away and the trip was amazing. After crossing the Golden Gate Bridge we had a very scenic drive through California's wine country. As the bus rolled on out into the country I started to wonder just where the base actually was. I had never been here before and had not researched it at all before making the trip. I just assumed since it was a Coast Guard base it was some place on the coast next to the Pacific Ocean. Finally after driving through the small town of Petaluma we drove out onto a winding country road surrounded by cow pastures. I was wondering, shouldn't there be water some place around here? And then we made a left turn into the base which was in the middle of nowhere. It was surrounded by farmland and not where I had expected a Coast Guard base to be located.

Although the facility was in the middle of nowhere it was state of the art and had all the newest barracks and furnishings. I was berthed in Horsley Hall and shared a room with another classmate. We had very nice individual wooden bunk beds with the desk below the top rack and a head in our room! The facility appeared to be almost brand new. This was a night and day difference from the facilities at Yorktown!

What made things even better was this was the base for the substance specialist school, better known as cooks, and the food was fabulous. On Fridays there was a line to get into the galley because they put out a sea food extravaganza, complete with lobster and king crab legs.

The SPOLAM class lived up to its name and was all about leadership and management. The class was actually easy and comprised of lecture upon lecture with minimal written assignments and homework. After class the only thing to do was head over to the club and drink. Going into town was an option, but it hinged on catching the liberty van back and forth. After several classmates passed the word that there wasn't anything to do in town, that cinched it for me to just stay on base.

My time at Petaluma was quiet, relaxing, and uneventful. But SPOLAM must have had an influence on me because on the 1st of August 1991 I was awarded the "Sailor of the Quarter" for E-4 through E-6 for the period from the 1st of April through the 31st of July 1991. I would be nominated several more times in 1993 and 1994, but this was the only time I was actually selected. This recognition demonstrated to me that with a little effort and more focus I could move forward in my career.

With the winds of motivation in my sails I began to study for the promotion examination for the prestigious rank of chief. This was a test given once a year in November and would rank me for promotion with my peers. Usually there were over 350 people taking the exam for MKC. My final score would be a combination of my exam, performance marks, time in grade/rank, time in service, and medals and awards. All of those scores were plugged into a formula and I would be given a final ranking. In 1992 I was ranked 130, and they selected 80. In 1993 I was ranked 138, and again they only selected 80. And finally in 1994 I was ranked 59, and they only anticipated selecting 16. Luckily they were just being conservative and ended up promoting just over 60, and I made it!

On the 1st of September 1994 I was promoted to chief petty officer. To the Coast Guard and Navy this is a huge milestone. As you can tell by the description of the chiefs on the *Sumac*, *Seneca*, and here at SCCB they are held to a high standard, given a tremendous amount of responsibility, and given special privileges because of their rank.

There is a process with being promoted to chief, and it's called the chief's initiation. It's unlike other promotions, which usually involve a quick pinning ceremony at quarters the day you're promoted. Instead, the chief's initiation starts about 30 days before you are actually promoted. The entire process culminates on initiation day, which concludes with a very nice formal dinner.

The process unofficially starts a few months before you are actually advanced when the selection list for the year comes out. If you're selected to be promoted, from that point on you start to take flak from the real, or initiated, chiefs. At this point you have to make a very critical decision, do I go through the chief's initiation or not? If you go through the initiation you are accepted into the supportive arms of the chief's network. If you decline, you're an outcast.

I saw the results of not being initiated right there at SCCB. Chiefs, who elected not to be initiated, or put it off, were shunned. I mean it's like they wore the scarlet letter "U" for uninitiated. Somehow chiefs knew you were an outcast and you were basically ignored and not welcome in anything involving "real chiefs." If that's the way it was on land I could just image how bad it would be afloat and in a chief's mess.

I had also seen chiefs go through the initiation and knew it was a hard and humiliating process. You never really knew what was going on because it is all quite secretive to a point. The official 30 days or so lead up was sort of in the open, but the day or two long initiation ceremony itself was behind closed doors. On the *Seneca* the chiefs had the yeoman first class (YN1), who was making chief, eating out of a dog bowl in front of the chief's mess for everyone to see. It put everyone on notice that you just don't pin on chief and walk through the chief's mess door, you had to earn it! At SCCB you would see those going through initiation standing at the front gate wearing what appeared to be Halloween costumes, waving to everyone coming to work. Another example to everyone that making chief is no free ride!

The chief's mess and retired chiefs formed the Chief Petty Officer Association who conducted the initiation. The Coast Guard was going through more changes in the early 90s, and cleaning up the chief's initiation was on the hit list. The Coast Guard was just enacting a new retirement policy known as high year tenure (HYT) for the enlisted force that would automatically retire you if you had over 30 years of service. This was a huge deal because there were folks in their 60s still on active duty. Of course these were chiefs, and if you were getting rid of all the old chiefs in the goat locker the thought was you may as well revise the chief's initiation. The revised process would take time and slowly took hold over the years. But those of us who were initiated by the old chiefs were typically initiated the same way they were.

There were many charges, or tasks, put on me once I accepted the initiation. Some of these were to know from memory the Coast Guard song *Semper Paratus*, the words to the Creed of the Coast Guardsman, the Coast Guard Core Attributes, and the list goes on. Probably the biggest charge was receiving a book that was to never leave my possession. In the book I would collect words of wisdom from all the chiefs I could find. The motivation was that the more words of wisdom I collected the easier the chiefs would be on me come initiation day. I was lucky that I was at a location that had a huge chief population and I received very good advice from the initiated chiefs. Between all of the active duty and retired chiefs stationed or working as civilians there at the SCCB, Yard, and surrounding commands I had no problem getting words of wisdom, and of course harassment!

Of course, I couldn't just walk up and ask a real chief to sign my book, I had to present myself. When I approached a chief I was to have a pen at the ready, ask them if I could get them a cup of coffee and how they would like it prepared, invite them to my initiation, and recite the following from memory; "Honorable chief, may I please have the honor of introducing my humble self. I'm petty officer one-and-a-half Edward Semler. I have been selected to become a member of the hollowed fraternity of the Chief Petty Officers of the United States Coast Guard. Whereas, I realize honorable one, that I am not yet wise enough to be called a chief, I ask of you and your honorable brothers and sisters that you indulge me with teachings from your vast storehouse of knowledge on all worldly things so that I may be mentally prepared to walk near your side. Honorable one, would you please do me the honor of making an entry in my charge book?"

Some of my entries were;

"Always believe in your abilities, never fear the unknown, be humble." David Bannon, MKC

"Don't expect others to listen to your advice and ignore your example." MKC D. E. Bartlett (Dan was my MK1 on *Seneca*)

"I truly wish you well as you enter the Chief's Mess and assume the responsibilities." CWO Bill Pitkin (This is MKC Pitkin who was the main propulsion chief on *Seneca*)

"Lead by example and just do the RIGHT thing. Remember the Chiefs that made impressions on you and helped develop you to what you are about to be." S.R. Twomey, MKC

"Chief, it is not just a rank title but a way of life. You will be looked upon to make decisions that will not only affect you but everyone around you. Don't be afraid to make mistakes, you will learn from them." MKCS G.E. Bailey

"Stand by your people always, right or wrong. They'll respect you for it. They may not always make the decision you would, explain it to them, and let them "learn" from the experience, but don't make them live in your "shadow." Continue the tradition, and make the words "Ask the Chief" meaningful for the people who work for you, with you, and for the people you work for." David Smith CWO3

Dave Smith, remember he was my MK1 on *Sumac* who took the time to engage me and motivated me to focus on becoming an MK and get serious about being in the service. He had made chief, promoted to CWO, and was stationed again with me at SCCB. He remembered our days on the *Sumac* when I was just the young fireman and wondered if he had been a good influence on me. He most certainly was.

On initiation day you go to court complete with a judge and defense attorney. The judge will decide if you will become a real chief or not. I had a lieutenant junior grade (LTJG) represent me as my defense. The initiation process is all about building humility and respect within you, the chief corps, and the officer corps. Since chiefs and officers work so closely together, the new chief and young officer are brought together during the initiation process to work together. They are put through a rough situation and are shown that if they are true to each other and themselves, they can succeed. The young officer is also given insight on what it takes to become a real chief. My junior officer was LTJG Mike Welch. He wasn't a Coast Guard Academy guy but a ROTC officer. Not that you could tell the difference unless they told you. He was a good man and a good officer. But he had no idea what he was getting himself into!

On the 9th of September I commenced my day of initiation. After a morning of making and serving breakfast to the real chiefs, we got down to business. We had changed into our costumes for the initiation and were held in a small room awaiting our turn in front of the judge. There were about eight of us going through the process. One by one we were led from the room, along with our junior officer, and taken in front of the judge. The judge turned out to be a tough master chief by the name of MKCM Arron Jones.

In appearing before the judge I was to be working off fines I had received during the lead up to the initiation. As I was interacting with the real chiefs over the past month, I was incurring monetary fines whenever I would falter in my charges. These fines climbed into thousands of dollars. Of course, unbeknownst to me, this was all made up.

As LTJG Welch stood before the judge I was on my knees, not worthy to stand in the judge's presence. LTJG Welch started out by pulling a pair of red briefs, or underwear, from his briefcase and proclaimed to the judge that he was going to "brief" him on the facts of the case. The judge, unimpressed, told me to put the briefs on over my coveralls! LTJG Welch and I presented our best defense but inevitably I would be charged with an infraction. My fines would increase instead of decrease, I would have to do a stunt, and we would both have to drink "truth serum!" This went on and on. The stunts weren't bad; it was the "truth serum" that got me. It was a mixture of hot sauce, fish, peas, and who knows what else. Actually I do know but I won't tell you!

Chief's Initiation
Left to right; MKCM Arron Jones (Judge), MKCS Harry Stevens,
LTJG Mike Welch, and MKC Ed Semler. In front of
the Judge drinking "truth serum"

The day concluded with a formal dinner and awards ceremony. I really didn't get to enjoy the meal because of the lingering taste of "truth serum" in the back of my throat! Of course while we were going through the initiation the guys would be telling their wives the amount of fines they had racked up. You can imagine how that was going over! While we were eating dinner, one guy's wife was getting a little tipsy. Through conversation she heard that MKCM Jones was the judge and in charge of the exorbitant fines. So, she got up and walked over to where he was seated at the head table. She commenced to let him have it about how she and her new chief husband could never afford such a huge fine! MKCM Jones played it off perfectly. He responded, "I'll drop the fine, now go back and enjoy your dinner!"

**Chief's Initiation dinner
MKCS Bailey, MKC Ruble, MKC Semler, and
MKC Dammon at awards ceremony dinner**

Upon being promoted to chief I received orders as the auxiliary chief aboard *USCGC Tampa (WMEC-902)* home ported out of Portsmouth, Virginia. In preparation for my departure, and still at SCCB, I commenced a series of pre-arrival training courses back in Yorktown, Virginia. These are known as "pipeline training" or "C" school. The courses were designed to bring me up to speed on the mechanical systems I would be in charge of on *Tampa* such as hydraulics, refrigeration and air conditioning, water making equipment, and heating and cooling systems. The courses were one week in length, with the exception of the air conditioning and refrigeration course which was several weeks long. In between attending the courses in Yorktown, Virginia I was out-processing from SCCB.

USCGC TAMPA (WMEC-902)

PORTSMOUTH, VIRGINIA

18 January 1995 – 19 July 1997

USCGC TAMPA (WMEC-902)
Moored at Portsmouth, Virginia

I reported aboard the *Tampa* while she was conducting a D1 North Atlantic patrol. I flew up to Portland, Maine after attending the last of my pre-arrival engineering courses and I waited for *Tampa* to pull in on a scheduled port call. She was a little late, and I ended up spending the night there at the Coast Guard Base. It was January, the temperatures were frigid, and the snow was piled up everywhere.

Like the *Seneca*, the *Tampa* was a 270 foot medium endurance cutter and had an all-male crew of 100, 14 officers and 86 enlisted. And Like the *Seneca*, patrols ranged from six to eight weeks underway and four to six weeks in port for maintenance. No matter what the ratio, it was mandatory to be underway at least 180 days a year. While underway on patrol we

207

would stop for two day refueling, supply, and liberty port calls every two weeks or twice a patrol. I would end up completing nine and a half patrols, to include one North Atlantic Fisheries patrol, Seven District 7 Caribbean drug and migrant patrols, and one District 8 Gulf of Mexico patrol.

Tampa was commissioned in 1984 and the second cutter built in the "Famous Cutter" class. She was named in honor of the first *Tampa*, which was in commission from 1912 – 1918. She was lost on the 26th of September 1918 with all hands while conducting convoy duty during WWI. As she transited the Bristol Channel, on the west coast of England, she was spotted by German submarine *UB-91*. The U-boat fired one torpedo, which sent her to the bottom with all 115 crewmembers and 16 passengers. Only four bodies were recovered.

The new *Tampa* was currently conducting fishery operations in the North Atlantic. We called it D1 because that area was controlled by Coast Guard District 1. When she arrived the next day I walked across the brow, saluted the ensign, turned and saluted the quarterdeck and reported aboard to the officer of the deck (OOD). I was a new chief and tried to carry myself with all the piss and vinegar the position granted me. But I remembered the tough time Chief Patton and Chief Hodgden had managing people, equipment, and the chief's mess. I was nervous about my new responsibilities, but unwilling to let it show.

I was shown my new home, a two man state room in the aft section of the main deck in chief's country. I shared it with the other MKC, Dave Gauthier. The state room I was to call home was simply identified as 1-199-2-L. Every compartment onboard Coast Guard vessels follow a number system to make for quick identification and location. You definitely knew what compartment you were in because it was painted all over the place with reflective glow in the dark paint. This is not only for daily use but, more importantly, in the event of a casualty such as fire or flooding. The system is broken down by the deck, frame, relation to center line, and type of compartment. So 1-199-2-L would mean it is located on the 1st deck, the forward most part of the compartment is at frame 199, the number 2 means it's on the port side ("1" would indicate starboard side and "0" would indicate center line), and the letter L indicates a living space. An "E" would indicate an engineering space, "M" ammunition storage and so on.

There were eight chiefs on board. We all lived in the aft part of the cutter on the main deck. We shared four staterooms, berthing two chiefs each and sharing two heads. Each head had two sinks, a toilet, and a shower. Our chief's mess was a small 10x10 room which was our dining and recreation area. You could just barely get all eight of us in there at one time. On my first day sitting in the chief's mess I noticed a bronze plaque commemorating the original chiefs that commissioned the *Tampa*. The name BMC Pawloski jumped right out at me! Remember he was the ass chewing machine from back on the *Seneca*. Since the *Tampa* was commissioned in 1983, and he was on the *Seneca* in 1987, he must have cross decked right from the *Tampa* to the *Seneca*. Commissioning two cutters back to back; no wonder he was always in a foul mood!

After two days in Portland we slipped our berth and headed back out into the Atlantic for five more weeks of patrol. It was in the middle of winter and the North Atlantic seas were rough with high seas and winds. We would stop in Halifax, Nova Scotia, Boston, Massachusetts, and again in Portland, Maine before returning to our homeport of Portsmouth, Virginia.

While in Halifax, Nova Scotia we moored at the Canadian Navy base. There were several Canadian Navy ships in port and our crew was invited over to tour them. The most unusual thing about the Canadian ships was that they served alcohol on board daily! That was unheard of on American military vessels. Of course we all drank like fish and liked to live up to the description, "drunk as a sailor" when we hit a port call. I just kept thinking; wow that would be very dangerous for us! But the Canadians had controls in place and they were allowed to drink as long as it was done responsibly. If you didn't, you had your rations cut off.

I felt technically confident being assigned the auxiliary position because I had spent three years on the *Seneca* in auxiliary and knew all the systems like the back of my hand. The current A-gang chief was MKC George Enos, a happy go lucky kind of fellow. He was on his last patrol when I met the *Tampa* in Portland and he would turn everything over to me during the remainder of the patrol. He was ready to move on after suffering a major casualty to a piece of his equipment. It was a simple mistake but the event was weighing on him.

On the previous patrol he had blown up the truck sized emergency generator and was catching a lot of heat for it. It was a simple mistake. He was trying to resolve an issue with the engine coming up to speed. Engine speed is controlled by a fuel control rod, which in this case is made with a slight curve to it. The overall throw, or travel, of the rod is only about a half inch from idle to full speed. George thought if he straightened the rod a bit it would help with his speed problem.

The generator was started and it immediately came to full speed, locking the fuel rod into an over speed condition. All attempts to secure the generator failed. The emergency generator is in the aft steering space, below the fantail. Now when that truck sized generator starts up in that enclosed compartment, with you standing there, it will scare the crap out of you on a normal day. You can imagine how George felt with that thing screaming at over speed. When he realized the danger he was in he turned to run out of the compartment. He was just heading out the hatch when it blew, sending metal engine pieces everywhere. We are talking hundreds of thousands of dollars in damage. It was all put back together before I arrived and George was happy to be putting this all behind him.

MKC Dave Gauthier was coming on board the same time I was and was to take over main propulsion. He was a small boat station guy and nervous about taking over the huge engine room. The Engineering Officer, Lieutenant Bob Breese, knowing that I had already served on a 270 asked if I would trade with Dave and take over the more complicated main propulsion. I had no previous schooling on the equipment in the engine room, but did stand countless hours of watch over it on *Seneca*. I left my comfort zone and agreed to take main propulsion. It turned out to be a good decision.

As the main propulsion chief I was proud of the engine room because it represented me. Fortunately, my tour was an uneventful one for major machinery casualties like George endured. Of course we had the occasional problem here and there but nothing major. Most of my issues were with my fellow chiefs. The chief's mess was young, and we all thought we were gun slingers who knew everything. Most of us were new chiefs and this was our first mess. We were the new breed of young chiefs, the ones who were promoted when high year tenure cleared out all the old goats. Our leader, and the *Tampa's* Command Enlisted Advisor (CEA), was Radarman Chief (RDC) Mike Matthews.

Chief's Mess
Back row left to right; EMC Joe Gardner, BMC Bill Leahy, RMC Ron Pridgen, MKC Dave Gauthier, TCC Lee Halyard
Front row left to right; SSC Dave Timko, BMC Lee(?), RDC Mike Mathews, EMC Willie Volante, MKC George Enos, MKC Ed Semler

The CEA position was an extremely important position at every command, and was usually the enlisted person with the most seniority. But this wasn't a set rule and the CO could choose another chief as the CEA if he wanted to. But, as important as the position was, it was still a collateral duty here and the CEA needed to balance this responsibility with his primary job. The CEA was the liaison between the CO and the crew, serving as an advocate for the 86 or so enlisted personnel. This would consist of advising the command on matters affecting morale, welfare, work environment, and assignments. Inevitably you became the mediator for every enlisted issue from so and so doesn't like me to whether a person should be brought up on charges for an infraction.

Mike was a great CEA who was passionate about his responsibilities. He also had a lot of energy and was easy to wind up. And I mean he could get wound up in a matter of seconds. For the most part he kept us focused in the mess, but being chiefs we all wanted to do things our own way!

My usual run-ins were with the Electricians Mate Chief (EMC), Joe Gardner. He had just as much energy as Mike, and could blow his top twice as fast. He was a great electrician and he knew it. Joe and I worked close because we were in the engineering department together and he had a huge amount of electrical equipment in the engine room. We would have the usual arguments about whether a machinery casualty was caused by a mechanical or electrical issue, but that was normal with MKs and EMs.

Our main problem was that neither one of us was going to back down in an argument. It all came to a head one evening while I was standing engineer of the watch (EOW) in the engine room. We were under way and I had asked Joe to have his guys work on a controller that I was having a problem with. Days went by without it getting fixed, so I did it myself. One of the EMs must have told Joe I was working on the controller because he came storming down into the engine room control booth and started ripping me about getting into his controller. We had words, and I had had enough. I called the engineering officer on the phone and asked him to come down before things got out of control. By the time he got there it was too late. Joe and I had a death grip on each other, cussing, and trying to choke each other to death. Yep, it was embarrassing! The EO was such a great guy and I felt like an ass letting him see me stoop to school yard shenanigans. Joe and I gave each other a wide berth from then on until he eventually transferred out. He was replaced by EMC Willie Volante, and we got along fine.

The guys that worked for me in the main propulsion division were the best a new chief could ask for. Over my three year tour they rotated in and out, and the changeover was high, but I always seemed to get quality MKs and firemen. The petty officers were on three year tours like me, but most of us were on different rotation years. The firemen were with me anywhere from several months up to two years, depending on how fast they qualified for their rating "A" school.

Main Propulsion
Back row left to right; MK3 Rich Arms, MK2 Steve Norred, FN D'Amore, Front row left to right; MKC Ed Semler, FN Rob Chofay, MK1 Gary Robison, FN Jeff Brann, FN Saun McCollough

My MK1s during my tour, Clancy Hull and Gary Robison, were true leaders. Even though they were older than me, and had pretty much small boat station backgrounds, our working relationship was never awkward and they gave me everything they had.

Along with the MK1s I had petty officers like MK2 Jason Carlson, MK2 Steve Norred, MK3 Matt Winn, and MK3 Rich Arms who always gave me, and the cutter 110%. I can't remember a casualty that wasn't quickly resolved or maintenance ever getting behind schedule.

I also never expected my guys to do anything I wouldn't or couldn't do. An example was crawling under the locomotive sized main engines to clean the bilge. Definitely not for the claustrophobic! The bilge under these engines was dark, dirty, and in some places only 15 inches high. They said getting under there couldn't be done. One day I slipped on my coveralls and slid under the #1 main engine and wiped up the bilge, all the way under it from the front to the back. About at the half way point I wrote something on the underside of the engine with a marker. I told my guys that if they could tell me what I wrote I'd give them a day of liberty. Over my tour only one or two guys were able to tell me what I wrote. And of course once they found out what I wrote, they were not going to tell anyone else after crawling all the way under that engine!

I lived on board and worked in the engine room in the evenings. When my guys had duty they worked into the evening with me. In exchange for their devotion I had a standing rule that if you gave me 110%, I would give you twice as much in support and liberty. They all wanted liberty and extra-long weekends. Only the captain could authorize a day's liberty or liberty in excess of 24 hours, so I would be sticking my neck out if we got caught.

I had this agreement with the petty officers and would extend it to the senior firemen if they were responsible. I had one young fireman who was from the same part of Pennsylvania as me and wanted to go home for an extended weekend. Now to get from our home port of Portsmouth, Virginia up to the Franklin, Pennsylvania area, where he was from, was about an eight hour drive. I should have known better, but the kid was a hard worker and I let him go. Needless to say he didn't make it back in time for muster, and I wasn't able to cover for him at that point. I told my boss, the EO, that I had let him go, so I was in trouble along with the fireman. When he finally got back later that day I gave him twice the ass chewing I received.

On the 7th of July 1995 my path once again crossed with my old XO from the *Seneca*, Dave Ryan. Now Commander Dave Ryan, he was assuming the duties of the Commanding Officer of *Tampa*. It was underway for another Caribbean Sea patrol from July through September of 1995. We called patrolling down there D7 patrols. Just like D1, this meant working for Coast Guard District 7. On the way down we stopped in Nassau, Bahamas for fuel and a port call. We usually volunteered in foreign port calls to help out a charity, and on this occasion I volunteered with eight others to paint and repair the Nassau Children's Emergency Relief Hostel. I picked up trash, repaired some doors and removed some toys that had somehow been thrown up on the roof. It was rewarding. We were also challenged by the American Embassy to a softball game. I got three hits and we won 13-11!

This was primarily a migrant patrol and we picked up numerous Haitians trying to make their way to the United States. I had seen this before on the *Seneca*, and it was always a sad. Unlike in the *Seneca* days we were now coming across an increasing number of fleeing Haitians. The numbers had jumped from an average of 4000 a year to over 25,000 a year now! This huge increase was largely due to political unrest in Haiti, and it is estimated that interdicting Haitians in the early 90s was costing the Coast Guard over $45,000.00 a day. Their small boats were about 20 feet long and pack full with 50 or more people of all ages. They ranged from infants, pregnant women, women, men, and the elderly. Everything they had they sold to pay for the journey so they basically had nothing but the clothes on their back.

Usually by the time we stopped them they had been at sea for several days, had run out of food and water, and were sea sick. They could barely make it off their boat and aboard the cutter. We would bring them aboard, search them for weapons, interview them, provide them with toiletries, then feed and house them on the flight deck. Unlike the *Seneca* where we used the helicopter hanger to house them, on the *Tampa* we would set up a huge tent covering the flight deck to keep them out of the hot Caribbean sun. We held them longer than on *Seneca* and set up portable toilets and showers for them on the flight deck. We would feed them twice a day with a ration of beans and rice. I thought the food provided to them was a bit bland, but was told that the Haitians actually preferred the rice and bean diet over ours. Once we had about 100 or so aboard we would now take them into GITMO instead of back to Haiti. They were detained there until the U.S. government could determine if they were seeking political asylum. If they were determined to just be leaving the country they were taken into Port Au Prince, Haiti, and repatriated.

GITMO was having a tough time making space for the detained migrants. There were huge green Army tents everywhere housing the Haitians and every available space, including the golf course, was now a tent city. The Haitians were kept in the middle of the base and the Cubans and Dominicans on the far side. It was a mess! But this was how we would spend the next several years down there conducting AMIO and HMIO. We just kept bringing them to GITMO.

At the beginning of September we headed home. It was getting into the heart of hurricane season down there in the Caribbean Sea and it was nice to be clearing out. It turned out we got out of there just in time because category three hurricane Marilyn came swooping in behind us.

We headed back down for another D7 patrol at the end of October that lasted into December. This was a drug interdiction patrol and we spent our time patrolling in the western part of the Caribbean Sea, off the coast of South America.

We received imminent danger pay of $150.00 for operating around Cartagena, Columbia, even pulling in there for a port call! Well we actually anchored out in the harbor. That was probably a smart move! I did pull shore patrol and got the pleasure of riding around in a Columbian military truck with a bunch of Columbian Army guys brandishing semi-automatic weapons. We just drove around the city center pretty much making a presence. We never stopped or got out of the truck, just drove around. Cartagena was supposed to be semi-safe and was known as a neutral zone to the drug cartels operating in the area. That was fine by me. It turned out to be a good port call and I collected an extra $150.00!

Looking for drugs the cartels were running was always a priority for us. And as my old boss CWO Rufus Beard would say, "Sometimes you get the bear and sometimes the bear gets you!" It was the latter in the case of the *Fortuna Bay I*. We had intercepted her in the Caribbean Sea off the south western coast of Cuba and had intelligence that she was carrying drugs. The boarding team after an initial search could not find the drugs. This was partly due to the fact that she was so crammed with cargo that they could only conduct a partial search. It was determined that we would need to bring her into a safe port and unload her to be able to search her entirely. So we set a course for GITMO to unload her.

Unloading cargo from the *FORTUNA BAY I* in GITMO, Cuba

After arriving in GITMO our entire crew participated in unloading and sifting through her cargo, but we could not find any drugs. We had divers search under her and we even brought aboard canines specially trained to find drugs. This was my first experience with Coast Guard drug dogs. Though I wondered just how well trained they were after one of the dogs, while crossing the brow to the *Fortuna Bay I*, jumped into the water! I was watching it cross the brow with its handler and over the side it went. We had to send our small boat over to pluck the poor wet thing out of the water. After several days searching and coming up with no drugs the *Fortuna Bay I* was loaded back up and sent on her way. Drug runners hide their drugs in very clever places and in very clever ways, so we will never know for sure if she actually had drugs aboard or not. But we did such a thorough search I feel certain we would have found them if she did.

Searching through cargo on the *FORTUNA BAY I*

In February and March of 1996 we were conducting a Gulf of Mexico, or D8 patrol. This was a great patrol and we had the opportunity to steam up the Mississippi River and into the heart of the city of New Orleans for Mardi Gras. This was one of those once in a blue moon port calls when we would have a great berth right downtown, and not in the seedier part of the city like usual.

Getting up to New Orleans was a big evolution for a ship our size. It took several hours manning an all hands special sea detail. There are special details for every evolution at sea like flight operations, anchoring, war time steaming, and coming in and out of port. Special sea detail involves all hands manning various positions to ensure a safe transit without grounding or running into something. Transiting the Mississippi River in a vessel our size was tricky because the navigable part of the river is narrow and the current was against us going up to New Orleans. We made it without incident from the Gulf of Mexico up the mighty Mississippi River and moored right smack dab downtown at Waldenberg Park along with another 270, the *USCGC Northland (WMEC-904)*. We were one block from Canal St. and four blocks from famous Bourbon St.

Taking a break from the engine room while transiting up the Mississippi River with MK1 Gary Robison and MK1 Clancy Hull

As you can imagine the town was nuts. This was the heart of New Orleans at the start of Mari Gras. The *Tampa* actually kicked off the celebrations by having the first parade king, King Zulu, come aboard and get Mardi Gras officially started. From that point on it just got weird. I had duty the first day, which meant I was stuck onboard for 24 hours standing watch. Once liberty was granted the cutter was empty. After the evening meal I took my cup of coffee and walked up to the flight deck where the gangway was and watched the mass of people walking by. Every now and then people, especially women, tried to cross the brow and the quarterdeck watch stander stopped them and explained that they could not come aboard. As the night went on folks got drunker and drunker. One drunken lady upon being denied entry to the cutter raised her shirt exposing her breasts thinking that was the secret move that would get her on! Although a nice gesture, it didn't work.

The next day I had eaten breakfast and was drinking my coffee on the fantail, waiting for 0800 and my relief so I could go on liberty. There was a dense fog that had settled over the cutter and the park next to us. My relief came and as I was walking back inside the OOD asked if I had seen the two mess cooks who were supposed to be taking the trash out to the dumpster on the pier. I told him no, but since I was off duty I would walk out to the pier and see if I could find them. As I walked off the cutter through the fog, I could see person after person lying on the ground sleeping in the park. It was as if they had just gotten too drunk to go any further and just passed out. I walked a little further and I could make out a group of people standing in a circle. As I got closer I could see that two of the people were the mess cooks still clutching their bags of garbage. As I walked up to them I saw that the circle was formed around two naked people having sex, right there in the park, butt naked and all! I told the two mesmerized mess cooks that the party was over and to get back to the cutter! And no I didn't stick around to watch the big finally!

The following evening started out with the usual partying and once again, the cutter was empty. At some point after dark the word went out throughout all the bars and restaurants in the area that we had been recalled and everyone had to get back to the *Tampa* immediately! We were being recalled to get underway for a search and rescue case out in the Gulf of Mexico. Apparently there was an out of control fire on an oil platform. I couldn't help but wonder if there wasn't another ship already out there that was closer to the platform than us? After I got back to the cutter we were all thinking that we'll just get the cutter ready tonight and sail at first light. Special sea detail is never done at night, especially when trying to sail down the narrow Mississippi River with the fast moving current!

We were all surprised when Captain Ryan said we would shove off that night and to get the engine room fired up. What a crazy trip down river that was! On the way up river we had been very cautious and steamed at a snail's pace. We went so slow you would have thought we were navigating through a mine field. Now on the way back down river in the pitch black with the current pushing us it seemed like we were going at a full bell, speeding down the river without a care in the world. My billet for special sea detail was in the engine room so I didn't see much, but I had that eerie looming fear we were going to hit something at any given moment! Thankfully we made it down safe and sound and out into the gulf without incident. But before we could even start to plot a course for the oil platform we received word that the fire was under control and we were not needed.

After patrolling for a few more weeks we pulled into Key West, Florida for fuel, stores, and liberty on the 24th of February. That same day two small American planes were shot down near Cuba by Cuban Air Force fighter jets. Cuba claimed the two American planes had ignored their warnings and entered into Cuban air space. The two American planes were operated by Cuban-Americans who were trying to help other Cubans flee Cuba by spotting their escaping boats and directing them to America, which was only 90 miles away. We were directed to cut our port call short and head to the location of the downed American planes and aid in the search and rescue of the four possible survivors. The exact location of the American planes was unknown. But a passing American cruise liner, the *Majesty Of The Seas*, and an American fishing vessel, the *Tri-Liner*, reported they had witnessed the incident and had seen a smoke cloud as they passed Cuba in international waters just off of Havana, Cuba.

More than likely the wreckage of the two American planes had ended up in Cuban territorial waters, which reach out 12 miles from their shoreline. As we patrolled along Cuban territorial water, in international water, we were shadowed by small Cuban gunboats that warned us to stay out of their water. After an intensive search along the Cuban boarder, without finding any evidence of the two American planes, we were directed to get back on patrol.

Soon after the shooting incident we began steaming our way back home. Somewhere off the coast of Florida we had a major casualty with our #2 main diesel engine salt water pump, which put that engine out of service. This cut our speed in half and since we were on our way home the whole crew wanted that engine up and running. You could feel the tension of the crew grow as our arrival date was slipping away because of this casualty. After having a good look at the broken pump, and a check of our spare parts, we determined the pump was not fixable while at sea. Knowing the mechanical systems inside and out my guys and I came up with a way to block off the damaged pump and utilize another auxiliary salt water system, which got us back up and running. We made up the time and hit homeport on schedule!

We were underway again in May and June of 1996 for refresher training (REFTRA). The REFTRA facility, which used to be at GITMO when I was on *Seneca*, had been moved to Mayport, Florida. It was a much better venue in my opinion, but unfortunately training still included the same arduous routine and the same yelling riders. The training lasted from 13 May to 7 June and, unlike on the *Seneca*, I was a chief now and really got to know the Navy chiefs that rode us.

The Navy chiefs would hang out in our chief's mess waiting for us to get underway or preparing for drills. They were a rowdy bunch and on one occasion, when we were all packed in the mess, an argument arose between two of the Navy chiefs. They were going back and forth at each other about something stupid and one of them says, "So you think you got a bigger dick then me?" and he drops his pants and flops his junk out onto the chief's mess table! He then told the other Chief he is arguing with to do the same so we could all see who really did have the biggest junk! I immediately intervened, "We have seen enough dick for one day!" and he put it away. He made his point! After that incident we would always fight over who had to sit at that part of the table for the rest of the time I was onboard!

Our moorings were on a pier with several Navy ships that were either home ported in Mayport or conducting training like us. One day I was walking down the pier and happened to take notice of the Navy frigate moored a few ships ahead of us. It was the *USS Stark (FFG-31)*. The *Stark* had been patrolling the Persian Gulf on the 17th of May 1987 when she was hit by two Exocet missiles fired from an Iraqi jet, killing 37 and wounding 21. On fire and severely listing she somehow stayed afloat. Now almost nine years later I looked for the damaged areas but she looked as if nothing had ever happened to her. I was on *Seneca* at the time *Stark* was attacked and remembered feeling a connection with her crew. It was unsettling knowing a vessel could be damaged so badly. It was also a reminder that it's a dangerous world with an ever present enemy.

The lessons learned from fighting the numerous fires and keeping *Stark* afloat prompted sweeping changes in the way damage control efforts were conducted throughout the Navy and Coast Guard. In trying to prepare a crew for what *Stark* endured, REFTRA concludes with a final battle scenario similar to what the *Stark* faced, multiple missile hits causing widespread carnage. Seeing the *Stark* there on the pier was a sobering reminder of why we come to REFTRA and train. We finished REFTRA and did very well; ending up with a 98.86 percent, earning the battle efficiency ribbon for the cutter as well as the crew.

While underway on the 16th of May 1996 I was awarded my permanent cutterman pin, indicating I had five years at sea in the cutter fleet. At the time there weren't too many pins worn by Coast Guard members, maybe a half dozen, and the cutterman and coxswain pins were the two most prized. This was a major milestone for me and it meant I could now wear my cutterman pin while at shore units. More importantly, in my community it made me salty! In the community of maritime professionals sea time is what you're worth. The more sea time you have the more respect you gain. No one had time for the casual sea goer or personnel who avoided going to sea. We called them "passengers" and "sand peeps." In my rating the saltier you were, the better!

As a chief I always seemed to be navigating around things I needed to be involved in or things I needed to stay clear of. One day I ran into the latter. We were underway and I was going through the chow line and there was a third class petty officer ahead of me. He commented to the third class cook serving the meal that "This food sucks!" The cook replied, "Go fuck yourself!" The third class petty officer in line looked at me, and asked me "Chief, what are you going to do about the cook telling me to go fuck myself?" I instantly recognized this as a situation I didn't need to be involved in. I looked at the petty officer and told him "You can either book the cook (bring him up on charges) or go fuck yourself, your choice." And with that I kept moving on down the serving line. He must have done the later because I never heard anything of it.

This brings me to another chow line story, one in which I needed to get involved. We were in port and it was time for the evening meal. The only people onboard were those who had duty and those who lived aboard. I was in the chow line and talking to the cook as he fixed my tray. Living on board you just seem to get to know people better, and I knew all the cooks pretty well. He told me that he was stressed out and felt like taking the knife in his hand and plunging it into his chest. After sailing with folks night and day for months at a time you really get a sense of when they are joking or serious. I felt he was serious.

I walked back behind the chow line and took the knife from his hand and led him out to the mess deck. There were a few guys there and I had one watch him while I went for the XO, who I knew was onboard. He was in the wardroom and I relayed the story to him and recommended we call base medical. I wasn't really sure if the XO was joking, but he asked me if he was stable enough to finish cooking and serving the meal! I said I didn't think so and he called 911. An ambulance arrived a few minutes later to handle the cook. After an extensive psychiatric evaluation he returned back to the cutter fit for duty.

During our July to August 1996 patrol I had taken over as the CEA from Mike because he stayed back and missed the patrol. I don't think I was the senior man in the mess, probably the only guy who would take on the thankless job. We got underway around the 19th of July and didn't make our first port call until around the 8th of August in Key West, Florida. That was 20 days under way, and a long time to be at sea with 100 guys. My ears were ringing as the CEA!

We were involved in Operation Frontier Shield; the largest Coast Guard led multi-agency maritime law enforcement effort in recent history. We were working with 12 international partners in the Caribbean Sea to reduce the flow of drugs and migrants into the United States through the area known as the Puerto Rican arrival zone. The total operation would result in over 500 boardings, the seizure of nearly 14,000 pounds of cocaine, and disruption of 19 smuggling events. In addition the number of illegal migrants attempting to enter Puerto Rico was reduced by 75 percent.

During everything that was going on with Operation Frontier Shield, one of the enlisted crew members got in trouble and was being taken to mast. The issue was a hot potato in the chief's mess. A few of the chiefs thought the matter should have been handled by the chiefs. It wasn't a general rule, but sometimes menial offenses would be handled by the chief's mess. This would save any permanent entries in the offender's service record. The chiefs would usually have the member do extra duty to work off his offense.

Going to captain's mast was the last thing you wanted to do as an officer or enlisted man. Traditionally the term "captain's mast" referred to the captain of a ship conducting punishment or other duties at the main mast of the ship. Today going to mast is a term used to describe when an officer or enlisted person has violated the Uniform Code of Military Justice (UCMJ), been brought up on charges, and ordered to appear before the captain. The mast, or trial, is held by the captain and he evaluates the facts and determines the level of punishment, if punishment is even handed down. He could also just throw the whole thing out.

The Executive Officer, LCDR Dan MaCleod (who is not the same XO I wrote about earlier in the suicide cook story) was compiling all the statements and findings for the mast, and had asked my opinion as the CEA. I felt the incident justified the member going to mast. Like I said the chief's mess was divided on this, so I made the final call. The XO suggested it would be a good idea to have the chief's mess present at the mast to show support for the command's decision. I agreed and asked the chiefs to attend the mast. The mast was held in the wardroom and was open to the crew. This was typical in most masts so the event and process would be seen by all.

The enlisted man was found guilty and punishment was handed down by the captain, which didn't involve the chiefs. After the mast we piled into the chief's mess for lunch. RMC (Radioman Chief) Ron Pridgen was sitting in a chair across the table from me and he was pissed. He didn't like the fact that I had made the final call to send the crewmember to mast and felt that the chiefs had been manipulated in attending the mast. He assumed that by being there they would have input on the level of punishment. He was yelling at me and accusing me of lying to him. Words were exchanged, and he stood up and threw his chair at me. He literally stood up and threw his metal chair at me from about eight feet away. I don't know how he missed me! Ron was a good chief and we had our spat in the mess, but when we walked out of the mess we put it behind us; we were chiefs and acted as such-at least in public!

Speaking of the XO, LCDR MaCleod, he gave us quite a scare while patrolling off of Puerto Rico. He was a big man like Captain Ryan, but the XO looked like he rolled right out of the Montana Mountains. He was a big rugby player and his body looked like he had taken many a hard scrum. We were conducting a boarding on a small cargo vessel and the seas were stable and skies clear. I had come off watch and walked back onto the fantail to catch some fresh air and see what was going on. The cargo vessel was just off our port bow and I could see the boarding team's small boat hanging back behind it, waiting for the boarding team to finish. All of a sudden our ship's horn started blasting. The only time that sounded was when we got underway or when we were in dense fog. Something was not right. Then suddenly the cutter changed course and flight quarters was piped. Now something was really wrong. Someone came running by me and told me that the XO had passed out on the bridge, and they thought he was having a heart attack. Flight quarters was piped and manned to medevac him off to Puerto Rico.

We were all stunned and waited for several days for word of his condition. Turns out he hadn't had a heart attack but had some other sort of medical condition involving his heart. The XO ended up coming back to full duty several months later, but not to the cutter. I ended up serving with him later at another command and he seemed as healthy as could be.

In mid-September we were underway for another D7 patrol. This would be a long eight week patrol operating around the U.S. Virgin Islands and Puerto Rico. Around the first week of November we made a port call at the island of Sint Maarten, which is a constituent of the Kingdom of the Netherlands. They didn't have a big enough facility for *Tampa* to moor up to so we anchored out in the bay. This was always a pain on two fronts. On the liberty front we had to take the small boat back and forth to the island. With only two small boats, this took time. On the duty front only a limited amount of the crew could go on liberty. This was due to the fact that the crew had to man the small boats, anchor watches had to be set, generators had to be running and monitored, and so on.

On the first day I went into town and it was very relaxing. The people were friendly and it had that slow island tempo. On the second day a U.S. Navy frigate came over the horizon and anchored out next to us. I took the small boat into town, and when we arrived at the boat pier the Navy small boats were offloading their passengers. As soon as the boats hit the pier it was like watching mice jumping from a sinking ship, they scattered as fast as they could! Once in town the relaxing atmosphere I enjoyed the day before was replaced with the feeling of a town under siege! The bars were full and the slow island tempo was kicked into high gear.

Later that evening when I made it back to the small boat pier I was shocked to see rows of Navy sailors laying on the ground! They were being overseen by Navy shore patrol personnel. I asked what was going on and the shore patrol said they were passed out drunk and not in any condition to get into their small boats. They would just have to sleep it off there on the pier! Nothing like the Navy showing up to spice things up!

We completed two more D7 and D8 patrols in January to February and April to May of 1997, all part of Operation Gulf Shield. This was another multi-agency effort intended to deny the expanding narcotics and migrant smuggling route in the Gulf of Mexico along the Mexico and United States maritime boarder.

In July 1997 we were underway again patrolling the Caribbean Sea. It was my last patrol on the *Tampa* and I was busy conducting my final requirements for relief of the engine room. We had picked up my relief in our last port call in Barbados. The most important part of the relief process was the "full power trial" test. This involved running the main diesel engines at full speed for several hours and taking readings. If the readings were within parameters the engines were determined to be running correctly. On the 12th of July I conducted the test and passed. I signed the engine room over to my relief and was waiting for the patrol to end. I had orders to report to the Engineering and Logistics Center (ELC) back at Curtis Bay, Maryland.

I enjoyed being underway and I knew I would miss it. When I was assigned to a cutter I immersed myself. I lived aboard and the cutter was my home, making the crew like family. We were constantly standing watch, drilling, eating, working, and relaxing together. The cutter was always alive, day and night, with someone walking around on watch, machinery kicking on and off, and waves hitting the hull. The smell of the sea, coffee, diesel fuel, and the night baker making bread were all part of my day. That was the routine in port and underway.

Technology had come a long way in a short amount of time since my last tour on the *Seneca*. Smoking was pretty much banned from all internal spaces and the movie system was upgraded to HI8 video. We were provided with updated movies and usually ran one or two over the ship's entertainment system, which now allowed you to watch movies on the TVs in the recreation rooms. There was still no internet. Mail and phone availability in American ports and at GITMO was still the only way to stay in contact with folks back in home port. And if there was an emergency back home, the Red Cross was still the only way to get in contact with you.

Captain Ryan was due to rotate at the end of this patrol also. His change of command was scheduled and his relief was ready to take command. In our last port call in Barbados the CO had fallen and severely hurt his leg.

He was a tough guy and wanted to finish the patrol. But after a week of being out at sea and getting tossed around it took its toll on his leg and he couldn't take the pain anymore. It was decided he would be flown off in the helicopter to Puerto Rico and then home to Portsmouth. The new CO would fly out on the helicopter and take command.

Well I was thinking this was the perfect time and opportunity for me to leave! Heck I was just sitting around and somebody needed to carry the CO's bags. It was settled, I would fly off with Captain Ryan.

After all those years of refueling them on *Seneca* this was my first helicopter ride. On the 19th of July, after the new CO assumed command, Captain Ryan and I lifted off from the flight deck. As I looked down at the *Tampa* with her crew manning their flight quarters billets, I felt a pit in my stomach. It was as if I had lost something very special. The captain and I were flown to San Juan, Puerto Rico where we would catch a flight back to Portsmouth, Virginia and the next chapter in our respective careers.

ENGINEERING LOGISTICS CENTER

CURTIS BAY, MARYLAND

28 July 1997 – 18 October 1999

I was back at Curtis Bay, Maryland again. Only this time they had changed the name of the facility from SCCB to ELC in an effort to make it sound more modern and cutting edge. Lipstick on a pig as the saying goes! The military personnel had changed a bit, but this was a great place for homesteaders so there were still a lot of familiar faces. The civilians were just about all the same, just in better paying jobs.

What struck me the most about the civilians was that the family atmosphere and close ties I had enjoyed a few years ago had waned. Some of the civilians had moved on, but most were still here. What was also noticeably different was that everyone was split up now. We all used to work there at the Yard in one or two different buildings. Now people were spread out over several different campuses, miles apart. It was like when you left home as a teenager and came back years later, something was missing, and it wasn't like you remembered. It was a little depressing.

I had taken the MKCS (E-8) exam in November of 1997, was ranked 7th, and promoted on the 1st of March 1998. I thought I would be transferred with the promotion, but my assignment officer said since I had just come off a sea tour he would leave me where I was to finish my four year land tour. I was assigned the king of all desk jobs, scanning data bases to ensure the exact amount of toilet paper made it onto the new 175 and 225 class buoy tenders being built in Wisconsin. Actually it was a two part job. The second part was to go to the buoy tender and make sure the toilet paper dispenser was the proper one for the toilet paper I had on order! So my days were spent scanning parts and supplies and then going to the shipyard in Marinette, Wisconsin and making sure the stuff I was provisioning for on load was correct for what was actually on the vessel. Boring!

The best part about this job was my boss, CWO Greg Thiewes. What a character! The office consisted of two other warrant officers, a chief, and me. All of us were the wrong guys for this job. We all loved being wrench turning MKs and hated being at a desk. CWO Thiewes was in charge of me and the other chief, Tom Casey.

CWO Thiewes just didn't get that Tom and I were chiefs and tried to run us around like non-rates. Tom was a feisty Irishman from New York City and I was my typical stubborn self. We bumped heads with Greg constantly. And when I made E-8 it was even worse. But with all that tension Tom and I called him "Daddy T," and he would refer to us as his "sons." Our relationship resembled two teenage boys and their father with a heavy dose of dysfunction.

In his younger days Greg was what we called a heavy steamer, known in the civilian world as a drunk. He was notorious for getting drunk, blowing his top, and passing out. The trifecta of being a sailor! Another warrant officer in the office had served with Greg on the *USCGC Gallatin*, a 378 high endurance cutter out of New York City. A favorite story of his was when Greg reported to the cutter. The *Gallatin* was pulling in and Greg was supposed to meet them on the pier. He was there alright, passed out stone drunk with his sea bag for his pillow!

Booze wasn't a problem for Greg these days because he had stopped drinking. His problems now were his ex-wives. He had more of them then I had service stripes on my uniform! Women came easily to Greg because he resembled Clark Gable. Getting them didn't seem to be a problem, keeping them is where it all went wrong. I think his personal life was stressing him out because he was always blowing his top for some reason. It always started with him puckering his lips, opening his eyes wide, turning red, and trembling. But, even with all his baggage, the thing about CWO Thiewes that made him such a standup guy was that no matter what was going on in his personal life he was all in for his job and the Coast Guard. He knew his job and how to get things done. Tom and I respected that.

Tom was a no bullshit guy himself. He was a hard working guy with high ethics. But when he got worked up he would start to cuss like a sailor. We had this MK1 who worked in another office that was always getting under our skin. He was getting ready to make chief and start the chief's initiation process. Well he comes into our office and starts to bend my ear about not having to work when he makes chief, so I promptly sent him over to talk to Tom. Of course the MK1 got right under Tom's skin, and Tom started cussing. A couple of minutes into his visit the MK1 asked Tom if he would stop using profanity. Tom looked at him squarely and told him to "Get the fuck out of here and don't you ever come back!" Tom then turned around and went back to work. That was Tom!

CWO Thiewes came from a family of sea goers and had a brother and other extended family in the Coast Guard and Navy. One day Greg invited Tom and me over to a family get together they were having. I ended up talking with a relative of Greg's who was in the Navy during WWII. We were sitting around telling sea yarns, and as usual when you have Coast Guard and Navy guys talking, the conversation eventually turned to who was tougher.

So Greg's Navy relative says he sailed on a battleship during the war. Okay, that's tough. Then he says he had the battleship tattooed on his chest. Okay, that's even tougher. Then he says that he had open heart surgery and the only thing he was concerned about was when they went to sew him back up that they lined the two halves of the battleship up correctly. And then he took his shirt off and showed me the great job the surgeon did getting the battleship back together. Okay, I conceded that he was one tough ole salt!

Remember back when I was on the *Sumac* and I mentioned the Commandant at the time was Admiral Gracey, and later that his wife had commissioned the *Seneca*? I had the pleasure of finally meeting Admiral Gracey at a military forum in Washington, DC. The gathering had all the current heads of the armed forces and their senior enlisted advisors. It was an annual get together which entailed a briefing on the state of the armed forces and a question and answer session. Afterward there was a meet and greet social I attended with several of my chief buddies, including Tom Casey and Cliff Tice. As we were conversing I happened to notice an older Admiral Gracey standing off in a corner. He was in civilian clothes, but I recognized him at once. He seemed over shadowed by all the current admirals and generals who were getting all the attention. It was like he was banished to what appeared to be the land of the forgotten.

I commented to Tom and Cliff, "There's Admiral Gracey, we have to go meet him!" and we rushed over to him. He was a legend to us. He represented the old traditions of the Coast Guard, the Coast Guard when we were young and he was bigger than life! We enjoyed a good conversation with him and he graciously allowed us to have our picture taken with him. I would like to think we made his day as much as he made ours!

MKCS Ed Semler, Admiral Gracey,
MKC Tom Casey, and EMCS Cliff Tice

USCGC EAGLE (WIX-327)

NEW LONDON, CONNECTICUT

13 June 1998 – 15 August 1998

USCGC EAGLE (WIX-327)

Figuring out how much toilet paper and pencils needed to be on-loaded to those buoy tenders was getting to be so tedious and boring. So I started to keep my eye on the message board that solicited for volunteers to go on temporary duty assignments on underway cutters. This usually involved a cutter needing to replace a critical crew member on an upcoming deployment with a non-critical member on a land unit.

The only cutters that had a MKCS on them at the time were the 378 high endurance cutters, which deployed for about three to four months on patrol. One had come open and I submitted my name to the coordinator at headquarters. The coordinator called me right back and said the 378 was already filled, but he had a high priority fill for a MK1 on the *USCGC Eagle (WIX-327)* if I was interested. He said it was for three months during their summer cadet cruise to teach engineering fundamentals.

I thought to myself that doesn't sound right, an MKCS which is an E-8 to fill an MK1 which is an E-6 position? An MKCS is two ranks higher than an MK1. It seemed weird but, what the heck, I wanted out of there and this was an opportunity. This was on a Wednesday and they wanted me in San Juan, Puerto Rico to meet the ship Saturday! It would be one of *Eagle's* first port calls after leaving its home port of New London, CT.

I accepted the assignment and had to rush to get my command to sign off on my paperwork by Friday. My boss, Captain Cheever, was just with us temporarily while he awaited his next duty assignment. He was a salty old Vietnam veteran and a mustang. A mustang is a term used to describe an enlisted man who becomes an officer. Coincidently, I would go on to serve in two cutters that the captain had served on previously, the *Sherman* on which he completed a tour in Vietnam, and the *Dependable* where he served as the engineering officer. And like him, I would also later become a mustang. After I explained my reason for being in his office the captain coolly looked up at me and asked, "What does your wife have to say about you leaving in such a rush?" I replied, "Captain I'm not married." He said, "Even better, good luck!"

I flew out of Baltimore on Saturday the 13th of June and arrived a few hours later in San Juan. I was met by a surprised, and mournful, duty driver from the *Eagle* who had been assigned to pick me up at the airport. He was confused that I wasn't an MK1, and mournful of the recent death of one of his shipmates. I hadn't known about it, but one of the seamen aboard the *Eagle* had fallen to his death on the 11th of June. He was a skilled seaman aboard the three masted barque and was working up in the main mast rigging the day he died. The main mast is about 150 feet high. Stories vary, but he was last seen working about mid-way up the mast. The cutter had anchored out of San Juan to prepare the ship for the port call, which for the *Eagle* was always a public relations event. For some unknown reason he fell and hit his head, either on his way down through the masts rigging or on the ship's side, landing in the water.

Needless to say the crew was traumatized. The event weighed heavily on the crew for the rest of the trip. Of course there was an investigation. The crew, like the seaman's family, wanted to know what had happened and why he fell. Was it an accident, foul play, what? Not knowing the facts seemed to add to the pain. When we pulled into Boston, Massachusetts in the latter part of the cruise the seaman's family came aboard and there seemed to finally be some closure for them.

View from the *EAGLE'S* fore mast looking aft at crewmembers working in the main mast

When I arrived aboard *Eagle* I was welcomed and shown my berthing in the chief's mess. The chief's mess had relics in it as old as me. Hanging on the back of the door was a huge plaque of rope fancy work dated 1964, the year I was born.

The chief's mess had the usual accommodations and consisted of a 16 feet x 16 feet lounge and eating area and a 16 feet x 10 feet berthing and locker area with two high racks. The head had one toilet, two sinks and a shower to accommodate six chiefs. The overflow chiefs who sailed with the *Eagle* on cadet cruises berthed in other berthing areas in the same area of the cutter. I was happy to be berthed in the chief's mess.

USCGC EAGLE Chief's Mess
summer 1998 cruise

I met the senior enlisted and CEA, MKC Dave Fiore, when I arrived my first day. He met me when I first walked aboard and seemed confused that an MKCS was just going to teach general engineering. I sensed that he felt uneasy about now being outranked. I immediately reassured him that my only reason for being there was to teach the cadets basic engineering, nothing else. Chief Fiore was a machinery technician like me and we got along great for the whole cruise.

My next stop was the executive officer. He also seemed a little curious as to why they had sent an E-8 to do an E-6s job. It's not like there were a lot of E-8s around. Per federal law the Coast Guard could only have 3% of their total enlisted workforce as E-8s, so you didn't run into them that often.

Because of the investigation into the seaman's death everyone seemed a little on edge, and I'm sure the thought of me being an undercover Coast Guard investigator ran through the XO's mind. I was getting the feeling that he, along with the rest of the crew, thought there was something suspicious about an E-8 showing up a few days after the death of one of their crew. I can't remember anyone questioning me about being Coast Guard Intelligence (CGI) but I defiantly got the impression that some crewmembers were feeling cautious around me. I ran into the XO about a year or so later when the *Eagle* came into the Coast Guard Yard for some refitting. He told me that the thought of me being sent by CGI as an undercover agent did cross his mind! We had a good laugh about that and it was good to catch up on the chief's mess and wardroom again.

My meeting with the Commanding Officer, Captain Papp, would finalize my arrival. He was a well-respected man and would later go on to become the commandant of the Coast Guard. I had never met him before but had been told by my friend, Steve Twomey, that he was a good captain to sail under. Papp was the commanding officer of the *Forward*, a sister ship that moored up at Portsmouth, Virginia when I was on the *Tampa*. Steve Twomey was Papp's main propulsion chief aboard the *Forward*.

You couldn't mistake Captain Papp. He was an average sized man but he had what I guess was a medical condition that left him hairless, so he sort of stood out. I had dinner with the captain in his private mess which was in the aft section of the cutter. It wasn't like this was some special meeting. Captain Papp scheduled to have dinner with crewmembers just about every evening to introduce himself. It was his way of getting to know his crew in an informal setting chatting over the evening meal.

As I walked back to the aft section of *Eagle*, toward the captain's mess, lining the passageway were pictures of the previous COs, including the Germans. Yes, I did say Germans! The *Eagle* was a war prize from WWII. She was commissioned in 1936 as the *Horst Wessel*, named in honor of a Nazi movement hero who died in 1930, and was used by the Nazis as a naval training vessel. Adolf Hitler and Rudolph Hess were both present at the launching. Urban legend on the cutter had it that Hitler dined and slept aboard her in the admiral's cabin. She was used by Nazi Germany in WWII but saw limited combat. After the war she was refitted in war torn Germany and sailed from Bremerhaven, Germany back to the Coast Guard Academy as part of the spoils of war.

I experienced a real sense of history when I was on *Eagle*. There are very few opportunities these days to sail a true tall ship out on the open ocean. I felt I had been granted the rare experience of sailing as they did in the days of old. That feeling was especially vivid after spending the 4th of July in Savannah, Georgia. We set sail and steered a course headed north under full sail with two other tall ships, the *Libertad* from Argentina and the *Simon Boliva* from Venezuela. What a sight it was to be out at sea with two other tall ships under full sail, slashing through the water like a vision from an Edward Moran painting!

One of the first things you notice while underway is that unlike a conventional ship that cuts through the water on an even keel, the *Eagle* is always hauled over a few degrees due to the wind catching her sails. You have to sort of get used to walking and conducting your daily routine on an angle.

The *Eagle* adhered to many of the traditional maritime traditions that I had experienced on my previous cutters. One of the traditions that the *Eagle* took a step further was the ringing of the ship's bell every half hour. All the cutters I had been on before only rang eight bells at noon to honor the tradition. On the *Eagle* the bell was rung as it was in sailing days of old, at every half hour while underway. This was how the watch standers knew what time it was and when to relieve the watch. Watches are four hours in length. Every half hour the bell was struck and when eight bells were struck it was the end of the four hour watch.

A lot of time was also spent on the nautical past time of fancy work, which is working with rope. In the evenings some of the crew and cadets would sit up on the forecastle and tie all sorts of knots and make decorative artwork with rope. It was a traditional nautical past time that was interesting and beneficial to every sailor. There was also a lot of work done with an instrument called the sextant. This device is hardly ever used these days because of GPS and other electronic navigation equipment, but there was a time when this instrument was the only way to find your way at sea. The sextant enabled the mariner to navigate by celestial navigation, using the sun, moon, and stars to find his position.

My days were spent teaching the Coast Guard Academy cadets basic engineering, and not as some covert CGI agent. I taught engineering organization, watch standing, casualty control, tracing out and drawing shipboard mechanical systems, basic internal combustion engines, electrical power generation, and engineering safety. As we slowly moved up the east coast we would pull into various ports such as Miami, Savannah, Boston, Halifax, Nova Scotia, and finally the Coast Guard Academy in New London, Connecticut where the *Eagle* was home ported. In each port call we would receive a group of cadets, and the freshly trained ones would return to the academy.

I taught a fairly good sized group of about 30 cadets at a time. The classes ran from 0800 until 1600 for one week and then they would change out with another group onboard. My classroom was on the crew's mess-deck where I taught using textbooks and a chalk board. For actual hands on experience I would have my assistant, an MK2, take small groups to the engine room and other mechanical spaces so they could physically see the equipment I was describing. At the end of the week there was a mini test just to make sure the cadets had paid attention during the week!

When I wasn't teaching I would go help out on deck and spent a lot of time up in the rigging. I enjoyed climbing the masts and the views once high above the cutters main deck. I also would act as a safety observer when the crew was setting and dousing the sails.

Crewmembers working on sails

The cadets spent every day underway learning something. The majority of which was seamanship and teamwork. The crew and cadets were constantly setting sail, dousing sail, and maneuvering the cutter. It took a tremendous amount of work, and a lot of it was done 50 to 150 feet above the water. And the ship was by no means stationary; as you worked aloft she cut and listed through the water.

One of the chiefs on board who taught me a lot about the rigging and sails was actually a U.S. Navy chief, who was assigned as the weather man for the cruise. Weather is critical on a sailing vessel. You need wind to move, but you need to be aware of bad weather. A sailing vessel caught in a storm under full sail could have her sails torn, her mast broken, or even capsize. *Eagle* had an alarm that was sounded if her sails needed to be doused in an emergency. When that alarm sounded it was an all hands evolution to get her ready for heavy weather.

The Navy chief loved getting up in the rigging. He would swing around up there like a monkey, which was amazing because he had had one of his arms nearly blown off and sewn back on! He told me he was aboard a Navy ship out at sea conducting gun operations with another navy ship. He was up on the ship's bridge wing along with the ship's XO and a few other crew members. The other ship was off in the distance and firing its Phalanx CIWS system, which is a defensive weapon used to shoot down incoming missiles. It shoots 20mm projectiles at a rate of 3000 per minute and sounds like a buzz saw when it fires. Apparently the guns safety interlocks failed and it somehow sprayed the bridge wing area the Navy chief was on, nearly blowing off his arm and killing the XO standing next to him. He told me he spent a long time in a Navy hospital recovering.

The chief was a lively guy and we had a memorable July port call in Boston. We had moored up near the *USS Constitution* and found the city was bustling with summer activity and celebrating the *USS Constitution's* Bicentennial Salute. To honor the occasion we went out on liberty wearing our summer dress uniforms. For us it meant wearing our dark blue slacks, light blue shirt, and white hat. For the Navy chief, who we called "squid," it would be his dress white Cracker Jack uniform. The term "squid" was used for anyone in the Navy, just as they referred to us as "puddle pirates!"

Well, a group of us got out on the town and of course every bar we went to people bought us drinks because we are in uniform. As the sun set we were just starting to get primed, that is except for the squid who was already plowed! We figured we needed to get him back to the *Eagle*, but we didn't want to go all the way back and break our drinking momentum. So I decide to take the squid out and get him a cab. We were in the heart of down town Boston and the place was packed. I hailed a cab and threw the squid in the back seat, and he slumped over like a rag doll. The traffic was stopped waiting on the cab and beeping their horns. I asked the cabbie how much would it cost to get the squid back to the *USS Constitution* pier and he said $10.00. I handed him a $20.00 and he peeled out so fast I saw the squids head snap back! It's like a picture burnt into my brain; the taxi driver, with his arm still sticking outside the cab clutching the $20.00 bill, and the white mass of the squid in the back seat flopping around lifeless as the cab sped away! When we made it back to the *Eagle* in the wee hours and opened up the chief's mess door, there was a trail of the squid's white uniform items leading back into the berthing area. He had made it back!

In preparing to come to the *Eagle* I had made sure I had my best uniforms and my sea bag was totally squared away. The *Eagle* trained Coast Guard officers, and every officer I knew that came out of the academy was squared away. As I settled down into my normal routine on *Eagle* I found that she was just like any other cutter, with the exception that she was the queen of the ball and talk of the town wherever we went. She was a total public relations ambassador. Every ship I had ever served on usually pulled into the longshoreman's pier in the seediest part of town, with no one to greet us but the line handlers. When the *Eagle* would pull into port it was a circus! The harbor would be full of boats of every size out to greet us along with fire department boats with their water cannons spraying huge arches of welcome! The day would always end with a party aboard in the evening complete with alcohol, which the *Eagle* carried its own supply of.

She was of course a floating school and I did get the feel of being on a college campus as the cadets transferred on and off. The cadets were managed by senior upper classmen, who were supervised by a few officers on staff from the academy. As the cadets progressively rotated on and off at the various port calls the demeanor of the underclassmen became more lax. The cadets seemed to bring a typical college campus frat house vibe with them. When they went off the cutter on liberty they wore their uniforms, but I'm not sure they followed any sort of uniform regulation I was familiar with. I would say it was a mix of academy clothes and active duty uniforms.

As we were transiting along the coast one day I saw an unusual sight, a huge whale, probably 50 feet long, floating dead on the calm ocean. The sea state was what we called "flat ass calm" and it looked like glass. I have heard of ships hitting them every now and then, and the bridge lookouts were always scanning the horizon for them. The whale could have been a Humpback or a Right Whale, I'm not sure. It was such an unusual sight. They are something you don't see a lot of in the first place, but one floating on the water dead was a first for me.

After our last port call in in Halifax, Nova Scotia we headed home to New London. On Saturday the 15th of August we began our final transit up the Thames River to our moorings at the academy. We were under diesel power with the sails "harbor furled" tight to their yards. The masts and yardarms looked like bare tree limbs with the sails rolled up so tight. It was damp and raining and I could feel the slight chill of fall in the New England air. After we arrived in port I caught the Amtrak train from New London back down to Baltimore.

The *Eagle* was a refreshing break from the hum drum routine back at the ELC. I will never forget the great chiefs, eclectic cadets, and the sense of history I experience on board *Eagle*.

AIR FORCE SENIOR NCO ACADEMY

CLASS 99-D

MAXWELL AFB, GUNTER ANNEX, ALABAMA

10 May 1999 – 23 June 1999

I hadn't been at the ELC for very long before I was promoted to senior chief petty officer on the 1st of March 1998. The Coast Guard had just started to ramp up their Chief Petty Officer Academy around this time and was making it mandatory for all E-7s and E-8s to attend or they would not be allowed to promote. The chief's academy is a leadership course lasting over four weeks. Since I wanted to promote to master chief (E-9) I applied as soon as I made E-8. Then in July of 1998 the Coast Guard came out with a directive stating that it was no longer a requirement to attend the chief's academy in order to be promoted from E-8 to E-9. I thought great, I can cancel my request. Too late, I had just received orders to attend the Air Force Senior Non Commissioned Officers Academy!

The Coast Guard had an agreement with the Air Force and the Navy to cross train chiefs academy members. We would send several of our members to each of their academies and in turn would accept their members at our academy. It was a good way to interact and get to know our counterparts in the other services. Unlike the other services, the Air Force had a stipulation that they would only accept E-8s and E-9s. So that's probably why I was headed to Maxwell Air Force Base in Alabama with five other E-8 and E-9 Coast Guardsmen.

The Coast Guard's chief academy usually consisted of about 64 students and lasted 33 business days. The Air Force academy class size was 358 students and lasted 33 business days. I'm not sure why the Air Force had the requirement for us to send E-8s and E-9s. Their own requirement to attend was to be a master sergeant (E-7) or selected to be promoted to senior master sergeant (E-8), so most of their class was filled with E-7s.

The Air Force had three levels of leadership training: airman leadership school for E-4, NCO academy for E-6, and senior NCO academy for E-7 and E-8. Attending each course is a requirement to promote. Each class builds off of the previous class's curriculum until you reach the final leadership course, the senior NCO academy. At each school it's a big deal to be a part of the class leadership, the distinguished graduate, and the John Levitow award winner. These accomplishments mean better evaluations back at the individual's unit and better chances for promotion.

The John Levitow award is the highest and most coveted award at the Air Force leadership academies. It is named in honor of Sergeant John Levitow, who was at the time the lowest ranking enlisted person in the Air Force to be awarded the Medal of Honor. He received it for his action during the Vietnam War. On the 24th of February 1969 he was assigned as the loadmaster on an AC-47 flying gun ship with the call sign "Spooky 71." As the aircraft engaged an enemy position the AC-47 was hit by mortar fire and Levitow sustained 40 wounds to his back and legs. Overcome with pain and shock he noticed a flare about to explode in the aircraft. Knowing the extreme danger the flare represented he threw himself on the flare, covered it with his body, and crawled to the rear of the aircraft where he threw it out the open cargo door. The flare ignited soon after being discharged from the aircraft. If the flare would have ignited in the AC-47 it would have caused certain death to the crew and destruction of the aircraft.

Well the five of us Coast Guard guys come marching in the first day of class and we are senior to almost everyone in our Air Force 99-D convening class. So it's not surprising that out of the 358 students, the class president and vice president were Coast Guardsmen. They were Master Chief Dave Johnson and Senior Chief Bob Frith. Bob was also the flight leader of flight 02, Senior Chief Gary Jensen was flight leader of flight 05, and I was flight leader of flight 22. The only Coast Guardsman who didn't get a leadership position was Senior Chief Kermit Hanson. Kermit would become a good friend of mine. We met up a few years later when I was subsequently transferred to the *Sherman* on the west coast. He was stationed at the base *Sherman* moored at and we would hang out at the base's chief's mess. Kermit didn't want anything to do with Air Force leadership, and knowing him they probably selected him as flight leader of his class but he told them to shove it!

Each flight had about 13 people and was designated a color. I was the flight leader of flight 22, the green shirts. Because the leadership positions in the class were highly sought after, some of the Air Force folks didn't like the fact that the Coast Guard was sucking them all up. The position of flight leader didn't really mean much to me. As a matter of fact all of us Coast Guardsman would have happily turned everything over to the Air Force. We had our hands full with the curriculum!

Flight 22
Front Row left to right; MSGT Jeff McBride, SCPO Ed Semler, SMSGT Lloyd Johnson, MSGT Keith Williams, SMSGT Roger King, SMSGT David Forney Back Row left to right; MSGT Cari Kent, SMSGT Ron Walls, SMSGT Mike Hamilton, SMSGT Todd Fazekas, MSGT Tom Skala, MSGT Jana Alvertos, SMSGT Dan Lutat (instructor)

The Air Force folks had been preparing for this class in all their previous leadership classes. From writing style, reading requirements, to study habits. The Air Force is a highly educated branch of the service. At a class meeting in the auditorium they asked the 358 students to raise their hand if they had an Associate's Degree, and about 95% raised their hand. Next they asked how many had their Bachelor's Degree, and about 60% raised their hands. Finally they asked how many had their Master's Degree, and about 10% raised their hands. These people were no dummies.

I also noticed that just about everyone was wearing a Meritorious Service Medal ribbon. This is a high ranking award, no matter which branch of the service you're in. The only folks you see in the Coast Guard with one of these are the officers, usually officers who have commanded a cutter or large command successfully. I asked a classmate why so many Air Force enlisted had the award. I was told that basically as an E-7 and above you are expected to be awarded one after every tour you complete. If not, it looked bad for promotion. I thought this was really strange until I learned more about the senior enlisted responsibilities in the Air Force. They are serious managers. The officers pretty much fly the planes and the enlisted manage the logistics and people. And I'm not talking about the 10 or 20 people a Coast Guard chief would be responsible for. I'm talking 30 to 100 people and huge amounts of equipment and supplies.

It was all new to me and my fellow Coast Guardsmen. I don't think any of us had a degree. And the last time I hit the books was in high school. Here we were hit with a stack of books, a lap top computer, and a paper due at the end of the week. So the last thing we wanted to do was hold a leadership position and manage people!

The Air Force living conditions were the best I had ever had. I was given my own room complete with a fully stocked kitchenette, cable TV, my own bathroom, towels, soap, shampoo, and a maid! It was way better than the apartment I was living in back at Curtis Bay. The disparity in living conditions reminded me of when I was at Yorktown, Virginia for a class as a chief. Yorktown was one of the Coast Guard's premier training facilities. The best berthing accommodations were at Cain Hall. This is where the chiefs, officers, and civilians were berthed. The rooms were a two man berthing set up with wooden lockers and single beds. There was a bathroom but you needed to bring all your own toiletries, including a towel. There was a TV but with only two local channels. They did have a service to clean your room and make the bed after you checked out so the room was ready for the next person.

If you were junior enlisted you stayed up at Lafayette Hall and the slums of four-man berthing with metal racks and lockers. There were no services and you were issued your linen when you checked in and had to return it when checking out. There was a TV down at the recreation room along with a microwave that was usually pretty nasty.

I was checking in at the front desk of Cain Hall and an Air Force guy was ahead of me. He told the civilian behind the desk that he had gone up to his room but someone was already in it. The civilian looked at him flatly and said, "That would be your room mate." I never really gave that incident much thought until after checking into the five star accommodations offered by the Air Force, and then it all made sense!

The galley at the Air Force NCO Academy was also five stars. They always had a variety of entre choices and it was damn good food. If for some reason you didn't like the galley there was the Falcon's Nest, which was an all hands club that served a variety of equally good food. I mostly ate at the galley. On one of my first days eating there I had looked for an open seat and happened to sit next to this Air Force guy who was in my class, but in another flight. The class was so big that our meeting in the galley was about our only interaction. We ended up eating together a lot and he turned out to be a very interesting guy. He was a normal looking guy, maybe a little shorter than most, and he had a Midwestern accent.

The galley was subcontracted to a civilian company and they had a huge contingent of Thai ladies working there. They worked behind the counter and out in the dining area cleaning tables and getting you refills on drinks. These ladies would be doing their thing and chattering away in Thai as they went about their work. My friend and I had been eating together for a while and one day he told me that the Thai ladies had been talking about us. I was thinking; we all have that feeling when someone is speaking a language we don't know around us. There were about three Thai ladies around us and all of a sudden my friend broke out in fluent Thai and started to talk to them. If you could have seen the look on their faces! Thai is a very difficult language to learn, let alone be fluent in.

Turns out he had worked at the U.S. Embassy in Thailand, was married to a Thai, and was obviously fluent in Thai. I'm not sure why he waited so long before speaking to the ladies, but I'm sure it had something to do with his security clearance. I guess he felt they were not a security threat to him and decided to interact. I'm glad he did because he was treated like a king from that point on. And since I was always sitting with him, I reaped some of the king's rewards!

Next to the academy is the Enlisted Heritage Hall. It is a museum dedicated to educate and enlighten Air Force enlisted members on their heritage. To drum up some money for the museum they were offering Prisoner of War (POW) and Missing in Action (MIA) wristbands for a donation. Each wristband had the name of a service member who was either a POW or MIA. I made a donation and was able to pick a wrist band. I saw one that had a service member from my home state of Pennsylvania and chose that one. My wrist band had the name CMS Gean P. Clapper.

On the 29th of December 1967 Chief Master Sergeant Gean P. Clapper and eleven other crewmembers with the 314th Tactical Airlift Wing lifted off in their C-130E Hercules aircraft from an airfield in Nha Trang, Republic of Vietnam. Chief Clapper was the radio operator aboard and his unit was involved in elite special operations. On this mission they would be flying into enemy territory at night to drop several million propaganda leaflets and to make a weapons resupply drop. Every 30 to 40 minutes Chief Clapper was to transmit a coded message on the mission's progress. Four hours into their mission, over hostile North Vietnam, Chief Clapper made his required radio communication. Subsequent transmissions never came and the C-130E never returned to Nha Trang. In the early 1990's a C-130E crash site was located in Vietnam and human remains turned over to the United States. It was identified as the C-130E that CMS Clapper was in, and it was assumed that the C-130E flew into the side of a mountain. It wasn't until 2000 that the remains of all 11 crewmembers, including Chief Clapper, were identified and buried in Arlington National Cemetery.

On the 23rd of June 1999 class 99-D held our graduation ceremony at the Montgomery Civic Center in Montgomery, Alabama with all the pomp and circumstance that could only be put on by the Air Force. As much as I was reluctant to come to the academy, I was now wishing my time there would last a bit longer.

USCGC SHERMAN (WHEC-720)

ALAMEDA, CALIFORNIA

20 October 1999 – 01 August 2001

USCGC SHERMAN (WHEC-720)
On patrol in the Bearing Sea

It wasn't long after I got back from the Air Force Senior NCO Academy that the tedious routine at the ELC caught up with me again. I cannot stress enough how painful it was to be stuck in an administrative position all day, every day. My heart just wasn't in it. So it was fortuitous timing that my old shipmate Captain Ryan called me out of the blue. He had just taken command of the 378 foot high endurance cutter *Sherman*.

She was the sixth cutter in the "Secretary" class of cutters and named in honor of John Sherman, the 32nd Secretary of the Treasury serving from 1877 to 1881. He would later go on to become the 35th Secretary of State under President McKinley from 1897 to 1898.

251

Sherman was an old cutter, commissioned in 1968, and highly avoided by senior MKs. The older 378s were a nightmare of mechanical problems due to their age. This class of cutter was so dreaded by my rating that every year during transfer season several MKCS would elect to retire instead of accepting orders to them! And it just wasn't the MK rating that avoided them. Most Coast Guardsman didn't want anything to do with getting underway for four months at a time. So filling the billets on this class of cutter was usually pretty tough.

Captain Ryan started his conversation with his casual, "Spuds, how have you been?" and explained to me that he had just relieved his current MKCS who was in charge of main propulsion. I would later find out the previous MKCS had gotten pretty drunk in a small Alaskan fishing village and caused some property damage. That along with some other issues required the captain to relieve him and remove him from the cutter.

I kind of got a feeling where this conversation was headed. He eventually came to the point and asked me if I would be interested in short touring at the ELC. He wanted me to come out to the *Sherman,* which was home ported in Alameda, California, to take on the job as his MKCS. I still had two more years of sitting here on the beach at ELC, but the job was so boring. Without hesitation I told the captain I would do it. It would be the beginning of a most enjoyable assignment.

On the 18th of October, after getting my affairs in order and placing my house hold goods in long term storage I caught a flight to Anchorage, Alaska. I was to meet up with the *Sherman*; she was out on a normal four month patrol of the Bering Sea. After arriving in Anchorage I was told she would be pulling into Dutch Harbor, Alaska and I was to meet her there while she was on a two day port call and to take on food and fuel. Dutch Harbor is a tiny island out on the Aleutian Island chain with a population of about 3500 people. It was used by us and the fishing fleet for fuel, stores, and liberty. There wasn't much there but they did have a hotel with a bar and an airport. It does have some Coast Guard historical significance. The Coast Guard song "Semper Paratus" was written in Dutch Harbor in 1927. Captain Francis Saltus Van Boskerck wrote the music to the Coast Guard song with the help of two others on a piano in Dutch Harbor. That piano is reported to still be on the island.

On my first attempt to fly into Dutch Harbor the flight was cancelled due to bad weather in Dutch Harbor. On my second attempt I boarded what appeared to be a normal sized commercial jet. We boarded from the rear and to my surprise there were only about 10 rows of seats, and then there was a bulkhead. I learned the rest of the plane was converted to haul cargo. As I settled into my seat the pilot came on the announcement system and explained that we would take off and head to Dutch Harbor, which was 800 miles away, and he would make the call once we got there if we could land or not. Flying in Alaska was appearing to be totally dependent on the weather.

The airport runway in Dutch Harbor is very short. Three sides drop off into the water and the remaining side is against a steep hill. You need perfect conditions to attempt a landing in an aircraft as big as the one I was in. After several hours we arrived at Dutch Harbor and the pilot announced he would attempt the landing. As he banked the aircraft and we came in, it looked like we would be landing on the water! Suddenly we hit the runway and I was immediately thrust forward as the engines were thrown into full reverse. It felt like a crash landing to me, but it was in fact a normal landing for Dutch Harbor.

I was met at the airport by the *Sherman's* duty driver and taken to the cutter. She sat moored up to an old wooden pier all by herself and looked like a fine lady with the picturesque Alaskan wilderness behind her. I walked up the brow, saluted the national ensign, saluted the quarterdeck watch stander, and reported aboard. I was shown my stateroom in the chief's berthing area, up on the 02 level on the forward end of the cutter. I was given a top rack in a four man berthing space complete with one toilet, sink, and shower. It was getting late and I stowed my sea bag, made up my rack, and hopped in it. It was 2200 and I listened to the low pipe on the intercom system, "Taps, taps, lights out, maintain silence about the decks, now 2200, now taps." I closed my eyes and wondered what I had gotten myself into. I awoke to the loader pipe of "Reveille, reveille, reveille, heave out and trice up, now reveille!" And another tour had begun!

Trice up is the term used to tie up the bottom rack in a berthing area to enable cleaning under it. Almost all the berthing areas, except for the senior officers, have racks two and three high. In-between these rows of racks there is usually only two or three feet of space. The bottom rack is lifted up and hooked to the rack above it. When I was on the *Sumac*, it was common to trice guys up in the rack so they could get a nap during the work day without being seen!

I settled into my new home aboard *Sherman* and began working on my damage control and engineering watch qualifications as we continued on with my first patrol. The qualifications on *Sherman* were typical for a larger cutter. It would take me about two months to complete my damage control and six months to complete my engineering qualifications. There were also my primary duties in the engine room to manage and collateral duties such as boarding team member.

Sherman was currently patrolling the Bering Sea conducting fishery law enforcement. This involved patrolling primarily three areas; an allocated fishing zone known as the "Donut Hole," exclusionary zones where fishing is not allowed, and regular fishing grounds. There are also international and domestic laws that forbid some types of nets used in the fishing industry, and we would enforce these laws. We were the "park ranger" of the Bering Sea. And of course there were the endless number of fishing vessels in distress, sinking, or sunk to keep us busy.

Boardings out in the frigid and rough waters of the Bearing Sea were tough. Wearing your cold weather survival suit, gear, and weapon, you had to be lowered in the small boat from *Sherman*, transit the rough freezing water, then scale a ladder up onto the fishing vessel. Once you were finished with the inspection you had to make it off the fishing vessel, transit back, and finally get back aboard *Sherman*. It was very hard work and accomplished several times a day depending on how many fishing vessels we came across.

Patrolling out in the isolated frigid water of the Bering Sea can get very boring. We were pretty much confined to the inside of the cutter because it's just too cold to go out on the weather decks, which are secure most of the time anyway due to heavy weather. So the only thing to look forward to was liberty in Dutch Harbor and the occasional, very traditional line crossing ceremony.

Boarding a fishing vessel in the Bearing Sea

Conducting a boarding on a fishing vessel in the Bearing Sea

There are several, centuries old, naval traditions that are observed to this day that revolve around sailing through certain areas of the seven seas. The open water is King Neptune's kingdom, and all sailors must pay respect to his highness. If not, you're sure to be sunk and join Davy Jones at the bottom of the sea! Crossing the 180th meridian, also known as the international dateline, is one of those areas deemed sacred by King Neptune. When we crossed the 180th meridian we always held a ceremony to appease King Neptune. It turned Polly Wogs, those who have never crossed the 180, into Golden Dragons, those who have. It does not matter how long you have been at sea or your rank; if you have never crossed you're initiated.

On the 27th of October 1999 the *Sherman* crossed the 180th meridian at latitude 60 degrees 21.1 North. For this time honored ceremony Captain Ryan turned the *Sherman* over to King Neptune, and *Sherman* basically shut down for two days while the Polly Wogs were turned into Golden Dragons! I was thankful that Captain Ryan -who had gotten me into this mess - was also a Polly Wog like me. It was a relentless 24 hours of wearing my clothing backwards and inside out, and becoming a servant to the crew of already initiated Golden Dragons.

The first day was consumed with doing the Golden Dragons laundry, getting their chow, and any other menial task they could come up with. On the second day we went through the gauntlet that would deliver us to King Neptune and his court. We were all blindfolded and made to crawl the length of the ship and half way back again. It took about 45 painful minutes!

I started at the bow of the ship in the enclosed main deck. I was handed a biscuit, yes a baked biscuit, and told no matter what, do not lose the biscuit! I had someone guiding me along as I crawled my way down the passageway, which was filled with obstacles. My first stop was getting my hair cut, or so I thought. When you're blind folded you really don't know what's going on. While someone was running a comb through my hair, another person was running electric hair clippers without the blades though my hair, and yet another person was sprinkling fine paper cuttings on my neck. It felt like a haircut!

Next was reaching into buckets of muck and fishing out what I was told were fish eye balls to eat, I want to say they turned out to be just olives mixed in with pudding, at least that is what they tasted like. Then it was outside onto the 20 degree snow covered weather decks. The first stop outside was a mop dipped in freezing cold water placed on my head. Now that will wake me up! I made it back to the fantail and was led into the "whale's belly," which was a freezing cold 25 foot long trough full of weeks old food and water. Luckily the stench was subdued by the freezing temperatures. As I made my way through the trough I was told to submerge my head several times as I swam to the other end. The bitter cold was just shocking, but I still had my biscuit at the other end! After being led up to the flight deck I was hit by a stream of freezing cold seawater being shot out of a fire hose. I had to crawl 50 feet on the flight deck fighting the force of the fire hose. At least that had rinsed the rotten garbage off me!

Going through the whales belly and yes that's snow on the deck!

I finally reached the helicopter hanger and the King's court, where I was told to kneel and remove my blindfold. The King was seated to the left of me with his three minions in between us. I had to go down the line of them to get to the King. The first was the Royal Baby, who was really FTC (Fire Control Technician Chief) Dave Powers. He was a bald guy with a huge belly and totally in his element! Today his belly was covered in Crisco grease topped with a cherry. He had an assistant holding a mop handle with a skull perched on the end. He ordered me to kiss his skull

257

and then get the cherry off of his belly without using my hands. As soon as I got my head close to his belly he reached out with both his hands, grabbed my head, and smeared my face into his belly full of Crisco!

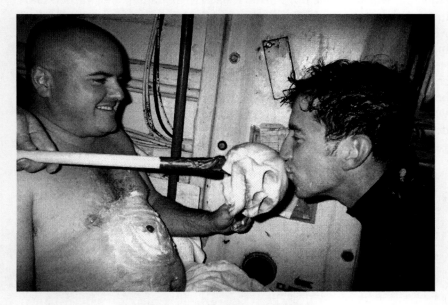

Golden Dragon ceremony in the Bering Sea
FTC Dave Powers as the Royal Baby

Next it was on to the Royal Hag, dressed as an old lady, who smeared a heaping spoon full of peanut butter in the palm of my right hand. Next was Queen Amphitrite, who had me first kiss her boot. She then asked me to produce my biscuit, which I proudly did! She then told me to place my biscuit in my peanut butter filled hand and then shove it all into my mouth. I did, and finally moved on to King Neptune. The King is the person on board who has the earliest date crossing the 180th meridian.

Kissing Queen Amphitrite's boot

Finally making it to King Neptune

The King on this occasion was an MK1, who I'm sure loved to see a MKCS in such a condition! So here I was soaking wet, freezing, clothes inside out and backwards, covered in Crisco, and a mouth full of biscuit and peanut butter. The King asked me, "Why are you here to see me?" I said, "Because I want to be a Golden Dragon!" He said, "Ok you're a Golden Dragon, now get on your feet!" And I sprang to my feet and I was no longer a Polly Wog! It took me weeks to get all that Crisco out of my hair and ears.

After almost three weeks underway we pulled into Victoria, Canada on the 8th of November for fuel, stores, and a break. Then it was on our way home to Alameda were we would spend the holidays. The *Sherman* had a crew of 167 and was the first cutter I had been assigned with a mixed enlisted crew of men and women. There were three E-8s, an MKCS, EMCS, and FSCS. I was the MKCS, Bob Cratty was the EMCS, and Ray Sturgess was the FSCS. The cooks changed the name of their rating from the last time I mentioned them, from substance specialist (SS) to food service (FS).

Bob was the senior of the three of us and the CEA. The CEA position, which was a challenge on any cutter, was an especially difficult job on this size of cutter because of the size and complexity of the crew. And don't forget that it's just a collateral duty. Bob also had collateral duty as the head of a boarding team along with his primary duty in charge of the electrical division. Bob Cratty was a true professional and a class act. As the senior electrician we worked very closely. If you remember back on the *Tampa*, electricians and I sometimes bumped heads. Bob on the other hand worked a lot of late nights side by side with me to resolve complicated casualties. He could care less if the problem was mechanical or electrical, it just needed fixed.

He knew he would be handing the responsibility of CEA over to me when he left. Not because I knew the CO so well, but because I was senior to his replacement and the FSCS position was downgraded to a FSC after Ray left. Bob mentored me in becoming a more rounded leader and better at handling issues involving a mixed gender crew. He had a special bond with the crew as the CEA, and that would eventually make it that much easier when I would take over a few months later in July of 2000.

There was no shortage of business for the CEA. It was always something from the mundane such as "I'm getting screwed over by my duty section," "My chief is out to get me," or "Laundry is not folding my clothes right," to more unusual accusations such as one from a few of the females down in female berthing.

The females lived just like the guys did; in a 21 man berthing area with their racks stacked 3 high. A few of the older and senior females came to me and stated that two of the younger and junior females were always in the rack together. They also stated that they were keeping them up at night with their giggling, moaning, and groaning. The senior females were insinuating that the two junior females in question were having sex.

Aboard Coast Guard cutters crewmembers were not to be sexually or romantically involved with each other. If the two were of the opposite sex, and on separate cutters, they could have a relationship within looser Coast Guard guidelines. Same sex relationships were a Coast Guard wide violation and fell under the "don't ask, don't tell" rule. Basically, unless you were caught red handed in a same sex relationship you didn't have to disclose it, even if you were asked. Leadership on *Sherman* didn't go around looking for people breaking any relationship rule, but once out in the open or brought to our attention we could not turn a blind eye.

The junior females in question were great workers and highly praised by their chiefs. Without any real facts or evidence of sexual misconduct, but not wanting to dismiss the matter at my level, I decided to go and talk to the captain and see how he felt about possible sexual misconduct. The captain's simple message was, "Spuds, don't ask and don't tell." After all, as far as we knew they could have just been in the rack together with the curtain drawn watching movies on a laptop computer. Not something guys would do, but not out of the ordinary for women. However, I still had the issue with them keeping the rest of the berthing area awake with their activities. I called the two junior ladies into see me and explained the noise situation, and they said they understood and would keep it down. That was the last I heard of that. That was until one of them came to me about a year later and announced she was pregnant, and would need to get off the cutter! I'll get to that later.

One of my more important duties was to advise the captain when an enlisted person was brought to mast. During the mast I would stand next to the captain while he sat at a table covered in green felt, another naval tradition. Most masts were for drinking infractions, drug use, sleeping on watch, failing to appear for duty, insubordination, and occasionally something unusual like having a loaded pistol in your locker!

The mast I felt the worst about was that of a male MK2 and Female quartermaster third class (QM3). A fireman damage controlman (FNDC) was making his appointed engineering security rounds one night while we were underway. This entailed inspecting all the engineering spaces hourly, taking readings on machinery, and checking for fire and flooding. He entered the damage control (DC) shop in the aft part of the cutter, turned on the light, and exposed the QM3 on her knees giving the MK2 a "sexual favor." The young FNDC reported this back to the engineer of the watch (EOW), not realizing that the EOW would have no other choice but to press charges. Hence the MK2 and QM3 were brought up on charges of having a sexual relationship, or fraternization, a violation of the UCMJ.

An officer was assigned to investigate the incident and the facts came down to a "he said, she said" between the FNDC and the MK2 and QM3. As the CEA, and knowing my long history with the captain, the MK2 and QM3 came to me and asked me what they should say when they were at mast. They wanted to take the position that the FNDC was mistaken in what he saw and it was their word against his. I told them to tell the truth, that the captain respected that, and if he caught them in a lie he would throw the book at them. I had been involved with numerous masts with the captain here, and on the *Tampa*, and knew he was fair. He leaned more on the lenient side when junior enlisted were involved. I felt confident he would let them off with a severe reprimand, maybe some extra duty, and an order to cease any personal interaction.

We went into the mast and I took my place beside the captain. The FNDC made his statement and the MK2 and QM3 stated that they were involved in a sexual act. The captain threw the book at them; reduction in rank, 30 days extra duty, and 30 days restriction! And they were told to cease any personal relationship that they had. I was floored! Afterward, in private, I told the captain I thought his punishment was too harsh. The captain was always gracious enough to let me plead my case, even though it was a moot point. Afterward I could see that he was making a statement. With a mixed gender crew there were always behind the scenes inappropriate relationships that you sort of had a feeling were going on, but just didn't have any evidence to prove. The captain was putting a shot across the bow of these relationships letting everyone know that they would not be tolerated.

The DC shop would later play a part in another ship board drama. We were underway and the captain had authorized beer to be broken out for the deck force division, who had participated in a huge tow job with a distressed vessel. Deck force had worked out in the cold for hours hooking up and tending the tow and the CO wanted to show his appreciation. Distribution of beer on a cutter was highly unusual. We did carry a small amount of beer on board for formal functions in various port calls but it was under lock and key. The captain authorized one beer per person involved with the towing evolution to be consumed in conjunction with a morale pizza party on the crew's mess deck. The beer was only to be issued to deck force and consumed on the mess deck.

I voiced my concern to the captain that it was going to be tough to only give beer to deck force, and that the remainder of the crew was going to be mad. I knew it would be seen as favoritism and as the CEA I knew I was going to get an ear full from the rest of the crew that they were not getting beer! The captain told me that deck force did an exceptional job and he wanted to reward them with a beer and that was that. After saying my piece I said, "Aye-aye" and beer was served on the mess deck to deck force only.

At some point a large amount of beer made its way back to the DC shop, which has no association with deck force. It's actually a part of the engineering department which is always at odds with deck force, sort of like the Hatfields and McCoys. Needless to say beer and pizza were consumed where it should not have been. It's not that anyone was caught; there was just a lot of bragging, or scuttlebutt, coming from the engineers. Well the captain got wind of it and he was not happy. Nothing really happed over the rumored incident, except that the engineering department moved up a rung on the captain's shit list!

The chief's mess consisted of 14 chiefs and was the biggest and one of the most eclectic I had ever been in. There were three four-man state rooms and one two-man stateroom. The berthing arrangements were always getting shuffled around. But for the most part the two most senior, who were males, had the two-man state room, the remaining males had two four-man staterooms and the females had one four-man stateroom.

USCGC SHERMAN Chief's Mess
Back row left to right; TCC Pam Arnold, ETC Dave Williams,
HSC Liz Beck, RDC Dennis Ferguson, YNC Mark Planitz,
SKC Ken Murrell Middle row left to right; FSC Tina Sondrini MKC
John Young, QMC Rob Eagleton, FTC John Spotts Front row left to
right; DCC Mike Dewitt, EMCS Joe Barthelemy,
BMC Phil Spurling, MKCS Ed Semler.

The chief's mess pictured above was our augment before sailing on our
six month out of hemisphere (OOH) deployment to the Persian Gulf and
circumnavigation of the globe in January 2001. We were a good tight
chief's mess. As with every cutter there was always a turnover of personnel in the summer months, and we had lost six chiefs that previous
summer; EMCS Bob Cratty, MKC Steve Underwood, FTC Dave Powers, FSCS Ray Sturgess, GMC Mark Riley, and DCC Ivan Adams. Those
were the chiefs who welcomed me aboard and made the mess feel like a
home and family.

We had a huge chief's lounge and eating area complete with our own
fridge/freezer, sink and prep area, and huge TV. As with the officer's

264

wardroom, we had a mess cook assigned to us to keep the place clean. Times had changed and that's pretty much all that we required of our mess cook. When our mess cook was done cleaning the chief's mess he spent the rest of his work day helping in the galley. We went through the chow line ourselves, made our own racks, cleaned our own heads, and sent our own laundry down to laundry facility.

One of my functions as the CEA was to spearhead the chief's initiations. Usually we tried to hold them in conjunction with the other units and cutters home ported in Alameda, but it was simpler to just hold them ourselves while underway. We sure had a big enough of mess to pull it off.

The charge I personally liked to give the prospective chiefs was one I picked up from an initiation judge while at the ELC. He would have them go around and present themselves to local community leaders like the fire chief, police chief, and mayor. The goal was to pose a challenge to the prospective chief and have them reach out and introduce themselves, and the Coast Guard, to the local community. The prospective chief was to set up an appointment, introduce themselves, explain the missions of the Coast Guard here at Alameda, get a picture taken with the community leader, and finally a signed business card. Hey, I needed proof they actually met the person!

This worked great and the prospective chiefs and community leaders received a better understanding of the roles we all played in the community. One of the more interesting officials I sent a prospective chief to see was the Mayor of Alameda, Jerry Brown. Mayor Brown was once the governor of California and a well know figure. As of the writing of this book he was once again elected the governor of California.

I sent prospective Chief Mike Dewitt to see him. Mike was a little hesitant because scuttlebutt was that Mayor Brown was not a fan of the Coast Guard. Story had it that he rode his bike up to the gate leading to the base one day and was turned away because he didn't have any identification. I thought this was just the guy who needed to have a face to face with the Coast Guard! Mike took the charge I gave him and set up an appointment with Mayor Brown. Upon his return he said he had a delightful meeting with the mayor. And that if there ever had been any hard feelings, they were mended and all was well between Mayor Brown and the Coast Guard!

The engineering machinery plant aboard *Sherman* was pretty much original from the 1960s. Although she had undergone a refitting in the late 1980s, her engine room machinery had only been overhauled and was still original. As a comparison, the U.S. Navy only keeps entire ships around for 20 years or so before they are deemed at the end of their service life and decommissioned.

The keystones of the machinery plant were the two main diesel engines and two gas turbines. The diesels were vintage Fairbanks Morse opposed piston engines, which were mostly used on train locomotives. The main gas turbines were 1960s era Pratt & Whitney FT4As, used mainly on jet aircraft like the 707 commercial passenger jet.

The design of having two different propulsion engines made the 378 a very flexible platform. Diesel engines were economical and well suited for transiting and idling around vessels while conducting boardings. Gas turbines provided the high speeds necessary for search and rescue (SAR) and for keeping up with Navy and NATO vessels.

Full speed on diesels was about 18 knots and on turbines it was 29 knots. But in the end it all boiled down to fuel consumption. The pair of diesels would run at around 300 gallons an hour where a single turbine could eat up 1000 gallons an hour! At a capacity of around 200,000 gallons, and no service stations out in the middle of the ocean, you had to use discretion when operating turbines.

The engine room on the *Sherman* consisted of three levels separated by grated metal catwalks. As you came down the ladder into the engine room you could see almost all the way down through the perforated catwalks. The catwalks surrounded the main engines and acted like scaffolding giving you easy access to work on them. As you made your way down into the depths of the space the catwalks became narrower while more and more machinery towered over you. Eventually you would end up all the way down on the lower level. On this lower level was a tiny compartment known as the Diesel Oil Purifier Room (DOPR) housing the fuel oil purifier. This is one place you did not want to spend a lot of time hanging out in while underway. If something bad happened in the engine room you could easily become trapped down there.

In 1985 the *USCGC Chase (WHEC-718)*, which was a sister ship to the *Sherman*, was heading home to Boston from REFTRA in GITMO. She was off the coast of Cape Cod, Massachusetts when she experienced an engine room fire. An MK3 was trapped down in the DOPR area and died from smoke inhalation.

During an in-port stop in Hawaii for REFTRA aboard the *Sherman* I happened to meet the MKCS aboard the *USCGC Rush (WHEC-723)*, another 378 class sister ship to *Sherman*. He relayed and incident to me about a time they were moored up at Dutch Harbor, Alaska concerning the lower level of the engine room. Dutch Harbor as usual it was freezing cold. Normal procedure when operating in that area is to start and warm up the main diesel engines every four hours to keep them warm and to keep the oil from thickening. For some reason the *Rush* machinery technicians had not kept the engines warm and were having a tough time trying to get them to start. MKCS says he went down to the lower level by the DOPR and was inspecting the oil filter housing, which is about four feet tall by three feet wide, and made of thick metal. It has a cover on it held down by several huge bolts. They were trying to crank the engine over and he said he turned away from the oil filter and that was the last thing he remembered. When he woke up he was covered in oil and being carried up the ladder out of the third level area. The oil filter housing had exploded and that thick metal lid had been blown off, huge bolts and all! Something had hit him in the back of the head and knocked him out. He told me that the review of the incident indicated that as the top cover of the filter flew off, it had just missed him. If it had hit him he would more than likely have been killed.

The engine room of *Sherman* also housed numerous pumps, purifiers, and an old flash type evaporator. The evaporator was for making drinking water. It ran off of steam and turned sea water into drinking water. With this class of cutter in order to stay ahead of the endless maintenance you had to have a devoted group of engineers, which by the grace of God I had. I lived on board and after working all day, I would relax for an hour or so while having the evening meal and watching the evening news. Then I would head down to my "garage" in the engine room and pass the evening working on anything needing attention. I also had a dedicated group of about 12 machinery technicians and fireman, ranging from E-2 to E-6, who worked tirelessly on maintenance and casualties.

My right hand man was MK1Patrick Dudley. He was a no-bullshit, tell it like it is enforcer who kept the guys focused and the day to day routine in the engine room on schedule. I really needed that after my second patrol when I relieved Bob Cratty as the CEA. I was distracted by the "Payton Place" of events going on elsewhere on the cutter. A junior MK1 by the name of Andy Vanderwalker, MK2 Joe Prince, MK2 James Stetson, MK2 Juston Thomason, and MK3 Alan Dowdall rounded out the rest of my crew of rated machinery technicians.

MK1 Patrick Dudley, CWO Bellairs, and MK1 Andy Vanderwalker standing watch in the engine room main control booth.

When I reported aboard, the engine room was just getting by and the operation of the gas turbines was questionable. One would run, but was not reliable, and the other was hit or miss even getting it started. The main diesel engines were in good running order but had a lot of exhaust, oil, and fuel leaks. When we started them up to get underway I had to have several guys out in the engine room with squirt bottles of water to put out numerous small fires! And the smoke would be thick enough to set off the fire alarm system.

We did have a good sized fire while underway one time just under the #2 gas turbine. The watch section for the engine room consisted of five people standing a four hour watch. You usually stood this twice a day. The watch section was headed by the engineer of the watch (EOW), and included a throttleman, oiler, generator, and security watch stander. The EOW and throttleman stayed in the main control booth located in the engine room, the oiler and generator were in the engine room space, and the security roamed all the other engineering spaces throughout the cutter.

I was standing the EOW, Ensign Heather Mattern was my throttleman, and MK2 Joe Prince was my oiler. Earlier that day the main propulsion crew had been cleaning up oil that had been collecting in a drip tray under the #2 gas turbine. They had piled all the oily rags in a location under the #2 turbine which appeared to be away from any danger. Little did they know that there was a condensation bleed tube that ran down from the #2 turbine exhaust just above where they had piled those oily rags. And the valve on this line, which is normally closed, was left open. If started, this tube would shoot extremely hot exhaust gas right onto those rags.

As fate would have, it I received a request from the bridge that they wanted to come off the diesel engines and shift to a turbine. Number 2 gas turbine was selected and we did our usual flying transfer and shifted from the diesel to the turbine without any reduction in speed. Captain Ryan had stopped down to have some face to face time with the watch section and he and I were talking while Ensign Mattern was stopping the diesel and throttling up the turbine. As Captain Ryan and I were talking we both suddenly saw flames jumping up from under the #2 gas turbine.

I immediately moved to the intercom system and called up to the bridge to set general quarters and sounded the alarm in the engine room, notifying anyone in the space that there was a fire. As I turned to make my way over to the fire control panel, which would supply the engine room with firefighting foam, I saw the Captain Ryan squeezing his body through the escape scuttle out of the control booth. This would put him up on the main deck and he could make his way to the bridge. MK2 Prince was no slacker, and once he had foam, he had that fire out in a matter of seconds. Before the CO could make it to the bridge the fire was out. There was no damage, just charred rags and a lot of embarrassed main prop MKs!

I'm sure our fire was nothing like the one in the spring of 1971 that destroyed half the engine room. The #1 gas turbine had a major failure and flew apart destroying it and setting the engine room on fire. *Sherman* was operating just off of her then homeport of Boston and made it back into port without any personnel casualties. With the fire long gone the evidence is still present on the side of the #1 main diesel engine's block, where you can see the dents left by the flying turbine blades.

As on *Tampa*, my rule was that if you busted your ass for me in the engine room I would stick my neck out for you and grant you extra liberty; off the record. The guys loved this because they didn't have to use leave and could get that extra day off when they wanted. Only the CO could grant a day's liberty, but I would bend that rule all the time. Like on *Tampa* I would pay the price!

I had a hard working fireman apprentice (FA) who was just out of boot camp. He sent a request up the engine room chain of command for special liberty, off the record, to go home to San Diego and pick up his car. MK1 Dudley came to me with his request but recommended I disapprove it because he thought the FA was too immature. I felt Dudley was being too harsh and told him to let him go. I should have known better, because if you remember, I had the same situation with a fireman back on the *Tampa* and I got burnt when he missed muster and I got my ass chewed.

San Diego was a good eight hour drive south, but the young FA assured me that he was catching a ride home with another shipmate going on official leave, was going to get his car, and come straight back. I told him he could have Friday, Saturday, and Sunday off since he didn't have duty and to make sure he was back on board Sunday night for work on Monday. Sunday night and Monday morning rolled around with no sight of the fireman apprentice. Of course Dudley was giving me the, "I told you so" look. I pulled up the FA's personnel record from the ship's office and found his parent's phone number. When I reached his mom and dad I asked, "Has your son been home?" And they said, "Yes, but only for a short while and he left." I asked, "Did he leave with his car?" And they said, "He doesn't own a car!" As I talked to the father it was clear that his son, my FA, was a troubled kid. He explained to me that they had pushed him into the service to straighten him out. Oh great, just what I needed to hear! At this point I had to go to my boss the Engineering Officer, LT Dave Socci, and explain what had happened. He in turn had to go to the CO and explain the matter. Not good for me and the FA.

The FA was listed as absent without leave (AWOL). Now the Coast Guard doesn't go and look for you if you go AWOL. We don't have the resources and pretty much hope you'll come back. Nothing is really done until after 30 days when you become a deserter. At that point you are placed on a report which will identify you if you are stopped by law enforcement for any reason. In which case you would come up as a deserter and they would detain you and hand you back over to the Coast Guard.

After about a week I received a call from the FA who was out running wild with his friends back home in San Diego. I was able to convince him that if he came back before 30 days were up he would be a lot better off and only face a captain's mast. If he waited over 30 days, he would be a deserter and go to the brig. He did come back and went to mast for being AWOL and got the usual 30 days extra duty and 30 days restriction. Soon after the incident he claimed he was sick and kept going to sick call. At first I thought he was malingering. After all, he had pulled one over on me before. But he kept getting sicker and sicker and finally he was moved ashore as he was not fit to sail. He was eventually diagnosed with a bad case of Crohns disease.

I felt sorry for him. Almost everyone runs a little wild or do something stupid when they are young. Lord knows if you've made it this far in the book you know I made my fair share of bad decisions. I ran into him after he was sent ashore and diagnosed with Crohns. I was doing my laundry at the base laundry facility and we bumped into each other and had a good talk. I think the whole episode was a growing experience for him and I could tell he wanted to stay in the Coast Guard. Unfortunately, the disease caused too much of a problem for him to be on active duty and he was eventually discharged from the Coast Guard.

His actions didn't stop me from taking care of my guys with off the record liberty. Even though I got reamed for the fireman apprentice taking off I still stuck my neck out for my guys just as much as they busted their butts for the cutter. I was even able to send one of my guys to Germany.

The USO was hosting a military appreciation event in Germany and was looking for service members to represent each branch of the military. I had a great MK3 by the name of Alan Dowdall and I submitted a nomination package on him to represent the Coast Guard. Dudley of course didn't think he was good enough material; he was such a hard ass! As I had hoped, Dowdall was selected and went to Germany for an all-expenses paid USO extravaganza. And best of all, I was able to give Dudley back the "I told you so" look!

Morale activities on the *Sherman* were pretty much the same as they had been on the *Tampa*. We had the HI8 video system and movies were shown throughout the cutter in the evening. You could also sign them out and watch what you wanted in your own recreation room. A lot of folks had personal laptop computers and watched movies or played games on them. There were also several video game systems on board. Internet was available but limited. No one except the senior officers had their own government computers. Everyone else used communal computers throughout the cutter. We all had our own email address, and when you wanted to send an email off the cutter you would type it up, hit send, and it would go to a holding area on the cutter's server. Because we were sending email through a satellite there were size restrictions on our messages, which limited us to text only. About once a day depending on weather, course, and satellite signal, the cutter would connect to the satellite and receive and transmit all of our email waiting on the server. It didn't take long to figure out when this happened because the cutter would come alive with chatter and you couldn't find an open computer! And then there were the times when we would go several days without a connection. It didn't take long before I was getting my ear bent by disgruntled crewmembers wanting to know why the CO wasn't steering a course to receive email!

We still had the regular mail call when we hit a port of call and phone service was a lot better in port because we hit a lot more American ports. Cell phones were becoming popular but had limited reception when we headed up north to Alaska and the Bering Sea.

We spent January and February 2000 conducting shipboard training in Hawaii. In route to Hawaii, which was about a seven day transit for us from Alameda, I decided to fine tune the #1 turbine's starter linkage. In order to accomplish this I would have to lie on my back inside the turbine enclosure and watch and adjust the linkage as the turbine started up. The turbine enclosure was a sound insulated steel container with a door on it which housed the gas turbine. Basically the turbine would start to spin, the two igniters would spark, the linkage would move to open the fuel valve and after a flame was detected the linkage would move to idle speed. At first it was a little scary because you felt like you were lying right under a jumbo jet taking off.

At some point in the tune-up process I decided to add oil to the starter gear box and I ended up spilling some of the oil on me and the deck. I had been covered in oil before and thought nothing of it and continued working until I had the linkage adjusted just right. Several days later, after we arrived in Hawaii, I started to break out in a rash all over my hands and arms. It was a really itchy rash and my arms and hands began to swell. The hot weather in Hawaii seemed to inflame it.

Getting underway every day from Hawaii and working in the 120 plus degree engine room didn't help. I had never had anything like this happen to me before, and it frankly scared me a bit. Eventually on the 15th of January I went to see the corpsman, Health Services Technician Chief (HSC) Liz Beck, who gave me some Benadryl. After a few days with the Benadryl having no effect, Liz sent me over to the Sand Island Coast Guard Base clinic on the 18th where I was administered a shot. The chief corpsman there, who I had known from my days at the ELC in Baltimore, made me feel a little uneasy when he said they had seen several cases like this before and never could figure out what it was!

Whatever they gave me at Sand Island didn't work and the rash and swelling was moving to my torso and legs. By now my eyes were swollen and my hands felt like I was wearing gloves, my fingers were so swollen. I was a swollen itchy mess and the heat of the engine room was making it even worse. When we pulled back into Sand Island after several days underway on the 20th, I told Liz I was going to the local military hospital which was Tripler Medical Center. I had the duty driver take me over and got there at about 1900. The doctor prescribed a steroid which did the trick. I noticed a difference almost immediately after taking the medication and it was such a relief mentally and physically. The event didn't shake me enough to stay away from oil and the turbines. But after that, if I was rolling around in turbine oil, I made sure to go get cleaned up right away instead of letting it soak in for a good while.

We returned to Alameda in late February. During our in-port I was sent back to Yorktown, Virginia to attend FT4A Gas Turbine School. By this time I had enough on the job training that I could have taught the school, but hey, it was a free trip back to the east coast.

In April it was time to shove off on our next four month patrol back up in the Bering Sea. We left Alameda the first week of April and pulled into Juneau, Alaska on the 12th for a briefing on our operations in the Bearing Sea. It was up into Kodiak on the 17th and then out on patrol for several weeks until we pulled into Dutch Harbor for a patrol break, food, and fuel.

On the 1st of May 2000, while on our patrol break, a Coast Guard C-130 aircraft out of Kodiak spotted the *M/V Artic Wind*, a Honduran flagged vessel, operating with illegal high seas drift nets. We were told to get underway from Dutch Harbor and diverted to intercept the suspected fishing vessel. High seas drift netting is a when a fishing vessel lays out a huge net that goes out for sometimes up to 20 or 30 miles, and it snags anything in its path. Its practice has been banned by the United Nations since 1992.

The last know position of the *M/V Artic Wind* was 850 miles from us, so it would be a good three day transit to get there with a good sea state. Now we are up in the Bering Sea, and anyone who has ever watched a TV episode of commercial fishing in the Bering Sea knows that there are no nice days up there! It took us three and a half days to get on scene and another day for the C-130 to locate the *M/V Artic Wind* for us.

On the 6th of May we intercepted the 177 foot *M/V Artic Wind* after chasing her over 1000 miles. We hailed her using numerous languages trying to get her to stop to no avail. By the time we had reached her she had painted over all of her identifying markings, including her name on the back of her hull, and flew no flags in an attempt to hide her identity. But we could tell who she was and could see her name through the bad cover up paint job on her stern. We even launched our HH-65 Dolphin helicopter and had it drop messages down to her and still nothing. She did not reply, and instead she cut her drift net free.

M/V ARTIC WIND in the Bearing Sea

We sent our small boat with a boarding team to try and board her and she made several aggressive course changes and radical maneuvers to prevent our boarding team from getting aboard. At one point she started to go in circles and then making high speed turns in the _Sherman's_ direction, as if to ram us. A request was made to Coast Guard Headquarters for permission to fire upon the _M/V Artic Wind_ to disable her. Permission was granted, making it the first time ever that Coast Guard Headquarters had authorized a Coast Guard vessel to fire on a civilian vessel for violating international agreements against the use of drift nets.

The captain had us point our 76 mm forward mounted gun at her along with our 25mm machine guns. We were close enough to the _M/V Artic Wind_ that her crew could hear the siren being emitted from our 76 mm gun indicating we were about to fire. A message came across the radio from the _M/V Artic Wind_ asking us, "What are you doing?" followed by,

275

"You wouldn't shoot us on the high seas!" Captain Ryan replied "Yes we will, we have permission."

The tactic worked and the *M/V Artic Wind* heaved to. Finally, she slowed and after a 27 hour chase we sent our boarding team over on the 8th of May. The crew who turned out to be Russian were arrested, the vessel commandeered, and crucial data was recovered, leading to the successful recovery of two deployed drift nets and four radio transmitter buoys. These nets contained over 600 salmon, 6 sharks, and dozens of albatross and puffins. One net was 5 miles long and hung down 300 feet into the water. It was reported that a Coast Guard aircraft had spotted a dead whale caught in one net thought to be from the *M/V Artic Wind*.

The *M/V Artic Wind* had only been at sea for several weeks on a six month scheduled voyage and had already processed and packed more than a ton of salmon. The boarding team manned the commandeered vessel and prepared to sail it to the closest U.S. port which was Adak, Alaska. With the *Sherman* following, the *M/V Artic Wind* was taken to Adak. The sea state was miserable, with 20 foot seas and 50 knot winds, and for most of the trip we only made about 8 knots an hour.

I made it up to the bridge with my video camera and documented the sea state. You could hardly see the *M/V Artic Wind* off our port bow as she plowed through the rough seas. At times she would disappear into the swells and sea spray. Up on our bridge it was all that I could do to hold on with one hand and film with the other. I can't imagine how my shipmates stood the pounding over on the *M/V Artic Wind*.

It was a slow eight day transit in miserable seas. On the 17th of May we finally pulled into Adak with the *M/V Artic Wind*. With all the time it took to find and commandeer the illegal fishing vessel, *Sherman* missed out on a once in a lifetime port call opportunity. We had been scheduled for a port call in the Russian city of Petropavlovsk. But now there was no time for it. The crew was disappointed, but not to worry, there were still some good port calls ahead of us. We finished up our patrol and started to head back home. On the 3rd of June we pulled into Ketchikan, Alaska for a brief port call and then it was on to Portland, Oregon to attend the Portland Rose Festival.

The Rose Festival was a huge port call for us. The city of Portland would be alive with festivities and there would also be a large contingency of

U.S. Navy and Canadian ships. The Navy always had a way of adding excitement to a port call! In route to Portland we stopped overnight on the 6th of June at the mouth of the Columbia River in Astoria, Oregon. We needed to prepare for the long eight hour transit down the river to Portland and we took on Navy League, Coast Guard Auxiliary, and Rose festival dignitaries for the transit down river.

While in Astoria a local bar owner came over to the cutter and handed out a bunch of free drink tokens for the crew. I had a look at one and they were actually old bus tokens from Ford City, a neighboring town back in my home state of Pennsylvania. I had a talk with the bar owner and he said he had relocated out here years ago and thought the old bus tokens would be a cool link back to his roots. We had a good conversation about Pennsylvania and it turned out my brother, who worked as a mail carrier, delivered mail to his old neighborhood. Small world isn't it?

Just off of Astoria and at the mouth of the Columbia River where it meets the Pacific Ocean is Cape Disappointment. It is an area regarded as one of the most treacherous river bars in the world. Because of the large number of shipwrecks near the river entrance it is often called, "The Graveyard of the Pacific." Because crossing a sand bar is notoriously rough, and dangerous, the naval community refers to passing over in death as "crossing the bar." This term is rooted in the poem "Crossing the Bar" by Alfred Tennyson.

After transiting down the river the next day we arrived on the 7th to a perfect berth right in the middle of Portland. Captain Ryan was the senior CO of all the ships attending, so we got the best parking spot! We were right in the center of all the action. The Navy League billed it as "the ultimate ship's party," and it was indeed a port call to remember! Being right downtown we were the bell of the ball and the Navy League, who was sponsoring the event, treated *Sherman* and her crew like the queen! They had reserved a hotel suite for the crew as a sort of hospitality spot to just hang out and relax in. I stopped by on several occasions and sat around with our gracious hosts, listening to sea stories from the older Navy salts. After spending several days in Portland we transited back up the Columbia River, past Cape Disappointment, and into the Pacific Ocean on our way to Seattle, Washington.

On the 14th of June we pulled into Seattle to meet with the crew of the *USCGC Midgett (WHEC-726)*, the 378 that had just returned from an out of hemisphere (OOH) deployment to the Persian Gulf. The *Sherman* was scheduled to make that same cruise. It would be a six month deployment and we were all pretty excited about it. This was our opportunity to sort of debrief the *Midgett* crew to get an idea of what we could expect. They provided us with many suggestions for making our deployment as smooth as possible. Surprisingly, their biggest complaint, and now our biggest concern, was the effects of the anthrax vaccination.

There was a major concern that Iraq would use chemical weapons such as anthrax against forces operating against them. Therefore, anyone who was getting ready to deploy to that part of the world was required to get the anthrax vaccination. The side effects had already been widely talked about in the other services, but hearing them first hand from these guys hit home. Most of their complaints were rashes and very sore limbs. Just what I needed, another rash! As fate would have it there was a shortage of the vaccine when we were preparing to deploy and we never received it.

After a few days in Seattle we hauled in our lines once again and finally made it back into Alameda the first part of July. In preparation for the upcoming deployment *Sherman* entered the shipyards in Alameda for major hull, structure, and machinery work. We would spend August and September in the shipyard.

Main Propulsion in the Alameda Shipyard

278

While at the shipyard Captain Ryan mustered the crew one day at quarters. Quarters was our daily gathering to pass the word of the day and make sure everyone was present or accounted for. The captain asked the crew if we would be interested in circumnavigating the globe in conjunction with our out of hemisphere deployment. He asked for a sign of hands in favor. Since a majority of the crew was young, adventurous, and single, the vote was a majority "yes" for the circumnavigation.

The *Sherman* hummed with positive scuttlebutt about the deployment as the day grew closer to departure. There was some dissention and it seemed to be driven by a contingent of disgruntled crewmembers' spouses. They didn't want anything to do with being without their loved one for six months or more. They put up a good fight and even lobbied the commandant of the Coast Guard wanting to stop the deployment.

Their argument stemmed around wanting to know why the Coast Guard was getting involved with actions in the Persian Gulf and why the Coast Guard was spending tax dollars on circumnavigating the globe. As the CEA I received a lot of complaints and even a call from the commandant's senior enlisted advisor, the master chief petty officer of the Coast Guard (MCPOCG). The MCPOCG wanted to make sure crew morale was up for the challenge in light of the concerns the commandant was receiving from the spouses. I assured him that the majority of the crew was excited and the dissent was a small minority.

I explained to the crew and their spouses time and again that the Coast Guard is part of the armed forces and is obligated to participate in actions in the Persian Gulf. It would also cost pretty much the same no matter what route we took to get there and back.

Before heading overseas we headed down to the U.S. Navy Base in San Diego in October to conduct more training for the deployment. On the way back home we stopped off at the U.S. Navy Base in Port Hueneme, California and the resort island of Catalina before reaching Alameda in November.

In Port Hueneme the Navy base CEA came aboard and asked if I needed anything. I told him I had a few chiefs getting ready to go through chief's initiation and asked if I could bring them over to his chief's mess so they could obtain words of wisdom. He graciously obliged and offered to have a get together at the chief's club there on base that evening. I took our chief's mess along with the chiefs going through initiation over and we had a great time. When I walked into the club the first thing I noticed was all these pencils stuck up in the ceiling. I'm talking hundreds of them! Turns out they were part of a money making game there in the chief's club. There were plate sized circles drawn on the ceiling, which was about 20 feet high. The ceiling tiles were made of a Styrofoam material and if you could throw a sharpened pencil up and have it stick inside the circle you won $50.00! It cost a $1.00 a try and the club made a lot of money off of us that night!

The Coast Guard was no stranger to the war, and follow-on action, in the Persian Gulf and had a permanent contingent in the area. Some of the assets were port security units (PSU) that ensured port security, and small patrol boats that enforced security and United Nations sanctions. Every year the Coast Guard sent one of its 378 class high endurance cutters to assist with the United Nations oil sanctions in the Persian Gulf. The 378 cutter class was the only Coast Guard asset able to handle the rigors of the deployment.

On the 13th of January 2001 *Sherman* slipped her moorings at Alameda and made her typical transit out into San Francisco Bay, past Alcatraz Island, and under the Golden Gate Bridge. Only this time she was steering a course for the Persian Gulf, and would make history becoming the first Coast Guard cutter since 1961 to circumnavigate the globe.

About three days out of Alameda we met up with the two much larger U.S. Navy ships that would make up our group for the transit to the Persian Gulf. They were the Spruance class destroyer *USS Paul F. Foster*, which was around 529 feet long, and the Arleigh Burke class destroyer *USS Stethem*, which was about 500 feet long. This was not our first time meeting the *Stethem*, she attended the Rose Festival with us in Portland.

We would from this day forward always stick out as the big white cutter amongst the fleet of grey Navy ships. Even though they were larger ships, we were commanded by a captain (O-6) and the Navy ships by commanders (O-5). This meant that we would lead the way to the gulf and at every port call we would have the choice berthing spot.

As we headed across the Pacific Ocean the sea state was rough, with huge rolling swells, due to a big storm north of us. We refueled at sea with the Navy oiler *USNS Yukon* and then pulled into our first stop at Pearl Harbor, Hawaii on the 19th of January.

On the 21st we left Pearl Harbor heading for the Coast Guard and Navy base at Guam. We steamed out of Pearl Harbor with the *USNS Yukon* and *SS Cape Girardo* along with the rest of our group. The *Yukon* and *Cape Girardo* sailed with us for about three days as we conducted replenishing at sea training with them. Once the training was completed, they were released to head back to Pearl Harbor after one more refueling from the *Yukon*. Heading toward Guam we crossed the 180th meridian on the 24th of January, which amazingly became the 25th of January, and we initiated all the Poly Wogs!

Before reaching Guam we crossed the Mariana Trench, also known as the Marianas Trench, on the 30th of January. The Mariana Trench is located in the western part of the Pacific Ocean and is the deepest part of all the oceans, reaching a depth of 34,240 feet or 6.5 miles. Of course we had to mark the occasion and a swim call was held for anyone wanting to swim in the deepest waters known to man. It was fun to watch the crew unwind and high dive off the flight deck, but I stayed on board nice and dry! The next day we pulled into Guam with our two other companion vessels.

Then it was on to Singapore on the 9th of February. It was a great port call with the exception of the first day, which involved resolving a huge personnel issue. One of the junior females, who I mentioned earlier in the berthing area incident, came to me with a male crewmember and they stated that they were in a personal relationship and she was pregnant! As big of a bombshell as this was, it meant foremost that I needed to get the pregnant female off the cutter before we hit the Persian Gulf. We couldn't sail into a hostile environment with a pregnant crewmember! Unlike the issue with the MK2 and QM3, if you came forward and notified the command that you were in a relationship with another crewmember before you were caught, no UCMJ action would be brought forward. The only downside for the crewmembers was that they would be separated. It is against regulations to have a relationship with another crewmember, so if they wanted to pursue the relationship one crewmember would need to be transferred off the cutter. In this case they wanted to have a relationship and it was obvious it would be the pregnant one leaving.

281

So I spent my first day of liberty making satellite phone calls from our communications center to assignment officers half a world away in Washington, DC. It was worth it because the two young crewmembers were good shipmates and I felt that I was doing something positive for them. With everything resolved the female crewmember was flown off from Singapore. I don't know how their relationship progressed from there, hopefully it all worked out for them.

After a nice break in Singapore it was on to Thailand on the 16th of February, and then on to the Persian Gulf.

On the 28th of February *Sherman* manned her war time steaming configuration and set battle stations as we entered the Strait of Hormuz along with the *Paul F. Foster* and the *Stethem*. This is the tiny entrance to the Persian Gulf connecting the Gulf of Oman with the Persian Gulf. The straits are lined by the country of Oman on one side and Iran on the other. To transit the strait we had to enter the territorial waters of each country. Iran likes to give U.S. Navy vessels a hard time and they tried to hail us on the radio as we steamed through with the *Paul F. Foster* and *Stethem*. With the *Sherman* leading the way we did not answer, and blew right through to the open waters of the Persian Gulf.

The Persian Gulf was a busy place and the *USS Harry S. Truman (CVN-75)*, an aircraft carrier, and her battle group were already operating in the gulf. On the 16th of February in support of Operation Southern Watch, her aircraft struck an Iraqi air defense system in response to Iraq firing on United Nation coalition aircraft. So the atmosphere in the Persian Gulf region was very tense when we arrived on the 28th.

For the next two months we, along with the *Paul F. Foster* and *Stethem*, operated under the U.S. Navy's 5th Fleet with Marine Expeditionary Forces 01-1 (MEF 01-1). Our mission was to enforce the United Nation's sanctions against Iraq and to participate in Operation Southern Watch. *Sherman* ended up conducting 219 queries, 115 boardings, and 5 diverts of vessels in probably the most dangerous maritime environment in the world. The *Stethem* recorded the third largest arrest of a vessel violating oil sanctions when she seized the *M/V Diamond*.

In November of 1999 I had taken the MKCM exam and was ranked first, meaning I was guaranteed promotion. I had also taken the exam for chief warrant officer that same year and was notified I was selected for promotion to CWO. I had to choose one or the other. Knowing I was number one on the MKCM exam I turned down the promotion to CWO. It was a difficult and consequential decision. An MKCM is an E-9 and the highest of the enlisted ranks. This is a prestigious rank across all the services. Chief warrant officer had promotion potential as an officer and eventually higher pay. But I didn't see myself staying in the Coast Guard much past my retirement milestone of 20 years. In addition I would also have to stay in at least 10 more years as a CWO to see any significant increase in pay. So on the 1st of March, while underway in the Persian Gulf, I was promoted to master chief machinery technician, (E-9). I was very proud to have Captain Dave Ryan, and the Engineering Officer, Lieutenant Dave Socci, pin my anchors on me.

Being pinned to Master Chief Machinery Technician
LT Dave Socci, MKCM Ed Semler and CAPT Dave Ryan

During our two months in the Persian Gulf we would take on all our fuel and stores while underway from U.S. Navy oilers and supply ships. Taking on fuel and stores was always an all hands evolution, and we would do it about every 10 days. The Navy oiler, which was around 670 feet long, would be steaming a steady course of about 15 knots. This is at the top end of our diesel speed so we had to come up on both turbines for the evolution. This was a very noisy evolution. When you walked out on deck during the maneuver it sounded like a jet plane taking off as we cruised along under turbine power. The oilers were busy and usually were refueling ships on both sides, so we would have to get in line and wait our turn. When the ship ahead of us would break away we would steam up alongside and match the oiler's speed. Once that was accomplished we would pass over the required lines and take on fuel and stores. We held over 200,000 gallons of fuel, so we would usually be taking on 100,000 gallons or so at a whack. The evolution would last a few hours. When we finished, and broke away, we would honor the oiler by blasting some rock and roll tune out over the intercom system as we sped off.

USCGC SHERMAN (WMEC-720) **taking on fuel from the Navy**
Oiler *USNS LEROY GRUNMAN (T-AO-195)*

Every Tuesday and Saturday we were visited by the Navy's "Desert Duck" helicopter. That was the generic name for the helicopter. The one that came out to us had the tail number 746 with "Mighty Duck" painted on its landing gear housing. This was an older Navy HH-3 helicopter that looked like it had been worked to death over the years out there in the Gulf. She would come zipping on up to us, hover over the flight deck, and drop off mail and small supplies. She would also take mail off and occasionally conduct passenger transfers. So the mail that the Mighty Duck would bring out to us was extremely important to our morale.

After Bob Cratty left he was replaced with an equally great EMCS by the name of Joe Barthelemy. Since Joe and I were the two senior enlisted, we shared the two man stateroom in chief's country. He ended up promoting to CWO while in the Persian Gulf and was flown off in the Mighty Duck to his next assignment. He later told me that his ride on the Mighty Duck was one he would never forget. He said the door wouldn't close, fuel oil and hydraulic fluid were leaking all over the place, and he feared for his life!

In the course of our two months in the Persian Gulf we only made two port calls, one in the third week of March and one in the first week of April. Both port calls were at the Mina Sulman piers at Manama, Bahrain. All of our mail, fuel, food, and everything else was either taken on underway from an oiler or delivered by the Mighty Duck.

While in port Manama, Bahrain I was frequently visited by the Navy's 5th Fleet Command Master Chief, MCPO Terry Scott. Whenever we pulled in he would be waiting on the pier to come aboard and see me to discuss any enlisted issues we had. He was always concerned about how we were getting along and if there was anything the 5th Fleet could do for us. He was very professional and I always felt he was truly concerned about our needs. I was not surprised when he later became the 10th Master Chief Petty Officer of the Navy (MCPON).

On one of our two port calls I had the privilege to tour a U.S. Navy Los Angeles class nuclear submarine, the *USS Alexandria (SSN-757)*. She was moored across the pier from us and I walked over to invite their chief's mess over to the *Sherman* for introductions. While there, the sub's CEA took me on a tour. The entrance to the sub was a small vertical shaft that was a bit tricky to get down. From there all I can say was that it was unbelievably cramped and not for the claustrophobic!

The enlisted slept up forward in three high racks that were on a movable grid system. This grid system allowed them to slide the racks around to enable them to load torpedoes into the front launch tubes. There weren't enough racks for the enlisted crew so they had to "hot rack." When you "hot rack" you basically share a rack with another crewmember. While you're working or on watch your rack partner sleeps, when he is working or on watch you sleep. There was one washing machine and dryer for the entire crew of 100. No wonder all they wore were one piece coveralls. The enlisted had one head as did the chiefs and officers. The chief's mess was about a ten foot by ten foot space that made our mess seem like a palace! I told the CEA his mess was more than welcome to come over and hang out in our mess whenever they wanted!

Sherman's initial job after entering the gulf was to provide watch over vessels being held for UN sanctions violations. There was a designated holding area in the gulf and vessels were held there at sea until they were cleared or directed to a port for disposition. Our job was to make sure they stayed in the holding area and to physically board and check on them daily. Oil samples were taken from these vessels and tested to see if the origin of the oil was from Iraq. If it was, that was a violation of the UN sanctions on Iraq and the vessel was seized.

During the patrol I augmented the primary boarding team several times. Boardings were always dangerous so I wore the usual bullet proof vest and I carried a 9mm Beretta pistol. I usually went over to help conduct health and well-being inspections with HSC Liz Beck. We inspected the boarded vessel for any health risks and to make sure they had enough food to last them if we were holding them.

The vessels barely had any food on board and we had to load them up with meals ready to eat (MREs), which were the new version of "C" rations. On one occasion I opened up this huge freezer to find a solitary frozen chicken, which looked like it had been in there for several years. That was all the food they had on board, or at least that I could find. On another vessel the boarding party had gathered the crew back on the fantail questioning them, and one was running around yelling his head off. When I asked what his problem was they said he was getting ready to pass a stone. I told Liz that it looked like she had a customer!

**Conducting a boarding on a suspect vessel in the
Persian Gulf**

While boarding another vessel I was asked to try and figure out if there
was any liquid loading information aboard. Liquid load data describes
how much fuel, oil, and water they are carrying. I went aboard and figured out who the engineering officer was. I asked him "Do you have any
liquid loading information?" And he said "No." I asked him "Can I look
around?" And he showed me to his stateroom. He had his own stateroom,
which was simply furnished, and I notice he had his liquid loading information right there on his bulkhead! I'll give him the benefit of the
doubt. He spoke English but it was broken and maybe something got lost
in the translation.

It seemed to me that most of the vessels I boarded had crews that spoke
broken English. The engineering officer, who had just shown me his
stateroom, and I sat down to eat MREs together. As a good will gesture
while conducting boardings on legitimate vessels we always tried to get
to know the crew and would break bread with them. He and his crew
seemed to really enjoy the small bottles of hot sauce in the MREs and he

asked if I had more. I really didn't like hot sauce and had a bunch of left over bottles in my back pack and gave them to him.

He was an interesting Iraqi man who was obsessed with the cost of goods in America compared to Iraq. In our conversation he was determined to convince me that Iraq goods were cheaper than goods in the United States. He seemed to have pleased himself when he asked me how much a chicken costs in the United States, and I gave him my answer of about $3.00. He said in a proud voice that it was much cheaper in Iraq! With all the sanctions and turmoil I wondered to myself, how good could an Iraqi chicken look! But I let him have the small victory as I radioed the liquid load information over to the *Sherman*.

Waiting for the RHI to pick us up from a suspect vessel in the Persian Gulf. Notice the bars on the port hole. MKC John Young sitting next to me

I knew that the boarding mission was dangerous but I never felt like I was in imminent danger. Getting from our cutter, via small boat, over to the suspect vessel was always a challenge. The suspect vessel would by no means stop or slow down. Sometimes the vessel's crew would lower down a ladder, but they were usually not happy to see us and let us fend for ourselves. To get onboard we would have to throw up our own rope ladder, time the swells of the water, and then jump onto the ladder to board. Once on board we had to secure the vessel and its crew.

When we entered the gulf we had to be prepared to make a non-compliant boarding. This meant boarding a vessel without their approval. Since the smugglers knew we were out there trying to stop them they welded their doors shut, welded bars over their port holes, and made any access into the skin of the vessel as difficult as possible. They also maneuvered their vessels erratically making the boarding process very dangerous. Their goal was to deter us long enough for them to get their vessel back into Iraqi or Iranian territorial waters where they were safe from us. Our goal was to get aboard, access the skin of the vessel, make our way to the pilot house, and seize the vessel. In preparation for this type of non-compliant boarding our boarding teams were trained using tactics provided by U.S. Navy SEALs.

Things got heated in the middle of April.

We had taken custody of the *M/V Zainab* in the Persian Gulf and had placed a custody crew aboard while *Sherman* headed off to relieve the *Stethem*, who was watching another seized vessel. The *M/V Zainab* was loaded down with over 3800 gallons of illegal Iraqi oil and was headed out of the Persian Gulf to Pakistan when intercepted.

On the 14th of April, while still in control of a one seized vessel, *Sherman* conducted a morning boarding on another suspect vessel and I was a member of that boarding team. The vessel was cleared as having legitimate cargo and I returned back to *Sherman*. Later that day the *M/V Zainab* and the custody crew along with another Navy vessel, the *USNS Catawba (T-ATF-168)*, were slowly making their way to our location. Unknown to the custody crew, the captain of the *M/V Zainab* had been pumping sea water into the ship thinking we would release his vessel if we thought it was sinking.

As the *M/V Zainab* got closer to us you could see she was very low in the water and was producing a large sheen of oil. She was about 200 feet long and an average size for an oil smuggler. *Sherman* immediately sent over a damage control party to assess the situation. Upon investigating below decks they determined the vessel was sabotaged and flooding. The damage control party quickly set up dewatering measures to slow the flooding.

I was actually really tired from the morning boarding I had gone on and went to my stateroom to try to take a nap. The event with the *M/V Zianab* was being broadcast over the ship's TV system and I watched the events unfold from my rack. For several hours the repair party, crew, and boarding team, tried to dewater the vessel but the flooding was too bad and finally took the vessel over. When all hope of salvage was lost we pulled the vessel's crew, boarding team, and damage control party from the vessel. Moments later we watched the *M/V Zainab* roll to her port side and her bow start to go under.

The *M/V ZAINAB* taking on water in the Persian Gulf

It didn't take long for the *M/V Zainab* to sink like a rock. After she went down she left behind a pretty good sized debris field of anything that would float. To limit the navigational hazard this floating junk may cause, *Sherman* opened up on the junk with machine gun fire in an effort to sink the bigger items.

M/V ZAINAB **sinking in the Persian Gulf**

The *M/V Zainab* is now a permanent fixture at the bottom of the Persian Gulf under about 100 feet of water, 20 miles off the coast of Dubai.

We lost the *M/V Zainab* but we still had our hands full. We still had the other seized oil smuggling vessel in custody, the one we relieved from *Stethem*. We placed a custody crew aboard the smuggler and left it to the watchful eye of the *Catawba*, and we steamed off to intercept several suspect vessels trying to sneak out of the Persian Gulf. We had been tracking them for several days and they were running in Iranian waters, headed for the Strait of Hormuz.

When we neared the strait Iranian gunboats come out to meet us since we were hugging their territorial waters waiting to pounce on the smuggling vessels. The gunboats came right up to us in a threatening manner and we set general quarters. As they shadowed us we saw that they had their guns covered, so they posed no immediate threat. Never the less we stayed prepared and they shadowed us until we reached the strait, at which point they broke off and we made it out into the Gulf of Oman without an incident.

The smugglers had made it out of the strait and into the Gulf of Oman as well, and we were gaining on them. But as soon as we started to close the gap they split up. Since we didn't have any back up we had to try and catch them both on our own. Our plan was to track one down, board the vessel, quickly leave a boarding team on board, and *Sherman* would sprint to catch the second vessel. Since we had already left a boarding team on the vessel with the *Catawba* and had two suspected vessels in our sights, I would be next up for a boarding. It was getting late when we came up on the first vessel, the *M/V Georgios*.

My boarding team was notified to get ready. This would be a long boarding and I knew I would be onboard for probably a few days until *Sherman* came back for us. I donned my bullet proof vest, took my contacts out in exchange for glasses, put my coveralls and camel pack canteen on, and headed for the boat deck. There I was issued my 9mm Beretta, inserted the magazine, chambered in a round, and holstered my weapon. We always carried our weapons with a round chambered and the safety off. All it would take to squeeze off a round was the pull of the trigger.

I loaded up in our small boat with CWO Paul Sepp who was the boarding team leader. He was the finance and supply officer and volunteered like everyone else to conduct boardings as a collateral duty. Once the boarding team was loaded in the boat we headed for the *M/V Georgios*.

The ride over was an adrenaline rush because we never knew what to expect! It was a clean climb up the side of the *M/V Georgios* and we scampered aboard her without an incident taking control of her and the crew. The *Sherman* immediately left us alone and took off after the other suspect vessel, the *M/V Kade Jah,* which was about 100 miles away. They finally caught up with her off the coast of Pakistan and took her under custody and headed back to us and the *M/V Georgios*. As we waited for the *Sherman* to return, we just held our position, made rounds of the vessel, and guarded the crew. Thankfully, the crew of the *M/V Georgios* wasn't interested in much more then sleeping.

What a sight for sore eyes when the *Sherman* returned! There is never a better sight then to see your ship coming over the horizon after you have been on a dirty, cockroach infested, scow of a ship, for a few days!

With the *M/V Georgios* and *M/V Kade Jah* in custody we headed back into the Persian Gulf to hand them over to an awaiting Navy vessel. Our boarding team that we left behind about a week ago with the *Catawba* had taken that vessel to a holding area. After dropping it off they spent some time in Bahrain waiting to rejoin us. Eventually they were flown out to another Navy vessel and then transferred back to us. With everyone back on board we finished up our last days in the Persian Gulf without incident.

Once again we transited the Strait of Hormuz and started the two month trip back home alone. The *Stethem* and *Paul F. Foster* escorted the *USS Harry S. Truman,* who was on her first deployment, through the Strait of Hormuz. Then they headed back home. Of course, instead of going back the way we came, we continued on our around the world journey and plotted our course for the African continent.

On the 4th of May *Sherman* crossed the equator heading south. In recognition of the equatorial crossing King Neptune visited us once again as all "Poly Wogs" became "Shellbacks." Like all line crossing ceremonies *Sherman* shut down for a day to conduct the ceremony. After stops in Victoria, Seychelles, and Port Louis, Mauritius we steamed for Madagascar.

We arrived on the 18th of May in the northern port town of Antsiranana, Madagascar, known as Diego Suarez prior to 1975. Madagascar was the 4th poorest country in the world at that time and it looked it! The people were fabulous but the infrastructure was a total mess. Part of our visit was to provide humanitarian supplies, mostly medical, to the local community. We didn't have much but every little bit helps.

The people of Antsiranana had not welcomed a United States ship since 1984 when a Navy vessel deployed there to provide aid after a cyclone. The first day I walked around with a few of the chiefs and we ended up in the city center which looked like a war zone. I commented to my buddy QMC Rob Eagleton that, "It looks like someone shelled this joint," And Rob replied, "Yeah, too many incoming rounds!" We laughed but it was sad. The people were so nice but had nothing. They obviously didn't even have basic garbage service because everyone just dumped it in any vacant space they could find. Goats and chickens roamed around the streets. All I knew was that I wasn't eating or drinking anything here…except beer.

On the first evening we held a reception for the local dignitaries on our flight deck. It was a nice event and I had the opportunity to meet a few young American girls who were there as Peace Corps volunteers. They were so excited to see Americans! As we talked and got to know each other they had a strange request, they wanted to take a shower and use the toilet. They told me that they had been there for six months and had not taken a hot shower or used a proper toilet since they had arrived! They said they were stationed out in the rural area of town and it was rough. Just from seeing how bad the town was from my walk earlier in the day I couldn't imagine it being any worse! I graciously provided them with my stateroom and told them to take their time. About an hour later they came out looking very refreshed and thanked me!

On the 20th Captain Ryan and I were invited to brunch at the Venilla restaurant by the General of the Brigade Raharijaona, Joseph Marie. The United States Ambassador to Madagascar, Shirley Elizabeth Barnes, would also be attending. The captain and I arrived at the Venilla, which was in the area Rob and I had visited earlier. I couldn't imagine how this place was going to look on the inside. I was pleasantly surprised. As we entered, the general and his staff were there and we exchanged courtesies. There was a language barrier so we did a lot of smiling back and forth.

Our hosts were very gracious and made us feel right at ease. There was a large table set in the sort of open air restaurant. The ambassador arrived and we were seated. The food was brought out and it consisted of a plate of mixed cold cuts! I was thinking, where in the hell did they get cold cuts and how have they been keeping them cold?

I was starting to get worried because I didn't want to eat, and I knew this would offend my hosts. This plate of cold cuts could probably feed a family of six for a week here. The captain was sitting next to me and said, "Spuds, you're not eating?" I took his comment to mean, "Spuds eat because you're offending our hosts!" Of course the old man had never seen a plate of food he didn't like and was busy plowing through his as was the ambassador.

I was thinking, how bad is the case of worms I am going to get from this going to be? One of our hosts sitting next to me asked if my meal was suitable in broken English and I said, "Yes, but I'm not a big meat eater." I made it a point to eat the greens and pickled vegetables so it seemed like I was eating something. I'm sure when my plate of uneaten cold cuts made it back to the kitchen it didn't go to waste. In the end, I lived to tell the tale!

We set sail on the 21st of May and headed for Cape Town, South Africa. The trip started to get nasty on the 26th of May as we ran into rough seas. As we neared Cape Town on the 27th of May we received a distress call from the 500 foot car carrier *Modern Drive*. She was in fear of running aground off of East London, South Africa near the Cape of Good Hope.

Modern Drive was huge, with a capacity for carrying up to 4500 cars. She was sailing from Freemantle, Australia to Brazil when she went adrift in 30 foot seas with 35 knot winds and an air temperature of about 50 degrees. Apparently, several of the 2000 cars she was carrying broke loose during the rough weather and crashed spilling gas. The gas ignited and caught the ship on fire. The crew activated the installed firefighting system which extinguished the fire. However, smoke had been sucked into the engine room ventilation system which led the crew to believe they had an engine room fire. Before they realized their mistake, they activated the installed engine room firefighting system which also disabled their main engines.

Sherman arrived on scene and stood by the *Modern Drive* in miserable weather until daybreak when we could at least see what we were doing. The *Modern Drive* was about three miles from land and we could see the shore line and buildings of East London. We decided to get a tow line over to her hoping to at least hold her in place until a sea tug could come out and get her. She was about 10 times our size, so holding her was going to be about as big of a challenge as getting a tow rope to her. As we took heavy rolls we managed to get the small boat into the water and the boarding team arrived alongside her. They would assess the damage on *Modern Drive* and assist with the tow rope hook up. She was listing pretty heavily, about 20 degrees, to her starboard side and the *Modern Drive* crew had put down a rope ladder for our boarding team to scale.

It was about a good 60-80 foot climb for the boarding team; consisting of LT Strickland, CWO Bellairs, and BM2 Alberici. Watching from *Sher-*

man's deck I could see them struggling to make progress up the ladder. With the winds blowing them around, wearing cold weather gear, and the weight of their equipment, they would go about 10 or 15 feet and have to stop and rest, just dangling there. Eventually they made it and the next step was getting the huge eight inch thick tow line over to them.

Sherman maneuvered as close as possible in the rough sea state to pass the tow line messenger, which is a smaller line used to haul the bigger eight inch line over. When we swung around to pass the tow we were only about 50 yards from the *Modern Drive* and she towered over us. The gunner's mate fired over the messenger which is shot out of a rifle. We were able to get the tow line set up and keep her stable as we waited for a local sea tug to arrive and take over. After about 30 hours of keeping the *Modern Drive* stable, and away from shore, the sea tug *Pentow Salvor* arrived on scene to relieve us of the tow. We were now free to head into to Cape Town for our port call a day late on the 29th of May.

Cape Town was a great port call and probably my favorite stop on the trip. One of the highlights for me was taking a tour of the Bergkelder Winery, a famous South African winery located in the historic town of Stellenbosch. Another highlight was visiting the local South African Navy who invited us to their base at Simons Town, just south of Cape Town, for a tour. Of course after the tour we ended up at the various junior and senior enlisted clubs for drinks and plenty of sea stories!

**South African senior enlisted with HSC Liz Beck and me at
Simons Town Naval Base, South Africa**

After Cape Town we headed up the west coast of Africa and crossed the
equator at the Prime Meridian. King Neptune granted us the status of
Emerald Shellback, the rarest of the Shellbacks because of its odd location. It's tucked up on the west coast of West Africa near the countries of
Nigeria and Ghana.

Next it was on to the island country of Cape Verde and the port city of
St. Vicente, just off the west coast of Africa. Then it was across the Atlantic for stops in Barbados, West Indies and Aruba, Dutch Antilles.

While in Aruba I took the time to initiate several prospective chiefs who
had been promoted during the trip. I knew once we got back to Alameda
everyone would be going on leave or departing, so I needed to do it before we reached homeport. We rented out the conference room of a local
hotel and conducted the ceremony. A 378 class cutter can actually put on
a great initiation. Not only did we have the chief's mess but all the warrant officers and several of the commissioned officers had been initiated
chiefs. Captain Ryan, who always supported the chief's mess, would also
be attending along with CWO Paul Sepp who would be the judge. CWO
Sepp was an initiated SSC, a character, and perfect for the job. While on

the *M/V Georgios* he kept our spirits up with his nonstop humor; even the smugglers hated to see him go!

CWO Sepp was known to tie one on occasionally and he tied one on the night before the initiation. I was up early preparing for the day's festivities and not worried about CWO Sepp until someone mentioned to me that he had been out late. When I went to his stateroom to see if he was ready to head over to the hotel, at about 0800, he was still fast asleep! I got him up and he said he would meet me on the pier. It was a rough morning for him. As he climbed into the van with his coffee he promptly spilled half of it down the front of his dress uniform! We finally made it to the ceremony and he was in rare form, half hung over and half awake. It all made that initiation one of the more memorable ones I have attended!

Next it was on to transiting the Panama Canal. We arrived at the entrance to the canal at 0600 on the morning of the 2nd of July. We waited our turn and then were directed to enter the first lock. The Panama Canal is a series of locks and as we were transiting from the Caribbean Sea to the Pacific Ocean we needed to go up in elevation, and this was accomplished via the locks. Although it would take us about 20 hours to transit the canal, the alternative was to sail all the way around the southern tip of South America, which would add weeks to our trip.

We were towed through the locks by locomotive engines on a rail system. We hooked up to locomotive PCC #57 and started our journey through the first set of locks known as the Miraflores Locks. At 0110 the morning of the 3rd of July *Sherman* sailed out of the Gatun Locks, the final locks on the Panama Canal, and into the Pacific Ocean. In transiting the Panama Canal we earned the "Order of the Ditch" certificate, another nautical milestone.

As *Sherman* headed northwest off the west coast of Central America on the 3rd of July the lookout spotted black smoke on the horizon. We quickly moved in that direction to investigate. When we arrived on scene we found the Costa Rican *M/V Ingrid* adrift. They had lit blankets on fire to get our attention. She had been adrift for 10 days after losing power and had been at sea a total of 20 days. Her crew had been surviving on fish and what little water they had brought with them when they had set sail.

She was a small 70 foot white and blue fishing vessel and was weighed down with nets and fishing buoys. We provided the crew with food and water and took her in tow and headed for Costa Rica. Ironically, the Costa Rican Coast Guard came out to retrieve the tow on the 4th of July in an old U.S. Coast Guard 82 foot patrol boat we had given them. She was in great shape with a new paint scheme and they had renamed her *Santa Maria (82-2)*.

With the tow completed it was on to one more stop in San Diego. And finally on the 13th of July 2001 we arrived back in Alameda after circumnavigating the globe and traveling over 38,000 miles. This feat would earn us the prized, "Order of Magellan" from King Neptune! There was no initiation because there was no one aboard who held the designation to conduct the ceremony it was so rare. *Sherman* was the first Coast Guard cutter to accomplish the feat since the *USCGC Eastwind (WAGB-279)* accomplished it back in 1960-61.

As we passed under the Golden Gate Bridge that foggy morning I stood out on the starboard weather deck by the MSB small boat. I knew that this would probably be the last time I would see these wonderful sights; looking up at the Golden Gate Bridge as we passed under her, the skyline of San Francisco, and Alcatraz Island. I also had the feeling that this would be my last time underway. Of course I would be wrong!

We arrived in Alameda to a warm welcome of friends and family waiting patiently on the pier. It was the biggest crowd I had seen there waiting for us after a patrol.

MKC John Young and me at our homecoming reception

This was it for me on the *Sherman* and this would also end my seagoing relationship with Captain Ryan. After arriving back in Alameda I passed on my responsibilities to MKCS Belcher who was replacing me as the main propulsion chief. I had received orders to Boston and would leave in a few weeks.

NAVAL ENGINEERING SUPPORT UNIT

BOSTON, MASSACHUSETTS

05 August 2001 – 05 June 2003

I reported into Naval Engineering Support Unit (NESU) Boston in August of 2001 after a lot of negotiating. My detailer had wanted to send me to the *USCGC Polar Star (WAGB-10)* which is an ice breaker out of Seattle. I had actually wanted to go to the Maintenance Logistics Command (MLC) in Norfolk, Virginia but the MKCM coming off the *Polar Star* had a higher transfer priority. He took the billet at MLC in Norfolk, kind of like when I bumped the other MK1 back at SCCB, which left me headed straight for the *Polar Star*! But after the *Sherman* I needed a break, and getting underway for 6 to 12 months to the polar caps wasn't going to cut it for me, I was burnt out. It was a last minute vacancy that landed me happily in Boston.

The MKCM that came off the *Polar Star* and bumped me from MLC was a great guy named Kevin Winter. He would later become a very good friend as his job at MLC, and mine at NESU, had us often working together. Sadly he would retire and suddenly "cross the bar" from the effects of cancer in 2011.

Just after arriving at NESU I was sent to attend a week long course at the Coast Guard Base in Portsmouth, Virginia on the duties of being a port engineer. I was attending the course with a shipmate of mine, who was a chief warrant officer, and a new arrival like me. He was a gruff sort of a guy from New England, a chummy I do believe, and he always looked like he was going to take a bite out of someone's ass!

September 11th fell on the second day of our course and we were pretty much stranded there in Virginia. We were told to stay put and not to try get back to our unit in Boston until they figured out what was going on. With pretty much all modes of transportation shut down we really didn't have a choice. So we continued on with our course and monitored events closely just like everyone else.

A few days later the CWO and I were riding into the base from our hotel rooms and we were talking about the recent tragic events. He had never talked about anything personal to me before, but the attacks of September 11th had dredged up memories of a dark event for him, and he started to relay a story to me about when he was an MKC aboard a 110 foot patrol boat.

On July 17th, 1996 his 110 foot patrol boat with a small crew of 16 were scrambled to get underway. They were directed to conduct search and rescue efforts on the downed TWA flight 800, which had exploded in midair above the Atlantic Ocean off the coast of Moriches, New York. As the MKC he was the senior enlisted aboard and much older than the two officers in command. As they arrived on scene he said they just kept pulling body after body out of the water. When their cutter couldn't hold any more bodies they would transfer them to another vessel to take them ashore, and then they stayed on scene picking up more bodies.

He said it was very surreal because most of the people looked like there was nothing wrong with them, as if you could have just shaken them and they would have woken up. Some had a reddish tint to their skin, some were in pieces, and sometimes there was only an arm or a leg. This went on for several days, pulling whole bodies and parts of bodies out of the water. The young crew began to break down emotionally. The CWO explained that he was having a tough time of it as well, but he had to keep it together for the crew because he was the chief.

The crew had emotionally had enough and things came to a head on the aft part of the cutter, where they had been staging the bodies. The crew was shutting down and the chief, who was stressed himself, lost it. The crew seemed fixated on a finger lying on the deck near the edge of the cutter and the chief stormed over and kicked the finger into the water and yelling at them, "Snap out of it and get back to work!" It was a rash and unthoughtful action, but it worked! The crew refocused on their job and they all got through it together. Although his actions got his crew back to work, the CWO confessed to me that he will always feel the deepest remorse for kicking the finger into the ocean.

My primary duty at NESU was the port engineer for the small aids to navigation boats in the New England area, from Maine to New Jersey. These boats ranged in size from 49 to 65 feet and worked the navigational aids such as buoys and markers on rivers, lakes, and the Atlantic Ocean. I made sure their major maintenance and haul outs were set up and arranged.

Hauling these boats out of the water for maintenance was a major evolution and took the vessel out of commission for several weeks. I would work very closely with MKCM Kevin Winter at MLC during these projects because he managed the all-important money! Kevin would always meet me at the boat's home port for budgeting and scheduling meetings leading up to the haul out. And we would spend a few days going over everything with the crew.

Kevin was a model master chief and didn't cut corners. His appearance and uniform were always squared away, complete with shined boots. He looked like a master chief, with a high and tight haircut and a chiseled face. When Kevin was walking toward you, you knew he was somebody important just by the way he looked and the way he carried himself. I on the other hand rode the line of just staying within regulation. But then, I liked to consider myself a wrench-turning master chief.

Well I had seen this neat master chief belt buckle at the exchange one day. It was brass and had the master chief emblem of a Coast Guard shield, anchor, and two stars on it. I bought it and started to wear it with my uniform. Only a plain brass belt buckle was in regulation and this one with the emblem was intended to be worn with civilian clothes. I didn't care, who was going to tell me to take it off? All the places I visited had at the most a senior chief or very rarely a junior officer. They weren't going to tell me to do anything.

I was at a haul out meeting with Kevin down in New Jersey and he saw my belt buckle. Being the professional Kevin was he didn't say anything until we were alone. Then he said, "Ed you know that belt buckle you're wearing is not in regulation." I said, "I know." That was it, we didn't say anything else. Later that evening I thought about what Kevin had said and the way he had said it. I didn't wear the buckle in uniform again. I had that much respect for him.

Port engineering duties were very independent. I would usually spend a week in the office and the following week I was on the road visiting the cutters under my charge. My units north ran up to Southwest Harbor, Maine, south to Bayonne, New Jersey, and west to Burlington, Vermont and Lake Champlain. I would make a north visit, return to Boston, then make a south visit, and return to Boston. That was the plan, unfortunately it seemed like I was always running from Maine to New Jersey resolving one emergency after another. Office time got shorter and shorter as time went on and it seemed like I was living on the road. I had a lap top computer and a cell phone so my office was always "with" me in any case. If the CO needed me he would call and redirect me to where he wanted me to go.

The units I managed were for the most part out in the middle of nowhere in some small fishing town, and it took time to get to them. Even though I was based about midway between my northern and southern most units it always seemed that when I was at one end, I needed to be at the other. My assets ranged from 1960s vintage 65' WYTL tug boats to newer 49' BUSL buoy tending boats.

The other MKCM in the office was Frank Tatu. He was an older and highly respected man, and I think he made master chief around the time I came into the service! Frank reminded me of Popeye and he sort of resembled him. He definitely had the strength of Popeye and was an unbeaten arm wrestler. It was always fun to see him take down the young officers in the office who were half his age. They looked at Frank and thought "easy pickings!" Oh the look on their face when Frank would take them without breaking a sweat!

Frank managed the fleet of 41' and 44' utility and surf boats. They were the backbone of the search and rescue boats at the Coast Guard's small boat stations. We worked really well together and if needed we would handle issues for each other. This worked out well. If I knew Frank was up north and I had a problem I would call him, and he could look into the matter for me, and I did the same for him.

The drive up north through Massachusetts, New Hampshire, and Maine was always beautiful. My northern most unit in Southwest Harbor, Maine was in the Acadia National Park and was worth the drive. It was nice to be able to see the port towns of Bath, Portland, and Rockland by land instead of by sea for a change. But the weather up in that area was always unpredictable. There was one time on my way back from Southwest Harbor when I stopped for the night in a small town before reaching Rockland. The evening was nice and clear. When I woke up the next morning I was snowed in!

My southern units went all the way down to Bayonne, New Jersey. I had several 49' BUSLs and two 65' WYTLs at the Coast Guard Base in Bayonne, which was out on a peninsula that looked right out onto the Statue of Liberty and the New York City skyline. I also had several shipyards that did a lot of work for me in Brooklyn and Staten Island. One of the shipyards in Brooklyn did a lot of work for me, so I spent a lot of time there. The shipyard was family run, small, and you really got to know the management and workers. These guys were good people and I never worried about the quality of work they produced.

When a 65' WYTL was taken there for its four to six week haul out, the boat's crew of about eight settled right in with the workers in the boat yard. Crews always took the opportunity to do their own maintenance on their boat while it was in dry-dock and worked alongside the yard workers. The workers at this particular shipyard were a bit eccentric and consisted of a few Jamaicans. These guys raised a little garden in the back part of the shipyard and seemed to always be keeping the Coast Guard guys entertained with their island stories. This was Brooklyn and it was rough around the edges but all in all a good place for getting a boat worked on.

So I spent a lot of time down in this area transiting in and out of the greater New York City area. These shipyards not only did a lot of the scheduled haul out work for me but they also handled emergencies.

A typical emergency would be like with the *CGC Bollard (WYTL 65614)* which was home ported out of New Haven, Connecticut. I received a call from the boat's CO one day telling me they had a huge vibration coming from their propeller or propeller shaft. This could be caused by something being wrapped around the propeller or shaft, or maybe they hit something and bent the shaft or propeller. Either way it needed fixed. I made arrangements to have her hauled out at the closest shipyard that could handle her over in Staten Island. I dropped what I was doing and drove down to the shipyard to meet her arrival. When she arrived we hauled her out, made the repairs, and sent her back on her way. I then went back to what I was doing.

**Hauling out the 65' *USCGC BOLLARD (WYTL-65614)*
home ported in New Haven, Connecticut**

That's about how my schedule played out. With all the operational assets I was managing there was a guaranteed casualty at least once a month. They didn't stop in the winter either. The 65' WYTLs broke ice on the Hudson River and many inlets, so they worked year round.

On another interesting venture I was tasked to go down to the Coast Guard Academy in New London, Connecticut and inspect four 65' WYTLs that they had down there for teaching seamanship and navigational skills. I had been sent down to the Massachusetts Maritime Academy a few months earlier to look at their 65 footer, so I guess that made me an expert on academy boats. The problem with these boats was that they were not maintained or centrally funded by the MLC or NESU. Therefore, they were considered non-standard and basically received little maintenance or upgrades over their life span. My sole purpose for inspecting them was to determine how far out of standardization they were. And they were way out of standardization! They would need huge amounts of money to bring them up to speed. In both cases the money was never allocated and the vessels stayed in their original 1960s vintage state.

One of my more unusual assignments in August of 2002 was to inspect a piece of equipment for NESU Seattle which was located all the way across the country in Seattle, Washington. They had a sea strainer off of a 378 class cutter being repaired at a facility in New Jersey. Apparently it was critical to get this thing inspected and flown back to NESU Seattle so the 378 could get back into an operational status. I was diverted from my northern operating area and drove 500 miles south to inspect the strainer and get it shipped out. I was later told by my CO that getting that strainer inspected quickly saved the Coast Guard over $700 thousand dollars!

The NESU was commanded by Commander Bill Krewsky who was a great down-to-earth guy. He was cut out of the same cloth as Captain Ryan. They were sensible men who looked out for their people, worked hard, and played hard. Most importantly they seemed like they could care less about promoting. I say this meaning that their decisions always seemed Coast Guard driven and not personally or politically driven.

After September 11th the Coast Guard was moved from the Department of the Transportation, where it had been since 1967, to the newly formed Department of Homeland Security. During this shift in departments it was determined that there was a need to increase the Coast Guard's work force significantly, especially its officer corps. The fastest way to do this was through various officer accession programs that drew from the Coast Guard and the other services' officer and enlisted ranks. Basically the Coast Guard solicited people who held degrees and offered them a commission. Since the entry level junior officer makes roughly the same amount of money as the most senior enlisted man, and the most junior officer outranks the most senior enlisted man, this was very appealing.

I was beginning to feel like I was topped out as a master chief. Most of the jobs were white collar, and out of the 33 job openings only a few interested me. Just getting this job at NESU was tough. And I knew when it was time for me to transfer it would be just as tough to find another good job. There were always the two ice breakers in play, no one wanted to go to them. Most of the problem was the fact that there were only four or five master chiefs in my rating moving around every year. So there were only four or five job openings to choose from. Slim pickings!

With that in mind I decided to give the direct commission officer (DCO) accessions program a look. Since I had my Bachelor's Degree, and was just below the age cutoff, I qualified for the program as a direct commission engineer. I had received my Associate's Degree while on the *Sherman* and my Bachelor's Degree while there at NESU. I completed my degrees by taking college level examination program (CLEP) tests on land and at sea.

When I first started my Associate's Degree at the ELC in Baltimore they didn't offer CLEP exams, so I had to drive down to Coast Guard Headquarters in Washington, DC about an hour away and take them there. Later I found out that they offered them at Fort George Meade Army base, about 20 minutes away, and I took them there. On the *Sherman* I took them whenever we pulled into a Coast Guard or Navy base that offered them, including Bahrain in the Persian Gulf. I finally completed my Bachelor's degree by taking seven upper level CLEPs there at NESU.

I had known several warrant officers who had gone from warrant officer to lieutenant over my career and it was a very impressive accomplishment. As I looked more and more into it, CDR Krewsky and the other officers at NESU really encouraged and supported me and I decided to apply. I got the impression that a few of the master chiefs in the Coast Guard were not happy with me, a master chief, converting to a junior officer.

By law there can only be 1% of the total workforce promoted to master chief petty officer, the highest enlisted rank. So with about 30,000 active duty members there could only be 300 master chiefs. The rank is highly coveted. In my own rating machinery technician, which was one of the biggest in the Coast Guard, there were only 33 master chiefs. The scuttlebutt with the other master chiefs was that I was selling out the rank of master chief. I'm sure I wasn't the first guy to shift from master chief to an officer, but I knew it was rarely done. Maybe it wouldn't have been such a big deal if I was being offered a commission as a lieutenant (LT). But I wasn't. I was being offered a commission as a lieutenant junior grade (LTJG). There is a big difference between a LTJG and LT, even though they are just one pay grade apart. To shift over to LT from master chief would be a lot more respectable then to a lowly LTJG.

I debated this with headquarters and their reasoning concerned future promotion potential, or in their view lack of potential. They were finding that lieutenants that are brought over through direct commission were having a tough time when it came to promoting to the next pay-grade of lieutenant commander due to a lack of an officer evaluation report (OER) history. As an officer you are promoted by a board that reviews your OERs and personnel record against your peers. They felt that if they were to start bringing people over as LTJGs they would have a better OER history and could promote with their peers more easily. Hey it made sense to me. My own experience over the years had shown me that few warrant officers to lieutenant made lieutenant commander.

I accepted the commission as a LTJG and took my oath of office given by CDR Krewsky on the 10th of March 2003 there at NESU. Just after being promoted I was sent down to the Coast Guard Academy in New London Connecticut on the 16th of March for three weeks to attend Direct Commission Officer School, better known as "knife and fork school." The curriculum was based around learning how to become an officer and a gentleman, complete with etiquette training.

I was berthed in Munro Hall, a relatively new building, which housed personnel attending direct commission and the chief's academy course. The accommodations were nice, with two man rooms with an attached head. Meals were taken at the permanent party galley in Chase Hall where the academy staff and chief's academy students also dined. It was a huge building and part of it was also used by the cadets. Our galley looked out onto an enclosed courtyard. The courtyard was used by the cadets to march off demerits they had received for sub-standard performance. To work off the demerits they "marched them off." As I ate my meal in the comfort of the warm galley I watched them solemnly "march off" demerits around the square courtyard in their dress uniform, most likely wishing they were someplace else. It was a daily reminder of where I was at.

If you remember I also stayed in berthing named Munro Hall while in boot camp at Cape May, New Jersey. The name Munro is well known in the Coast Guard and there are numerous buildings, awards, and even a cutter named for the man. This is because Douglas Albert Munro is the only Coast Guard member ever to receive the Medal of Honor, our nation's highest military award. Signalman First Class Munro lost his life in the battle of Guadalcanal during WWII. On the 27th of September 1942 Munro was the officer-in-charge of a group of landing craft assigned to retrieve marines from a beach. The marines were being attacked by an overwhelming enemy force. Seeing that the last group of marines trying to get off the beach was in extreme danger, Munro placed his landing craft between those marines and the enemy so they could be safely evacuated. He took this action knowing he was putting himself at great risk. He was fatally wounded. It is reported that Munro's last words were, "Did they get off?" That is why the name Munro is revered in the United States Coast Guard. His actions epitomize what the Coast Guard stands for as a lifesaving service.

Since Munro Hall was also being used for berthing the chief's academy students it provided the opportunity for me to run into an old shipmate, Mike Bogue. He was the fireman who almost had his fingers severed back on *Seneca*. He had made damage controlman chief and was attending the chief's academy. It was nice to run into him and share a few sea stories!

The Coast Guard Academy is a huge 103 acre facility with 26 buildings dating back to 1931 and set alongside the Thames River. It has over 1000 students enrolled in its four year degree program and graduates about 200 ensigns, the lowest ranking officer, into the Coast Guard each year.

The campus was in session when I was there and the place was bustling with activity. It was interesting to see the cadets go through their daily routines and it brought back memories of when I sailed on *Eagle*. Their behavior was the same as I remembered; with the under classmen smoking and showing a bit of rebellion and the upper classmen settling into their military curriculum and taking ownership of their responsibilities.

My classes were held at Yeaton Hall and made up of a small group of eclectic guys totaling about 15. They consisted of U.S. Army cobra helicopter pilots, U.S. Navy pilots, and Coast Guard electronics and engineering guys like me.

Basic Officer Training class aboard *USCGC EAGLE*

The Army pilots had all been recruited by the Coast Guard while they were still in the Army and were basically lateralling over. They said they had become tired of the constant training and few opportunities to fly meaningful sorties in Army helicopters. They were warrant officers in the Army and now Coast Guard commissioned officers, not a huge increase in pay but enormous promotion potential.

The Navy pilots lateralling over had also been recruited while still on active duty. These guys had also become dissatisfied with the constant training and lack of meaningful sorties just like the Army guys. But in the case of these Navy guys they were taking a pay cut of around $800 a month to come over! They had been LCDRs and would now be LTs. It didn't matter to them, they loved the new opportunity.

We had a free weekend in the middle of our two week class and I invited three of the Army pilots to come up and tour Boston. They would crash at my apartment, which was right in the middle of downtown next to the famous old North Church. It was a great time seeing the city and closing the bars in Faneuil Hall. Most of us had made sacrifices to get here and it was nice to spend time socializing and talking about our personal decisions to take commissions. On the 4th of April we graduated and went on our separate ways. Unfortunately, I never crossed paths with any of my classmates again.

I knew making the transition from master chief to lieutenant junior grade was going to bring me some humiliation. But it hit me a little faster and harder than I anticipated. The week before my commission date I went over to the base parking and ID center to get a new parking pass, as mine had expired. I walked straight up to the third class petty officer working the desk and he was more than happy to drop what he was doing and help out the master chief. He was very accommodating and solicitously asked if there was anything else he could do for me.

Three days later I had my new LTJG bars on and walked up to get my new ID card from the same office I received my parking pass. I walked up to the desk and the same third class petty officer gave me a quick look and asked me to have a seat, he would be right with me. When he was finished with what he was doing he asked me what I needed. I told him I needed a new ID card. His reply was, "Sorry sir we only do those on Tuesdays and Thursdays." My reply was, "Okay, I'll be back on Tuesday." As I turned to leave the petty officer asked, "Sir, this may sound weird, but weren't you a master chief last week?" I replied, "Yes but I took a commission and was promoted today." The young Petty Officer said, "I'm sorry master chief, I mean sir, I can get your ID card for you today." And that's about how it would be for the next four years!

One of the neat things about being an officer is that I now had the authority to re-enlist folks. Before leaving NESU Boston one of the junior enlisted on the 65' WYTL home ported there asked if I would re-enlist him. It would be my one and only re-enlistment and I did it right there on the cutter as they were moored up in Boston.

I finished out my tour at NESU as an officer, and then reported to my new assignment aboard the *USCGC Dependable (WMEC-626)* home ported out of Cape May, New Jersey.

USCGC DEPENDABLE (WMEC-626)

CAPE MAY, NEW JERSEY

5 June 2003 – 01 June 2005

USCGC DEPENDABLE (WMEC-626)
Port call Boston, Massachusetts

I arrived aboard *Dependable* on the 5th of June 2003. She was conducting a normal two month D1 patrol of the Atlantic Ocean and had pulled into Boston on a port call.

The *Dependable*, a 210 foot medium endurance cutter, was commissioned in 1968 and home ported in Cape May, New Jersey. She was the 12th in the "Reliance" class of cutters and had a crew of 75, 12 officers and 63 enlisted personnel. It was an all-male crew with the exception of two female junior officers.

I was also now a junior officer and assigned a berthing space forward and below the main deck. I shared it with another officer and the room had its own shower, toilet, and sink. The berthing accommodations were some of the best aboard. Only the captain, executive officer, engineering officer, and operations officer had their own staterooms. The eight chiefs slept in two separate four man staterooms and shared a head with two sinks, toilets, and showers. The enlisted were grouped into 10-12 man berthing areas with attached heads containing several sinks, toilets and showers.

The CO, Commander Mike Christian, ran a fast paced operating tempo. I had never been on a cutter which conducted more boardings, migrant interdictions, and drug busts. As you read the patrol summaries which follow you'll see this cutter meant business! And this was only a 210 foot medium endurance cutter, the smallest law enforcement cutter I had served on.

CDR Christian respected me for the rank I once held, something he didn't have to do. Over my two year tour he would interact with me more as an experienced senior enlisted man rather than a junior officer. I appreciated that. He noticed that the shift from senior enlisted to junior officer was tough for me. A true mentor, his guidance helped me get through my first tour as an officer.

My primary duty was as an engineering officer in training (EOIT), but I would assume the duties of the damage control assistant (DCA), and electrical and damage control division officer. As I finished my qualifications I would assume other collateral duties such as civil rights officer and voting officer. It was a small crew and everyone had to take on extra duties.

One of the other collateral duties I would be assigned from time to time was that of the investigating officer for individuals brought up on UCMJ charges. The process would start with an individual having a form CG4910 written up on them formally charging them with an offense. The slang term for this was "booking" someone. The XO would receive the CG4910 and assign an investigating officer to ascertain the facts and to see if the charges and facts met the requirements for an offense per the UCMJ manual. If they did, the matter was taken to mast. If not, the matter was dropped or handled with a verbal or written reprimand.

There were two incidents that were sort of typical of the charges brought up to mast here on *Dependable*; drugs and alcohol. I was assigned the perfecta of what started out as an alcohol incident and turned into an alcohol and drug incident.

A young seaman from *Dependable* was driving through the front gate at Cape May Training Center, where *Dependable* was moored. He was maneuvering his vehicle around the jersey barriers leading up to the gate when he ran into one. The civilian officer at the gate walked up to the seaman's vehicle to investigate and found the seaman to be drunk. He was taken to the police station on base and given a breath test which he failed. He was brought up on charges, which were forwarded to the *Dependable*, and his car was impounded.

The XO assigned me as the investigating officer. The case seemed pretty cut and dry. I called up to the warrant officer in charge of the base police detachment and he said he would compile the paper work on the incident involving the seaman for me. He called me the next day and asked me if I wouldn't mind coming up to his office, he had something to show me. I arrived at the police station and the warrant officer handed me his file folder and a stack of pictures. He said, "We arrested him for DUI but you may be interested in these pictures we found in the vehicle's glove box." As I shuffled through the pictures they were all of the seaman and other people smoking pot, or some sort of drug, out of a makeshift pipe. Needless to say the case went to mast and the seaman was found guilty of drug use and discharged from the service.

It got me thinking back to a time about 19 or so years earlier. On this same base I was caught on a urinalysis drug test and charged with the use of marijuana. My punishment then was working on base until I cleared my drug tests. After that I was sent on to the *Sumac*. Oh how the times had changed. I appreciate that the Coast Guard had taken the time and made the effort allowing me a second chance. I would like to think they got a good return on their investment.

I was later assigned the case of another seaman involved in an alcohol incident. This one demonstrates the double jeopardy members face in the military judicial system that is not allowed in the civilian system. In this case, a seaman was on leave driving a vehicle with several of his civilian friends as passengers. The group drove by a policeman who had another vehicle pulled over. As they drove by, one of the seaman's friends yelled out the window something to the effect of, "Fuck you pig!" The police officer got into his cruiser and pursued the seaman's vehicle, pulling him over. The seaman was given a breathalyzer test, which he failed. He was arrested and once the police discovered the seaman was in the service our command was notified. I was the investigating officer and I called the police officer who arrested the seaman and he informed me that the local police were going to press charges. I relayed this to the command, hoping we would drop our investigation. The command directed me to file a CG4910 on him and if my investigation turned up enough evidence to charge him, we would take him to mast.

The seaman was found guilty in the civilian court and had to pay fines. I found his actions in violation of the UCMJ and he was taken to mast where he was found guilty, received 30 days confinement, 30 days extra duty, and 30 days loss of pay from the Coast Guard! The 5th Amendment to the United States Constitution, which addresses being punished twice for the same crime, only applies to judicial criminal proceedings. The military loop hole is that all the punishment handed down at captains mast is deemed non-judicial under the UCMJ. This punishment can be handed down legally in conjunction with a civil conviction or a military judicial court martial.

Another interesting incident worth mentioning occurred when I was making rounds of the vessel with Captain Christian while underway. One evening after the nightly department head evening report was given to the CO at 1900, he asked me to accompany him on a round of the cutter. We were underway so all the main hatches leading below the main decks were secured and we had to open the small scuttles to transit into the lower spaces. Everything was going fine until we started to head toward engineering berthing, and I got a sudden feeling of dread in the pit of my stomach.

I just remembered that the engineers were planning a sombrero party for one of the guys leaving and I knew it was against regulations. I know my story is starting to sound like an episode of McHale's Navy and I'm LCDR McHale, but the crew had to have ways of blowing off steam while underway and this was truly a harmless tradition. The Coast Guard at the time was going through a hazing witch hunt and just slapping someone on the back to say welcome aboard was deemed a hazing infraction!

A sombrero party was a simple going away event in which a member transferring off the cutter was tied down, covered with shaving cream, and had a sombrero placed on his head. A picture was always taken and given to the departing member as a souvenir from his shipmates.

As the CO spun the handle on the scuttle to enter the engineering berthing space below I was getting nervous. As soon as the CO climbed down through the small opening I hurried down the ladder behind him and shouted attention on deck to try and warn the unaware engineers of the pending danger.

It didn't work, and the CO came face to face with an engineer lying on the deck, wire tied to a table, covered in shaving cream, and wearing a sombrero!

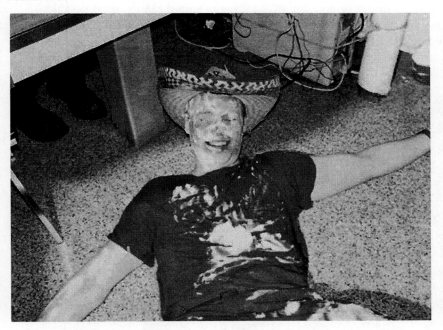

Sombrero going away party

If I were to say that the CO was pissed that would be an understatement! He wanted heads to roll and the usual engineering suspects, consisting of two of my electricians, EM3 John "Hank" Dudley and EM3 Matt "Juice" Lesniak, were brought up on hazing charges and taken to mast. They asked me to act as their defense council at mast and the investigating officer duties were handed off to another junior officer. With a lot of fast talking, and pleading for compassion, I managed to get their charges reduced and they were placed on probation.

Getting back to my normal duties; as the DCA I was responsible for the overall firefighting, damage control, fueling, training, and stability of the cutter. To learn my trade I was sent to the Navy's damage control assistant (DCA) School in Newport, Rhode Island from the 5th of January 2004 to the 19th of February 2004. DCA School reinforced what I had already experienced over the years being assigned to repair parties and firefighting teams on previous cutters.

During a casualty at sea which sent us to general quarters (GQ) such as a fire, collision, flooding, or attack, I manned and ran the total casualty response from a location known as damage control central (DCC). This location was in the aft part of the cutter, but if it was compromised I had various fall back points containing all the ship's diagrams and communication systems I needed to direct a response.

**Damage Control Central with my sound powered
phone talkers EM3 Dudley and OS3 Bevilacqua**

In DCC I had a diagram of every system on the cutter along with a communications system comprised of two sound powered phone talkers. You can see the sound powered devices around the necks of my two phone talkers in the photo above. Basically, the devices worked like tin cans and a string - they needed no electronics to work. My phone talkers were in contact with the various repair lockers and the captain on the bridge.

Through these phone talkers I received information on the casualty and was able to disseminate a plan of action.

Let's say we had a fire. General quarters would be sounded and everyone would man their GQ billets. Once I received the manned and ready from my repair lockers I would order the nearest repair locker to the fire to set the required fire boundaries, provide routes for the fire team to get to the fire, and identify any problems that may arise because of the location of the fire. Don't forget we were a military vessel and carry lots of ammo! As the repair locker set boundaries and fought the fire they would report back to me on their progress every step of the way. If the sound powered phone circuit would go out, written messages would be used via human runners. Redundancy was built in to everything we did.

Like every other cutter I had served on we trained in damage control several times a week in port and underway. At least one day a week was dedicated to all hands drills. Every evening the duty section trained in damage control.

While underway it was my daily responsibility to calculated all the liquid loads and weights above the main deck and provided the captain with the stability curve for the cutter at the 1900 evening report. This curve basically told him what the cutter's maximum degree of roll would be before capsizing. This was obviously very important in rough seas.

As the electrical officer I was in charge of the five man electrical division. They had a real chief, EMC Terry Collins, so I just signed paperwork and represented them at mast!

I would make eight patrols on *Dependable*; three in the North Atlantic and five in the Caribbean Sea. Because I experienced more of the operational tempo aboard *Dependable* then on other cutters I'm going to outline my time a little differently, providing more of a running timeline of events. Here we go!

We slipped our berth from Coast Guard Base Boston at 1700 on the 6th of June and headed back into the Atlantic Ocean. Patrol break was over and it was time to go to work.

On the 9th of June 2003 while on patrol in the Atlantic Ocean, in D1's operational area, we were diverted to the disabled fishing vessel *M/V*

319

Rachel T who was near Cashes Ledge about 90 miles off the coast of Maine. The *M/V Rachel T* had sustained an engine room fire and was disabled at sea. We took her under tow and brought her into Portland, Maine where the tow was transferred to a commercial tug to take her into port.

19th of June, received a search and rescue (SAR) call that a fisherman had fallen overboard from the Canadian fishing vessel *M/V Atlantic leader,* about 50 miles from our location. We came up to a full bell of about 18 knots and headed toward the SAR area located about 150 nautical miles east of Cape Cod. We arrived on scene just as I was getting off of engine room watch at 0330. I stayed awake along with the rest of the crew searching the waters and horizon without luck. The water temperature was about 50 degrees, which would give the missing fisherman about an hour of survival time in the water without a protective suit. We never did find the fisherman.

27th of June, escorted a fishing vessel deemed un-sea worthy into port. The boarding team, while conducting normal fisheries inspections, found the vessel to have numerous fuel and oil leaks in the engine room and no fire suppression equipment aboard. We took the vessel in tow. As we dropped the vessel off in port we received a distress call from another vessel about 30 miles away taking on water. We were in route at best speed, which in the sloppy sea state was about 15-16 knots per hour. We arrived on scene with the disabled vessel two hours later at 1325 and sent our rescue and assistance (R&A) team over. A HH-65 helicopter had dropped the boat a P-1 dewatering pump that helped out with their water issue until we arrived. Our R&A team got the vessel's batteries charged and they were able to start their engine. The *USCGC Sanibel*, a 110' cutter, arrived on scene to assist. We left the fishing vessel with the *Sanibel* and continued on patrol at 1545.

8th of July, one of the female ensigns aboard had her appendix burst. The weather was really bad with a high sea state and driving winds. Her condition had worsened and we didn't know if we would be able to get a helicopter out to our location to medevac her off. The officer's wardroom was readied in case an emergency operation was required. The wardroom is actually designed as a make shift operating room, complete with operating lights and table. Luckily the sea state calmed and a helicopter was able to make it out to us and pick up the ensign. Since we didn't have a doctor on board, only a corpsman, I'm sure the ensign was relieved she didn't have to hang around and have him perform his first ever appendectomy!

9th of July, we were diverted to the 44 foot sail boat *Alegrea* that was about 170 miles south of Nantucket, Massachusetts to assist with a crewmember suffering from severe abdominal pain. While in route to the vessel a Coast Guard helicopter arrived on scene and picked up the sick crewmember and flew him to shore for medical treatment.

16th of July, I was awaken at 0215 for a SAR call 40 miles from our location involving five people who were in the water after their fishing vessel sank. We had been idling around in dense fog for the past several days so the transit to the distressed vessel took longer than normal. We arrived at the last known location of the fishing vessel *M/V Iiha Bravo*, which was 69 miles east of Chatham, Massachusetts. A Coast Guard helicopter had arrived before us and had hoisted the five crewmembers into the helicopter flying them to safety. There was no sign of *M/V Iiha Bravo* when we arrived on scene and she was presumed to have sunk.

We returned to our home port of Cape May on the 28th of July for our scheduled in port period.

On the 13th of September we shoved off for the Caribbean Sea. We would be patrolling off of Honduras. On the 15th we conducted helicopter operations and embarked our helicopter for the patrol. We didn't have a permanently assigned helicopter. Every patrol a different helicopter and crew was assigned to us from a rotating pool.

17th of September, we stopped in Key West, Florida for fuel and stores. We had a fireman who was restricted to the cutter due to punishment he received at mast and he needed to go to the exchange to purchase toiletries. No one wanted to be bothered with him. I was heading that way and said I would escort him. I was always willing to give these young guys the benefit of the doubt; probably because I saw myself in them. Heck, I did just as many stupid things as they did when I first came in the service. If MK1 Smith had not taken the time to interact with me, where would I be now? In my position I felt obligated to try and mentor these guys. Sometimes I got through to them and sometimes I didn't. But at least I tried. The exchange was about a mile walk through the Coast Guard Base and onto the adjacent Navy Base. I struck up a conversation and we chit chatted about general stuff along the way. As we came out of the exchange I walked over to the paper machine to get a paper. When I turned around he was gone! I was thinking; no way! I walked around the corner of the exchange and there he was smoking a cigarette. I guess I should have had a little more faith in the kid.

It reminded me of another story salty Gil Parks had told me. Now this story was from sometime in the 50s or early 60s. He told me that he was detailed to drive a prisoner up to Fort Jay, the Army prison on Governors Island, New York. On the drive up the prisoner said he had to take a leak, so Gil pulled the car over to the side of the road and let the prisoner out to do his business. Gil said he sat there in the driver's seat and lit a cigarette. He looked into his rear view mirror to check on the prisoner, who should have been in the bushes taking a leak. Damn if the guy wasn't about 50 feet from the vehicle and hitch hiking! Before Gil could get out of the vehicle and grab his prisoner, the first car that came along pulled over and picked him up, probably because he was in uniform. Gil tried to wave the car down but the car sped off. Gil hopped back into his vehicle and began to chase them. He caught up to the car and honked and waved until the car with the prisoner pulled over. He eventually got the prisoner back into custody and off he went to Fort Jay!

19th of September, we departed Key West and had just hit the sea buoy when we were given custody of a Cuban migrant who was picked up off of Key West. The local small boat station had intercepted him and we were tasked with transporting him to GITMO. On the 22nd we pulled in to GITMO to disembark the Cuban and take on fuel and stores.

26th of September, I was awakened by the announcement on the intercom system for my roommate, ENS Jack Sauder, to report to the boat deck ASAP! This was around 0500 and with all the noise I decided to get up. I headed up to the wardroom to get a coffee. Scuttlebutt in the wardroom was that we had intercepted a "go-fast" boat. The term "go-fast" is used to describe a drug running speed boat. I pulled back the curtains on the wardroom porthole and there, about 200 yards off the port beam, was this huge Navy frigate with a helicopter hovering around it. I decided to get a better look and took my coffee out to the weather deck. There, about 50 yards in front of *Dependable*, was the go-fast surrounded by our two small boats and one from the Navy frigate. Later that evening as I was coming off of my four hour engine room watch, I stepped out onto the weather deck to get some fresh air. It was dark out, a thunderstorm was brewing on the horizon and you could see the lightning in the distance.

The fantail light was on which is unusual at night because we steam in a darkened ship status to avoid detection.

I walked back toward the light and saw we had prisoners from the go-fast and they were lounging around while being guarded by some members of our crew. As I walked back forward I could see our small boat was alongside of the cutter disembarking passengers. A few people got off and they headed toward me making their way back aft to the fantail. More go-fast prisoners, wow we must have made another bust!

The go-fast is hard to catch. They run at night at high speeds with no lights and during the day they stop and throw a big blue tarp over themselves so you can't see them. They also have what are known as "mother ships" stationed on their drug running route that provide them with fuel. They have quite the logistical set up!

Captured "go-fast" boat running drugs

15th of October, we had pulled into Guatemala for a few hours for fuel and to remove garbage. We were patrolling in the northern part of the Caribbean Sea. Things were slowing down and we were getting ready to pull into GITMO for a patrol break. Early in the morning on the 24th of October we were informed that there was a go-fast operating in our area and we were to intercept it. We launched our helicopter and began the search. The go-fast was spotted by the helicopter and the chase was on. Needing fuel the helicopter returned to the cutter and was quickly redeployed to track the go-fast. As we neared the go-fast our small boats were deployed and we closed in on her with the helicopter in the air and small boats in the water.

As we closed in, the crew of the go-fast started to throw bales of drugs overboard to lighten their load so they could make better speed. Each bale weighed about 75 pounds which was causing a considerable drag on the boat. Eventually the helicopter was running out of fuel and the small boats were slowing to recover the jettisoned bales of drugs. We needed to break off pursuit, recover the helicopter, and relieve the small boats of their cargo. Despite all our efforts the go-fast was able to escape. But we had recovered over a ton and a half of cocaine with an estimated street value of $75 to $100 million dollars!

Recovered cocaine worth an estimated $75 to $100 million dollars

1st of November, we rounded the sea buoy and returned home to our moorings in Cape May for our scheduled in port.

16th of December, we hauled in the brow and set a course out into the Atlantic Ocean on what would only be a seven day patrol for me. The rest of the crew would be at sea for Christmas and New Year's.

20th of December, while conducting fisheries inspections off the coast of Long Island, in D1's operation area, we were dispatched to a SAR case involving a sailing vessel. The weather had gotten really nasty with high winds, 13-15 foot sea state, and 38 degree water. The fishing fleet had huddled together for safety and we had closed in to keep an eye on them. One of the fishing vessels became unsafe and we began to escort it into New York harbor. On the way into New York we received a distress call from the 40 foot wooden sail boat *Gaucho*, which was near our location. I was told the vessel had an interesting history; it was once owned by President Franklin D. Roosevelt.

We diverted from our escort and headed toward the location of the *Gaucho*. Upon arriving at 0200 in the morning we found the *Gaucho* was out of control and floundering in the wild sea state. The story was that there was a crew of two, a husband and wife aboard. The husband had fallen overboard attempting to fix something on deck and the wife, unable to help her husband, became hysterical and fled to the safety of the inside of the boat. A Coast Guard helicopter had beaten us to the scene and had plucked the husband out of the water and was taking him to a hospital ashore. The weather was too rough and the wife too distraught to attempt to remove her from the vessel by helicopter.

As we assessed the situation nothing was working in our favor. Initially we thought that we could wait the weather out and then get a boat in the water and rescue the wife. This idea was soon not viable when the weather and sea state put the boat in jeopardy of sinking. We had to somehow get our small boat in the water and get it over to the floundering sail boat before it sank along with the wife. After getting the cutter in the best leeward position to lower our small boat, we launched our RHI along with a small boarding crew.

It took the RHI and her crew about 30 minutes to get to the *Gaucho* which was only several hundred yards away. Try after try failed to get the RHI alongside and a crewmember aboard. Finally a heroic seaman, SN Benjamin Murphy, coaxed the RHI coxswain to get the RHI close enough for him to make a jumping attempt to get onto the *Gaucho*. As the RHI neared the *Gaucho* SN Murphy leaped aboard. If he had missed,

325

he could have been crushed by the two boats slamming against each other. Once on board he located the wife huddled in the lower cabin and administered her comfort. He then managed to pull two more of our crewmembers on board directly from the RHI to assist him. Together they doused the sail and started the trolling motor, which would got the boat somewhat under control.

Once these tasks were accomplished and the situation stabilized they were able to transfer the wife to the RHI and then to the cutter. The three Coast Guardsmen stayed aboard to hook up the tow rope. The sea state was so bad that they had to stay aboard the *Gaucho* overnight until daylight when the towing attempt would be safer. Once the *Gaucho* was in tow we headed into Long Island, New Jersey.

I had the morning watch the next day and entered the wardroom for breakfast. The sea state was still rough and just walking to the wardroom was a challenge. While having my breakfast the wife from the *Gaucho* walked in and sat down. I started a conversation and we talked about her ordeal. She said she and her husband were taking the *Gaucho* south for the owner when they ran into the bad weather. Her husband had gone topside to take care of some rigging and had fallen over board. She did not know how to sail and could not get the boat to come about to try and pick up her husband. She dispatched the distress call and the Coast Guard helicopter came out and picked her husband out of the icy cold water.

They both were wearing the appropriate cold weather suits and she thought he would be okay once the Coast Guard helicopter picked him up. I reassured her that everything would be fine and we would get her reunited with her husband as soon as possible. She left the wardroom and the XO came in. I asked the XO if he had heard anything concerning the husband and he told me to keep it hush-hush but he had passed away on the helicopter in route to shore.

On the 23rd of December we pulled into the inlet at Sandy Hook, New Jersey and transferred the tow of the *Gaucho* to another Coast Guard cutter. I was getting off the cutter to attend damage control officer school and escorted the wife ashore via a Coast Guard small boat from station Sandy Hook, NJ. By this time the CO had informed her that her husband had passed away, so the boat ride in was very somber. We sat next to each other but I didn't try to make small talk. I just left her to her

326

thoughts. When we arrived I escorted her to the station's mess deck where her family had gathered. It was an emotional meeting as expected. I was relieved to be able to hand her over to the good care of her family.

The patrol was over for me and I headed to Newport, Rhode Island to attend Surface Warfare Officer Damage Control Assistant School until the middle of February. After I graduated on the 19th of February I caught up with *Dependable* back in Cape May.

On the 14th of March 2004 we hauled in our mooring lines and headed once again for the Caribbean Sea. This would turn out to be an action packed patrol with illegal migrants and drugs.

We made our transit into the Caribbean Sea and refueled in San Juan, Puerto Rico on the 18th before slipping out into our operating area.

4th of April, we ran into our first yola - a small open boat - of Dominican migrants and they were not happy to see us. They were illegally headed to Puerto Rico with hopes of getting to the U.S. mainland from there. We followed the yola and tried to stop it using our small boats and boarding teams. As the small boats neared the yola the migrants started waving machetes and other weapons to scare off our teams. When the small boats continued their approach the migrants then began to throw their shoes and personal belongings at the boarding team members! Entangling devices were deployed by the boarding team, fouling the propeller of the yola, forcing it to stop. Luckily there was a Dominican Navy vessel in the area and it had come over to assist in the detention of the migrants. The migrants were handed over to the Dominican Navy vessel and I'm glad they had to deal with them instead of us!

It didn't take long to run into more migrants. The very next day while patrolling off the coast of Puerto Rico we intercepted a 30 foot yola carrying 121 illegals from the Dominican Republic off of Borinquen, Puerto Rico. The yola refused to stop and we followed it as it headed back to the Dominican Republic. Once in Dominican waters the yola was stopped and boarded by a Dominican Navy vessel. Later on that day two more yolas were spotted off the coast of Desecheo Island, Puerto Rico. We stopped them and took 63 Dominicans into custody for illegally trying to enter Puerto Rico. We later took them into the Dominican Republic and repatriated them back to their home country.

6th of April, we were diverted to an incident involving a 23 foot yola carrying 38 illegals, 24 Dominicans and 14 Peruvians, off the coast of Punta Boqueron, Puerto Rico. The yola was stopped by another U.S. vessel and three illegals had jumped into the water. The three drowned before we arrived on scene. The remaining 35 illegals were taken aboard our vessel. Later that day we offloaded the 35 migrants in Myaguez, Puerto Rico.

6th and 7th of April, we intercepted another three yolas. The first was at around 2230 on the night of the 6th, again off the coast of Punta Boqueron. The 20 foot boat was carrying 18 Dominicans, 12 male and 6 females. In the meantime two smaller Coast Guard cutters intercepted two more yolas containing 27 migrants on one and 54 on another. These illegals were transferred to us for a total of 134 illegals onboard *Dependable*. We later repatriated them back to the Dominican Republic on the 10th.

Once we intercept a yola and offload the migrants to our vessel we destroy the yola. It's burnt at sea or fired upon until it sinks. This is done for a couple of reasons. First, we just have no way of towing all these yolas behind us. Second, they are in such bad shape they are not sea worthy.

Yola being burnt and sunk at sea

Dominican migrants on our flight deck

11th of April, we took on more illegal migrants. As we were due to pull into San Juan, Puerto Rico that day for a patrol break we transferred the migrants to another 210' cutter operating with us, the *USCGC Resolute*, and pulled into San Juan.

18th of April, as the patrol was winding down we were operating in the area of the Caribbean Sea known as the Mona Pass, which is between the Dominican Republic and Puerto Rico. While monitoring the suspected vessels list we came across the *M/V EL Conquistador* and boarded her. The boarding team found 4,840 pounds of marijuana in a concealed compartment worth over $10 million dollars. The drugs were seized and five people arrested. The next day we pulled into San Juan and turned over the drugs and prisoners to the Drug Enforcement Agency (DEA).

Our boarding team apprehending
M/V CONQUISTADOR

Captured drug runners from the *M/V CONQUISTADOR*

4,800 pounds of marijuana from *M/V CONQUISTADOR*

24th of April, we arrived back into our moorings at Cape May. It had been a long patrol. We had physically rescued 481 people from unsafe or sinking vessels from Haiti, Cuba, Peru, and the Dominican Republic. Most were dehydrated and sea sick. One migrant was in such bad shape we had to medevac him off the cutter. This also included 35 people who were stranded on the uninhabited Mona Island.

In all we had overseen the rescue of 899 migrants while supervising other Coast Guard assets and repatriated or transferred 752 people to the border patrol. All of this took place in the Mona Pass between the Dominican Republic and Puerto Rico.

Sailing the high seas had become a lot easier over the years and on *Dependable* we had all the comforts and conveniences of a modern ship. We had internet connectivity pretty much 24/7 and you could email when you wanted. There were still communal computers and an email size limit, but now you could email pictures. We also had satellite TV and Captain Christian always tried to steer a good course for football games on Sunday.

Mail call was usually in every port of call and the only thing limited was cell phone use. When we got underway cell phones had to be turned off so that their signal could not be traced. Every once in a while if we were close to shore, and within cell phone range, the CO would lift the cell phone ban and let the crew make calls. This was always a morale booster! Oh how the times had changed from the days of the *Seneca* and *Tampa*.

Dependable hauled in her mooring lines on the10th of July and set another course for the Caribbean Sea.

14th of July, we made a brief stop for fuel and to load our helicopter detachment in Key West and then entered the D7 operating area. We would be patrolling off Honduras and Nicaragua.

22nd of July, we pulled into GITMO for 19,080 gallons of diesel fuel, 433 gallons of aviation fuel, food stores, and then departed back into the operating area on the 24th of July.

29th of July, while patrolling about 30 miles off Columbia we boarded the Honduran flagged *M/V Miss Mery Hill*. We had received intelligence that the *M/V Miss Mery Hill* had left her homeport loaded with cocaine so we had been looking for her. She was heading on a northeasterly course when we picked her up and started to shadow her awaiting a Statement of No Objection (SNO) from Honduras. We could board U.S. flagged vessels at will but in order to board a foreign vessel we needed an SNO from the vessel's flagged country.

M/V MISS MERY HILL

The SNO was granted and we boarded her. The seas were calm, the weather very nice, and the boarding team had no problem making the transit and securing the vessel. They had been onboard for about 10 hours and had found nothing. The team was still hopeful because they were unable to account for space between some aft fuel tanks. These tanks hold thousands of gallons of fuel and we would need to pump the fuel out to be able to inspect inside them. Fuel, oil, and water tanks are tough to get dimensions on because they are built into the hull of the ship.

It was determined that the boarding team would pump one tank into another to empty it for inspection. As the gas free engineer I would go over and make sure the emptied tank was free of explosive gasses and safe for entry. I received the word that the boarding team was ready and I made

333

the transit over in the small boat with my gear, which consisted of an oxygen/explosive meter and an air tank; the type firefighters wear.

As the small boat pulled alongside I waited my turn and made the leap over to the *M/V Miss Mery Hill*. It was a typical Caribbean small fishing vessel about 80 feet long and rusting. I had to transit through the living area and you could see the boarding team had left no stone unturned. There were huge holes in the bulk heads, contents of every cabinet and drawer were emptied on the deck. The ceiling was torn down. The place was trashed with no sign of drugs. I certified several tanks gas free and let the boarding team go to work inspecting them. Since I wasn't one for hanging around half sea worthy vessels, I headed back to the *Dependable*.

The next day, the 30th, I was called back over to the *M/V Miss Mery Hill* to inspect several more tanks. I arrived onboard and made my way back aft. When I got back to the aft part of the boat I passed the six *M/V Miss Mery Hill* crewmembers who were under armed guard. I hopped down into a compartment to find one of the boarding team members, an MK2 who was on temporary duty with us, sweating up a storm while he was taking off the 50 or so huge bolts holding the cover on a fuel tank. I helped him remove the remaining bolts. When we finished removing the bolts we slid the 24 inch by 12 inch cover to the side. We were looking into an empty small bathroom sized fuel tank with two more tank covers on port and starboard sides of the tank. Now we were onto something!

The MK2 wanted to bolt right in but I put the brakes on him. If he were to just hop in there and there wasn't enough oxygen, he could just pass right out. If there were explosive gases he could blow us all up. I took a test and it showed good oxygen but borderline for explosive gases. I said I didn't feel good about him going in until it had been ventilated. Several of the boarding team members had come down and the adrenaline was really pumping. These guys had been here for over 20 hours tearing the place up with no luck and they wanted some justification for their destruction. Plus we had been told there were definitely drugs on board.

Caught up in the moment I decided to let the MK2 go into the tank before ventilating it. I had gotten to know the MK2 really well over the past month or so, standing watches in the engine room together, and knew that he was competent and would move quickly. And I would put my air tank on and be ready to go in and get him if something went wrong. Still, it was with some anxiety that I told him I would only give him time for one side, and he could pick. He picked the starboard side and went in. After about 20 minutes he had removed all the cover bolts and slid the cover plate off to reveal another empty compartment. He wanted to start removing the port side cover bolts but I told him we would need to let the first compartment air out before I would let him spend another 20 minutes in there.

The airing out process would take several hours. I hated being away from the cutter as you well know and told the MK2 that I would head back over to *Dependable* and come back in a few hours after the tank had time to vent. I hopped back into the small boat and told the coxswain to take me back over to the cutter. As I was jumping into the small boat my $100.00 flash light slipped out of my coveralls and fell into the crystal clear water. I cussed as I watched that $100.00 flash light sinking to the bottom. And with those clear Caribbean waters it was a long cuss!

When I got back over to the *Dependable* I made my way up to the bridge to brief the CO on what had happened, minus the borderline explosive gases part. About the time I got up there everyone on the bridge was really excited. Come to find out the MK2 and the rest of the boarding team hadn't waited for the compartment to air out. They had gone ahead and opened the port side cover as soon as I left. Inside the hidden compartment they discovered 64 bails containing 3,997 pounds of cocaine with a street value of $274 million dollars!

M/V MISS MERY HILL cocaine

The vessel was confiscated and the six crewmembers taken into custody.
While towing the vessel toward Honduras the *M/V Miss Mery Hill* began
to leak oil into the sea and the tow was transferred to a U.S. Navy vessel.
The *M/V Miss Mery Hill* was eventually determined not to be sea worthy
and sunk. The cocaine and crewmembers were later transferred to the
U.S. Drug Enforcement Administration.

This seizure added another drug bust sticker to the side of *Dependable's*
hull. This would be a snowflake indicating a cocaine seizure. Marijuana
would be indicated by a marijuana leaf. Like human active duty members, cutters are awarded medals and citations for their accomplishments
and they wear them on their hull proudly.

USCGC DEPENDABLE (WMEC-626) awards

We returned to GITMO on the 4th of August for a quick refuel and took on 18,097 gallons of diesel fuel. No liberty, just fuel. I had to go ashore to make sure the fuel delivery was arranged correctly and walked down the 100 yard pier where I could see there were some vehicles parked. As I got closer I could see several very good looking ladies standing around with a group of other people. Curiosity got the best of me and I walked up and said, "Hello." They replied "Hi, we're Miss Universe, Miss USA, and Miss Teen and doing a USO good will tour here on GITMO." I immediately forgot all about refueling!

I knew the crew would love to meet them and I asked if they would come aboard. They were most gracious and agreed. Needless to say they didn't need to be announced, because about half way down the pier the entire crew had noticed them! They were as gracious as could be and took the time to pose for lots of pictures.

GITMO with Miss USA, Miss Teen, and Miss Universe

After the USO good will group left we were back underway and in the operating area.

10th of August, category 4 Hurricane Charley caught us in the middle of the Caribbean Sea. We were lucky to be far enough east of it not to catch its full force. But the 50 mph winds and high seas still tossed us around. Our patrol break finally came on the 13th of August and we pulled into the island of Aruba for liberty and took on 16,979 gallons of diesel fuel.

As we set sail from Aruba we had another storm barreling down on us, tropical storm Earl. He was dishing out 50 mph winds and high seas right behind us. The storm was moving at 22 knots and we were doing 14 knots. He eventually overtook us and we were once again tossed around by the wind and the waves. It was a rough ride and there were a lot of sea sick Coasties!

On the 7th of September *Dependable* returned home to her moorings in Cape May until mid-October.

12th of October, *Dependable* once again slipped her moorings and entered the Atlantic Ocean on another D1 fisheries patrol. The patrol started off with a main engine casualty, which required us to pull into Portsmouth, Virginia for repairs almost immediately after getting underway. After several days of repairs and topping off with fuel we steamed back into the Atlantic Ocean.

The remainder of the patrol was quiet and only highlighted with towing a disabled fishing vessel into port on the 25th of November. Some patrols were like that; just sitting around out in the middle of the ocean waiting for something to happen. We made the best use of the time conducting damage control drills and performing maintenance. On the 1st of December we pulled back into our berth at Cape May to spend Christmas and New Year's at home.

17th of January 2005, we once again left Cape May and set course out into the Atlantic Ocean for another D1 fisheries patrol. It would be a short one as we were having trouble with one of our propellers. The propellers on modern ships operate on hydraulics that actuate each propeller blade. The system is known as controllable pitch propeller (CPP). When you want to go faster you increase the shaft speed and pitch on the propeller blades. When you want to slow down you decrease the speed and pitch.

We knew we had a problem with the hydraulic system on the #2 CPP blade seal, which holds hydraulic fluid in the system and keeps sea water out. The only way to gain access to the propeller blade seal is to haul us out of the water to affect the repair. So a dry-docking was scheduled and we headed to the Coast Guard Yard at Curtis Bay, Maryland.

The transit to the Yard was interesting. There are two ways to get there from Cape May. We could go the long way and sail into the Atlantic Ocean and up the Chesapeake Bay, or we could go the short way and sail up the Delaware Bay, transit the Chesapeake and Delaware Canal, and down the Chesapeake Bay. We did the latter.

I had transited the Chesapeake and Delaware Canal numerous times on other cutters and it was always enjoyable. It is 14 miles long and only 450 feet wide, lined with houses and small towns which made for a very scenic trip.

USCGC DEPENDABLE (WMEC-626)
Dry-docked at the USCG Yard in Curtis Bay, MD

After arriving at the USCG Yard we were hauled out and the CPP system repaired. It took less than 24 hours; we were back in the water the next day headed into the Chesapeake Bay and out into the Atlantic Ocean on patrol. The remainder of the patrol was uneventful and we bobbed out in the freezing Atlantic Ocean boarding and inspecting fishing vessels. The most interesting thing to happen was that I had received orders to Coast Guard Headquarters in Washington, DC. My replacement had arrived and I was starting to hand my duties over to her.

She was a young, newly commissioned ensign. As she delved into her qualifications she appeared to be grasping the fundamentals of engineering. Unfortunately, the more time we spent working together the more I began to see she was having difficulties. The fast paced engineering watch qualifications, deck watch qualifications, and the operating tempo, soon seemed to overwhelm her. All the qualifications are sort of like when a medical student interns at a hospital; a lot of work, no sleep, and high expectations.

Everything came to a head during a port call in Boston. I walked into a bar and sat down for my usual drink on the rocks. The bar was filled with *Dependable* crew, and as I look around I spotted her and another junior male officer from our cutter over at a table. I didn't think anything of it until they started to make out right there at their table! I hurriedly finished my drink and walked over to them and I nicely told her she was going back to the cutter with me, right now! If they were caught fooling around they would end up like the MK2 and QM3 back on *Sherman*!

As we walked back to *Dependable* she was obviously drunk and broke down crying. She explained how overwhelmed she was with all the qualifications ahead of her. She felt like she was over her head and out of control. This took me a little by surprise because everyone seems a little overwhelmed when they take on a new job but this didn't seem normal, and I was worried. After witnessing her setbacks in the watch qualifications process and now hearing how stressed she was feeling, I felt I had to talk to the command about her suitability for the job. Truthfully, I was half worried about her and half worried about having to stay aboard *Dependable* for another six months to a year while they figured out what to do with her. I had just signed all my responsibilities over to her and was getting the unwelcomed feeling that I would be taking them all back! The command, in an effort to ease her work load, shifted some of her responsibilities around until she could handle them and that appeared to have done the trick. During the time I had left on the cutter she seemed to be getting it together and I sensed the command had faith in her. But in the end I guess it was just too much for her. A short while after I transferred off *Dependable* I was told that she was also transferred ashore and then discharged from the Coast Guard.

Being assigned afloat can cause enormous stress. Some like the ensign who relieved me show it outwardly and some hold it in. Not too long after I left *Dependable* I heard that the operations officer, a lieutenant, took his life after he had transferred to a shore station on the west coast. He was a good officer, good person, and liked by the crew. It was very sad news to hear of his death.

On the 16th of February it was time to head home and we arrived back to cold and quiet Cape May with as much fanfare as when we had left; none. We were in home port for about six weeks before we set sail once again on the 3rd of April. This time we were headed for Little Creek, Virginia for TACT, the new acronym for REFTRA. When we finished with TACT we headed straight down to GITMO for fuel and into our operating area.

4th of May 2005, while patrolling 10 miles south of West Caicos Island in the Caribbean Sea we rescued 132 Haitian migrants loaded on a 50 foot boat. The seas were choppy and it was after dark when we spotted the Haitian vessel. The Haitians were transferred aboard our cutter via our two small boats and housed on the flight deck until we repatriated them in Port-au Prince, Haiti. The Haitians had been at sea for five days and were dehydrated and hungry. They had no food, water, or sanitary facilities on the dangerously overloaded boat when we intercepted them.

Interdicting a boat of Haitian migrants and taking them aboard the RHI

The process of interdicting migrants is an all hands evolution. My job was to film the whole process. As we came upon a suspect vessel I would start filming. The purpose of the filming is to document the entire evolution from interception to safely embarking them.

When you come upon a suspect vessel of migrants they are going to be either friendly or hostile. We have had them throw shoes and knives at us trying to get away and we have had them welcome us as their rescuers.

342

You have to realize that they have sold everything they own to try and make the transit to the United States and we have just shown up and stopped them. They can also become very excited to get off their boat, all rush to one side, and tip their boat over. A lot of migrants can't swim and many have perished due to their boat flipping over when approached by Coast Guard small boats. I was always told to never jump in after them because they can pull you down with them. The protocol was to throw life jackets into the water for them to grab onto until we could safely remove them from the water.

Once the suspect vessel has been approached, the occupants are calmed, and life jackets are distributed to all aboard. We then start the process of transferring them from their vessel to ours. All children and pregnant women are brought aboard first. As they are brought aboard they are frisked for weapons and given a blanket and simple toiletries. Medical personnel inspect them for any health issues and they are led to the flight deck. The flight deck is a huge area in which they can relax and be contained. Armed personnel are posted to guard them from harming each other, or us. Make shift toilets and showers are set up along with a huge tent to keep them out of the hot sun. They are fed three times a day and all meals consist of rice and red beans.

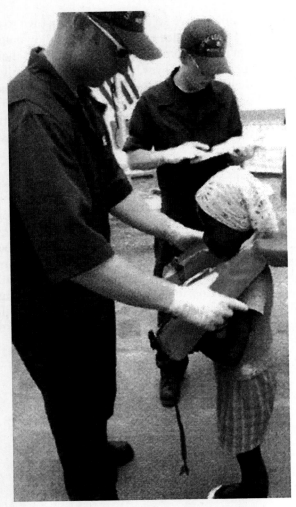

A Haitian child being taken aboard _DEPENDABLE_ and documented

12th of May, while patrolling 50 miles northwest of Mathewtown, Great Inagua Bahamas we rescued 116 Haitian migrants in another dangerously overloaded 50 foot boat. After removing the Haitians from the boat we destroyed it at sea. The 116 Haitians consisting of men, women, and children were taken into Port-au-Prince, Haiti and repatriated. From there we set a course for Key West to refuel and take on food stores.

On the 18th of May we departed Key West and commenced our eight day transit home. On the 26th of May we entered the channel into Cape May and made berth. That was my final patrol on *Dependable*, 53 days away from homeport. After liberty was granted I walked off *Dependable* for the last time. There was nothing unusual about the event, it was like every other time I had departed the *Dependable*. I walked back to the fantail where the quarterdeck was located, slid the lever by my name from green to red indicating I was ashore, saluted the quarterdeck watch stander, walked to the edge of the gangway, saluted the ensign, and walked ashore headed to my new assignment.

I was done making assumptions that this would be my last time at sea. I was an officer now with a lot of potential assignments ahead of me, on land and at sea. At this point well over half of my time in the Coast Guard had been spent at sea. But in the end this would be the last time I crossed the brow of a Coast Guard cutter. I would not go back to sea again. Walking off *Dependable* ended my time at sea; leaving me with my permanent silver cutterman's pin as an enlisted man, gold cutterman's pin as an officer, sea service ribbon with three bronze stars, and a whole lot of memories!

COAST GUARD HEADQUARTERS

WASHINGTON, DC

6 July 2005 – 30 November 2007

For as much power as it contained Coast Guard headquarters was a relatively small building. It was quite common to pass the commandant and other high ranking admirals in the passageways or in the elevator. It made the organization seem small and fraternal.

I was assigned as the enlisted force manager for engineering, logistics and the C4IT directorates. I was responsible for the strategic direction, guidance, resource distribution and life cycle management of enlisted personnel in nine Coast Guard ratings; electronics technician (ET), information technician (IT), electrician mate (EM), damage controlman (DC), machinery technician (MK), storekeeper (SK), aviation machinist mate (AMT) , aviation electronics technician (AET), and aviation survival technician (AST). This equated to 55% of the Coast Guard's entire enlisted workforce. I supervised eight E-9 master chief petty officers, 30 students in the advanced college education program (ACET), and managed a $5.6 million dollar budget for technical schools with a throughput of over 6454 students.

Now that was what my officer evaluation report (OER) said I did. What I really did, was cat herd eight master chief petty officers who were all gun slingers and wanted to do things their own way! They were like the *Tampa* chief's mess on steroids! This was the biggest grouping of master chiefs in the Coast Guard. They ran their respective ratings from recruitment, training, billet allocation, and rank structure, to future rate planning. I managed the money, their travel budget, and broke up fights.

It was sort of ironic that these were some of the very same master chiefs who had been so disdainful of my decision to take a commission as a LTJG when I was a master chief. Not all of them, but a few, and now I would be in charge of them as a lieutenant!

They were personally and professionally a great group of guys, but they never let me forget that in their eyes I had turned my back on being a master chief. I had served with several of them before. MKCM Kevin Winter and I worked together as master chiefs when I was at NESU Boston and he was at MLCLANT. And ETCM Daryl Bletso along with

SKCM Myles Shaw and SKCM Mark Ferguson and I were chiefs together at SCCB and ELC. Daryl was even at my chief's initiation and initiated me as a real chief.

I was of course their boss now and professionally we had a superior to subordinate relationship. I knew they didn't like taking orders and direction from a LT. To establish myself I put my foot down as soon as my predecessor had left. Like BMCM Nadeau from back on the *Sumac*, I had to establish authority from day one. When I arrived, the master chiefs all drew their travel money from a single fund which I managed. They had no self-control with their travel funds, they spent it as fast as they could and then look to me for more. I nipped this in the bud right away and split the travel funds evenly amongst them. I told them when it was gone they were done, even if the travel was critical.

Of course they thought I was joking and would give in. The first person who ran out of money was denied subsequent travel funds. Surprised, they scurried around to beg for money from one of their peers. Good luck with that! Because as liberal as the master chiefs were with other people's money they were frugal with their own!

My daily routine at headquarters revolved around commuting to work, meetings, lunch, more meetings, and commuting home.

Commuting was brutal. There were a limited amount of parking spots and they were awarded on a lottery system, unless you held high rank. And I mean high rank, just because you were a captain didn't guarantee you a parking spot. Headquarters had just as many civilians as military and they competed for parking just like the military. You could park on the street but that was dangerous and more trouble than it was worth.

Headquarters was located in one of the roughest neighborhoods of DC, and your car was fair game parked out on the street. And if you did dare park out there it was metered, and you had to constantly run out to pump the meter with quarters.

I lived outside the city, in Maryland, so I would have to drive from home to the commuter rail (METRO) station, take two different METRO trains, and then a shuttle bus to the office. On the way home I had to do the reverse. The major hold up was the shuttle bus. They only had two shuttle buses that held about 20 people each, and there would be a line waiting to catch them. It was common to wait 15 minutes for the shuttle. This was a far cry from my days on the cutters when all I had to do was wake up in my rack, open my eyes and I was at work. My toughest commute on a cutter was making my way to the galley for breakfast!

Once at headquarters I soon realized that a program known as Deepwater was consuming everyone's time and attention. It involved the future of the Coast Guard and its assets. For me it was meetings upon endless meetings about things that really didn't pertain to me. I was there just in case an issue involving my office was brought up, which rarely happened. Usually it was a few of us sitting in a room with five or six other people scattered around the country on speaker phone. Oh those meetings were so boring. So boring I would fall asleep! It was painful. I was a hands-on technician and now I was consumed with boring meetings. Like at the ELC, I was finding out really fast that I wasn't cut out for a desk job.

Meetings with Coast Guard Recruiting were about the only meetings that kept me awake. I could wrap my arms around the issues and could see immediate results, or the lack of. Once a month I would meet with recruiting to discuss the recruitment for my ratings. If the Coast Guard was low in one of my ratings, I would classify it as critical and request recruiting to fill those vacancies as a priority. Because these vacancies sometimes involved hard to fill ratings, it was common for recruiting to offer cash enlistment bonuses along with other incentives such as a guaranteed "A" school to entice prospective recruits.

That seemed pretty cut and dried, but recruiting and I always seemed to butt heads over their drive to meet monthly quotas and my need to fill critical vacancies. I looked at it like this; say I need ETs, so I designate them as a critical rate and pass that on to recruiting. Recruiting has a kid come into the recruiting office that meets the requirements of being an ET, but would rather be an MK, but MK is not critical. I believed they should tell the kid we can hire you as an ET with an incentive, but we are all full of MKs.

Recruiters looked at it like this, in my opinion; LT Semler has made ETs critical so I need to keep my eye out for kids wanting to be ETs. I have this kid in here right now that wants to be an MK and I might lose him if he can't join as an MK. I have a recruitment quota to meet and I'm running short this month, so I'll hire this kid as an MK so I can make my recruiting quota.

Of course that was my perspective. But it all boiled down to what was best for the Coast Guard, and we didn't always agree on what that was.

Recruiting always sent over some mid-level enlisted person, like an E-6, to basically recite their recruitment numbers and talking points. Of course I would get agitated when I would hear that instead of filling critical vacancies they hired into non critical positions. And of course the junior enlisted guy they had sent over couldn't answer any of my questions.

While it would have made me feel better, blowing up on the poor junior enlisted guy wouldn't have resolved anything. So, I had my boss relay to recruiting that they needed to send over someone of authority who could speak to my issues and hopefully get things moving in the direction I needed them to go. It was a slow process but we eventually came to common ground.

I worked with recruiting, and their parent command Enlisted Personnel Management (EPM), on other issues such as ASVAB waivers and the ACET program. In order to qualify for a rating you had to have the minimum qualifying ASVAB score for that rating. The more technical or complicated the rating, the higher the ASVAB score required. ASVAB waivers were approved by another office, but our ruling was the determining factor for their decision.

Commanding officers in the field and recruiting were authorized to grant a one point waiver, anymore and it needed to come through me. My rule was to have the ratings master chief look at each individual case and determine if the individual appeared capable of handling the rating. We had tried to lower the ASVAB scores in several critical ratings that were highly technical and found that these service members were failing at the ratings "A" school. So if you tried to cut a kid a break, you may just hurt him in the long run when he failed school, so we had to be careful with our minimum standards.

ACET was another interesting program. The Coast Guard had 30 active duty enlisted members enrolled in a two year degree program to attain their college degree. These students were selected by a board and were issued orders to attend civilian colleges of their choice for two years. Once in the program I monitored their progress and made sure they were not failing and that their tuition was being paid. It was easy and the program seemed to run on auto pilot once they were at school.

It took a lot of coordination with EPM to get these active duty students transferred to college and then have a place for them to go when they came out of college. The ultimate goal was to select a student who was coming up on transfer anyway and then find a follow-on assignment when they finished where they could put their degree to work for the Coast Guard.

On the 22nd of August 2006 I decided that the time had come for me to move on without the Coast Guard, and I submitted my letter of retirement to take effect the 1st of December 2007. I was able to retire with just under five years as an officer because I had declined to integrate. But I almost missed the deadline to decline integrations a few years earlier. That would have made it impossible for me to retire for another 10 years!

Back in April of 2005 when I was still on *Dependable* we had pulled into Key West for fuel. When we received our mail delivery there was a letter for me from headquarters stating that I was being offered an appointment as a permanent officer. For most people this is good news, because you are no longer a temporary officer and will now have more or less job security as a permanent officer. This wasn't good news for me, because when you accept a permanent commission you are also committing yourself to 10 years as an officer before being able to retire. I wanted the flexibility to leave when I wanted to.

The letter also stated that I had five days to decline. I looked at the letter head date and I had missed that deadline because we were underway and the letter had taken several weeks to catch up to me. After making a few frantic phone calls I notified HQ of my situation and that I would be sending back the letter declining integration. I had that letter in the mail to them that day in Key West.

That event was critical for me to be able to retire in 2007. If I had integrated as a permanent officer I would not be eligible to retire until 2015. I never would have survived the boredom of headquarters!

351

When EPM received my retirement letter in 2006 they called me and said there seemed to be a problem because their data stated that I had in fact integrated! After a few phone calls and emails documenting that I had declined integration, my retirement letter was approved.

God had been looking out for me the past 25 years. He provided me with plenty of opportunities to succeed, guided me in tough times, and placed good people around and over me. Over the years I have stayed in contact with many of the soldiers and shipmates I served with, and I am reuniting with others all the time. The bond of being in the service is so strong that we are able to just pick up right where we left off all those years ago. Sadly, some have already crossed the bar, though they live on in my memory.

Through the years, I have often recalled a sign on one of the cutter repair party lockers. Someone had put it up to help when you just felt totally stressed out while drilling and being underway. It said, "Go to your happy place." Remembering all those I served with over the years and the special times we shared takes me to my happy place.

"Fair winds and following seas"

ABOUT THE AUTHOR

Ed Semler retired from the United States Coast Guard in December of 2007 with over 25 years of military service in both the United States Army and United States Coast Guard. In the United States Army he was enlisted and was honorably discharged as specialist four (E-4). While in the United States Coast Guard he was enlisted, obtaining the rank of master chief petty officer (E-9), was commissioned as an officer, and retired as a lieutenant (O-3E). He currently lives in Butler, Pennsylvania with his wife Jana, a retired Air Force senior master sergeant.

His major awards which are shown on the following page are from top to bottom, left to right;

Coast Guard Officer Cutterman Pin

Meritorious Service with gold star and operational service device

Coast Guard Commendation with gold star and operational
Service device

Coast Guard Achievement

United States Army Achievement

Coast Guard Good Conduct with Silver Star

United States Army Good Conduct

National Defense with gold star

Armed Forces Expeditionary Service

War on Terrorism Service

Korea Defense Service

Humanitarian Service

Coast Guard Expert Rifle